GRACE FARM
ALWAYS AND FOREVER

Andrea Comer

Copyright © 2019 by Andrea Comer.

All rights reserved. No part of this publication may be reproduced, distributed or transmitted in any form or by any means, including photocopying, recording, or other electronic or mechanical methods, without the prior written permission of the publisher, except in the case of brief quotations embodied in critical reviews and certain other noncommercial uses permitted by copyright law.

Book Layout ©2013 BookDesignTemplates.com

Grace Farm – Always and Forever / Andrea Comer. -- 1st ed.
ISBN: 978-0-9953904-3-0

For Frank Hydrick, Linda Wilson, Andrea Casella, Dean Hughes, Peter Horton, Carolyn Mountcastle and Pat Flynn.

And for Lumen Grace, Lilly Rain, Amber "The Divine One", Steffy, Ruben John, Brian, Baby and Agnes Griffiths. I love you, I'm very grateful to have known you and I thank you for everything.

CONTENTS

Introduction
Always and Forever   1

Chapter one
Emily   15

Chapter two
Tommy   109

Chapter three
Lilly   175

Chapter four
Gerald   239

Chapter five
Horton   313

INTRODUCTION

Always and Forever

When I was thinking of a title for the second book in the Grace Farm series I didn't have to think very long or hard, the title came to me quite early on, even before I started writing this book. One thing I always do when a new pug joins our family is have what I call the "Always and Forever" talk. I will sit with the new little blessing on my knee, well that's if they are comfortable enough to want to sit on my knee and some of them are not because they are still a little shell shocked from what they have been through, at those times I will just go and sit next to my new little son or daughter. Sit as close to them as I can, look them in the eye and tell them that my home is now their home and I want them to treat it as such. "This is your home now" I will softly say, "This is where you are going to live for the rest of your life, you can relax now my love for you are home" I tell them that I am now their Mother, that I love them and that I am going to take real good care of them. I promise them that for the rest of their days I will love them with all my heart. I tell them that "Wherever I am they are going to be also", that I am never going to leave them, and I am never going to give up on them. I tell them that I am going to be here for them always and forever.

The reason I do this is because I think it's very important to let them know where they stand, I want them to know there will be no more moving on, no more being given up on and that whatever issues they have we will work them out together. I tell them they can trust me and that no matter what they throw at me I am never ever going to stop loving them. And some will be there on my knee looking up at my face as I speak taking every word in, some will be on my knee but looking at everything else but me and yet I still feel they are hearing all that's being said. And some will be just sitting by my side, eyes open or closed it doesn't really matter, they too will be listening to my words because that's what new dogs tend to do the most, listen to everything that's going on in their new surroundings because it helps them get used to things. I feel very strongly about having these little chats with them, it's vital to let them know where they stand because if I don't tell them and then follow through by showing them with my actions how else are they going to know these things. Dogs understand what we say far more than most people give them credit for. I do not want them thinking this is just another home in a series of homes they will be passing through. I want them to feel they are safe and secure here and once that's sorted out, I believe they relax a little bit, and all of this helps them on their road to being fully settled in.

Some may think I'm mad doing this, but I truly believe these little chats help and so time and time again I will give them. It's also a nice way of having a bonding time with my new family members. It's a special time for both of us. And I love taking in elderly pairs that have lived together all their lives and when this happens I'll go sit on the couch and have one at either side of me, I'll have an arm around each of them and my head will be going from one side to the other, so they know I am talking to both. I'd hate one to think that I was just meaning his sister or brother and have him sitting there wondering what is to become of him. So I speak softly but clearly and if I have given them a name already I will use it, if not I will call them by their old names as was the case with Tommy and Lilly and then of course when I change the name I'll go and give the new name talk. I say that I know you have been called by such and such a name for quite a long time, but I am going to call you this name now and I will go on to tell them why I am changing it, why the new name has been chosen and why I like it so much. I will explain to them what it means to me and in doing so what they mean to me. It's a pretty good way to start off a relationship I think. No better way then telling somebody exactly how you feel, exactly how much you love them. I know if I was in their position it's something I would really like to hear. And you can't fool dogs, they sense things about us, people get fooled by people all the time, it's like you think you can trust somebody and then it hurts your heart deeply when you find out you can't. With dogs it's different, they pick up on all sorts of things that human beings don't and it helps them read us. They get a feel for us quite quickly because we give so much of ourselves away without knowing we are even doing it. They can read us like a book, they'll have a person pretty much summed up right away, so they'll know whether to believe you or not. My dogs quickly know that they can trust every single word I say and so a connection begins. And it's special and it's beautiful and it's nice to see it unfold. The Always and Forever talk is the basis of which our relationship is built on. It's where we start. It's like we'll have our little chat and away we go. And the speed at which we go is always entirely up to them. It has to be because they have all been through so many different things, I have not walked the same path they have been made to walk and so I leave them to set the pace. It's always going to go at their pace anyway so it's good that I learnt this lesson early on and I did that by doing exactly what I had been taught by my dogs to do, to watch, to listen, to really see them and not just glance over them, to try and read them as well as they have been reading me. It was a handy lesson to have learnt from them and not the only one I've been blessed enough to learn along the way. It's quite amazing how much you can learn about somebody by simply watching them, their mannerisms, the way they react or don't react to certain things. A few days of observation helps me get to know them better and that in turn helps me help them, give them what they need, help them to heal. Animals can't talk so they can't tell you how they are feeling on the inside, but they will always show you. Then again, it's kind of the same way with some people, even though they can talk they don't because they aren't willing to reveal what's going on inside. Being an observer in a racing raging world is quite a handy thing to be.

Another reason I like the title Always and Forever is because of all the souls this book is dedicated to. For me titles and dedications are just as important as the book itself is. This book is dedicated to some beautiful individuals I have known and lost and so I feel this title is a nod to them as well. I feel those we lose never truly go away, they never fully leave us, in one sense they have done yes, but they are always going to be a part of us and will be forever in our hearts. So really it's like they are not so very far away from us at all. And you never forget them, ever, sure they are not forefront in our minds all the time, although you'll definitely have days where they are, but they come flickering across your mind from time to time. Like waves against a shore these memories will come. Sometimes they'll be loudly crashing, at other times slow, soft and gentle, just drift in and drift out very quietly and peacefully leaving you feeling the exact same way. And it can take the tiniest thing to trigger the loveliest memory. A sight, a sound, a smell, all these things will be able to take you back to a time and a place and the feeling you had when you were with them. And yes, there are times in your life where those memories will make you sad, especially in the early days of loss and the early stages of grieving. But as time goes on the memories we have can be so comforting and you'll find yourself laughing at something they did, or you'll recall a meaningful utterance. For me I remember all sorts of things about those I have lost, each one came, made an impact, taught lessons, gave me something, contributed to my life, and then left me with a little piece of themselves and I am forever grateful to them for doing so.

I remember many years ago when I was newly married, when I'd not suffered loss, you know before my world had been rocked by it. When you are so young that you think that you are invincible, you think that nothing can touch you, well I was still in that phase of my life and I was talking to David about people we knew who were going through some really hard times, they had lost, they had suffered heartbreak and were reeling from it and I was looking on at all of this and feeling completely helpless in a way because there was nothing I could do to help them and I found that incredibly hard. Oh of course you can be there for them to talk to, offer a shoulder to cry on, but you can't stop their hearts from breaking and you can't bring their loved ones back. I was talking to my husband one day saying how sorry I was for those friends of ours and I also made a quick comment about how we were very lucky because we'd not been affected by such things, but what I should have said was that we'd not been affected by such things "Yet" because they were certainly heading our way and when they hit they hit like a tornado. And then it was my time to be in agony and it was my friends that were now looking on helplessly at me the same way I had done with them.

I have seen a few paintings done where there are people and animals that are clearly in the land of the living and beside them in a sort of faded fashion are people and animals that have passed away, they are sitting or standing right beside their loved ones. Well sometimes I wonder what that image would look like if the artist was capturing my life, sometimes I will be walking round the farm with the pugs and I imagine all those I have loved and lost over the years walking along right next to us. It's quite a lovely image I have in my mind and it's both sad and really beautiful all at the same time. And if such a thing is actually happening well, I think it's good that we are walking around in that wide open space because there's plenty of room there for us all to walk side by side. But whether or not they are walking beside us, they are still, I feel, very much a part of us and who we are. They made us, through their love and through their special connection to us, the people we are today, I feel that very deeply, especially with my Mum. I don't think somebody who you love with that amount of depth and intensity, who made up such a huge percent of who you are, will ever be lost to you, how can you not feel them with you and within you after they have gone. And I believe that as you walk through your life you are always going to be able to sense their influence on you and in that they live on and on.

I have a few items I've kept that remind me of those I have lost, a few trinkets I'll never part with. One is a little ornamental shelf sitter, two strawberries with painted on faces and their arms wrapped round each other, they have long dangly legs and army type boots on, well at the start they had long dangly legs with army type boots on anyway but over time their legs frayed and so now they are legless and bootless but it takes nothing away from their cuteness, it improves it actually because they are now just two little life sized strawberries with faces on them. I remember the day my mother-in-law gave them to me, well more presented them to me actually on one of her visits to the farm. She smiled from ear to ear as she placed them in my hands, she knew I liked strawberries and she knew I liked ornaments, she knew with this gift she couldn't possibly loose, that I would love it and I did, loved it enough to keep it all these years later. I also have the last mug my brother-in-law sipped from when he came to stay. Yes, the handle is no longer there but the memories of his laugher are. Actually, that mug is a two for one deal when it comes to evoking memories. It is a green eggs and ham mug and so being Dr Suess it also makes me think of Horton as well. It now sits on my desk holding pens and pencils, I mean why have a meaningless pen holder when you can have a sentimental one. I also have a bluebird tea towel that my Mum loved so much she had it draped over her walking frame and took it wherever she went, when I look at that tea towel now I am instantly transformed to walking with her in the hallway of the nursing home. She liked to take me round and introduce me to her new friends. I'd be a few steps ahead of her waiting for her to tell me which room I should be walking into, I'd turn and see Mum, grey haired and smiling, leaning on her frame with the tea towel folded neatly over the main bar.

And if you peep inside my handbag, you'll see quite a few toys from pugs that have passed. Old, worn, chewed, well-loved toys that were special enough to be carried round in little mouths, each one brings a smile, each one triggers a memory, they are far more than tatty fabric, they are much more than gnawed on plastic, they are as precious to me as they were to the pugs that had chosen them to be their favourites. And to this day Horton's nappy bag still hangs on my bedpost, I don't notice it all the time, I'm so used to it being there now that it just blends in and becomes part of the bed. But when I do notice it, if I brush up against it and feel the fabric against my hand, it does make me smile and the memories of him start to flow. These are some of the special things I have kept and I've no doubt that you have items you hold dear as well. It's not like we need these things to make us remember them, it's just that they hold far too much sentimental value to ever be thrown away. And I don't know about you, but I like to talk about the loved ones I have lost because I think to not do so is a dishonour both to them and their memory. Some people may find it morbid. But I think to never say their name again is disrespectful. David and I have many lovely conversations about people and animals that are no longer here. And that makes me happy because if we were to never speak of them again it'd be like we were erasing the fact that they were ever here at all and that's not right. I don't believe any of us wants to be forgotten. Yes, they are gone but don't wipe them away forever by never mentioning them again, I don't think that gains you much, it lessens your life if anything.

I must talk a little bit about the cover of this book because it makes me happy every time I look at it. I remember this day so well. A few of the dogs had had a bath, it was a warm day, and they were out drying in the sunshine. I had wanted to get a photo of multiple pugs for the cover of my next book and with that in mind I'd taken quite a few photos over the previous months. Photos of the pugs walking around the farm was what I'd been concentrating on and that can be a hard thing to do because a lot of them stay near my feet and all you get then is an aerial shot. So I'd wait until David was home walking with us and I'd stand back and try and get a photo of the pugs as they all marched along after him. Time and time again I'd get some beautiful photos of the pugs but time and time again you could see David's foot stepping out of the photo. He would sometimes pause trying to get as many of the pugs as possible pausing behind him and then take off fast and I would try and get a photo before they took off after him but that really wasn't working out too well at all. I'd be able to get four pugs in the shot at most and that wasn't enough for me because I wanted to get as many of them on the cover as I could. So there we were in that beautiful treed part of the front paddock, which is actually one of my favourite parts of the farm, especially in Spring when the trees have woken up after a long cold winter and the grass is lush and green. Everybody was gathered together in the one spot because David and I had been standing there talking for a while and the pugs, as is often the case when we stop to talk, gather around our feet and wait until it's time to move on. Some were laying down having a rest, some of the blind pugs were hearing the voices over their heads and stood sniffing at the air and listening to the mutterings of their Mum and Dad. I like that one little girl is on her back, paw stretched out, trying to get her brother to play. The way some of the really old pugs are standing lets me know who they are even though I cannot see their faces because I can identify their bodies due to the way they hold themselves.

Lilly Rain is in the forefront of the photo looking to the side, not at anything in particular that was just her reflective pose, how she held herself when she was thinking. And the look on her face tells me that's exactly what she is doing. Amber "The Divine One" is standing in the middle of the group chilling out, little tail unfolded, the lower part of her body sinking down as she stood drying off. Steffy is standing in full sun, no doubt enjoying feeling it's warmth on her back like she always used to do. To date Steffy is the pug that has spent the most amount of time here at Grace Farm. We were blessed to have her loving, lovely presence for over a decade. And my big boy Brian is standing near Amber, looking towards Steffy, he is no doubt taking everything in in that calm peaceful gentle way he always did. Lumen Grace is towards the back of the group, freshly washed and amusing herself laying there watching a magpie in the distance, a thing she often liked to do when she was still alive. Well, it was actually a mother and baby magpie that she was fascinated with that day. I remember it because the baby was making a heck of a noise due to being hungry and his mother was feeding him some worms. And I looked at him and thought it odd because he was almost as big as she was, give him another week and he probably would have overtaken her, especially with the speed in which he was ramming those worms in. I thought he was definitely old enough to be searching for food on his own instead of wearing his poor old mother out. I had been keeping an eye on them because they can get quite nasty when they are raising their young, but these two were far enough away to not be a problem, and for magpies they were a pretty placid pair, I think they had more important things on their minds than interfering with us. The baby was the furthest one away and the mother kept sneaking in and out amongst the trees, hopping along searching for worms, she got closer to us than I thought she would at one time but the dogs didn't bother her and she didn't bother the dogs which is more often than not the case here but I always keep a close eye on them anyway just to be sure. Also, if you look real close one of the horses is grazing near the trees but I think you'd need a magnifying glass to see her. I only saw Whisper was there when I enlarged the photo on my computer. This day was a happy one, there was a light breeze blowing and the smell of coconut dog shampoo filled the air and that is why this photo touches my heart so much and that is why it was chosen as the cover. It was a lovely family moment for my camera to capture forever and I'm so glad I had my phone on me at the time.

We lost Lumen (17), Lilly (11), Amber (16 and a half), Steffy (15 and a half) and Ruben (16 and a half) while I was writing and editing this book and we lost Brian (13 and a half) a few weeks before I started doing the second edit. And then just before the book went into print, we lost our darling girl Baby (15 and a half) who we more often than not referred to as Baby Baby. You will no doubt have noticed their names in the dedications, and it is really nice to have all but two of them on the cover. When I first started writing Always and Forever I was living in a very different household to the one I was living in when I finished it. I wrote this book with Lumen, Lilly, Amber, Steffy, Ruben, Brian and Baby sleeping all around me. They were my little writing buddies and so they are very much a part of this book. They may not be mentioned on all the pages, but they are woven into this book in a very big way. Of course I wasn't trying to capture their essences when I took the cover photo but as it happened I did precisely that, one glance sums up everything they were and I feel for the rest of my days whenever I walk by this book I am going to pick it up and look at the cover and smile as I recall each individual little soul. The only thing I am a bit sad about is that Ruben John Comer and Baby Baby aren't on the cover. Ruben was up on the deck sleeping that day, I remember glancing up, making note of where he was, and he looked so happy laying in the sun so I turned and went back to having a conversation with the thought in the back of my mind to keep an eye on him in case he got too hot. Baby Baby was inside the house fast asleep in the middle of one of the big soft lush dog beds. I saw her as we all walked out the door, she was in a deep peaceful slumber and didn't even open that one little eye of hers as we all filed by and in not wanting to disturb one who looked so serene I left her where she was. I knew once she woke up she would woof for one of us to come and get her, so we were both listening for her call coming through the open windows. But she was still sound asleep when we all came back inside. But if I knew how things were going to go, I would definitely have gone and brought Ruben and Baby down to be with us because they both deserved to be on the cover of this book too and I did think about trying to Photoshop them in but I reckon that would look kind of tacky. The best thing I can do is put a photo of Ruben and Baby on the pages before the first chapter starts that way their faces will always be part of this book too just like all the others are and my heart sits right with that.

I hope you enjoy reading Always and Forever. From my home to yours I send you much love.

Andrea Comer

Ruben　　　　　　　　Baby

CHAPTER ONE

Emily

Time and time again I'd hear people telling me how beautiful Emily was. And I agree she was our best looking pug as far as "Judged by the world" beauty goes. She has a beautiful apricot tone running through her coat, her mask is jet black and she has a wonderfully shaped head and face, and her tail has that perfect curl that pug lovers adore and she is a good 6 years younger than Tommy and all but one of her sisters so she stands out for that reason as well. Emily is what I call a well-bred pug. Just stunning, stunning, stunning, I wouldn't have been surprised if there are ribbons in her history, watching her walk, the way she holds herself I'm certain she would have been a hit in the show ring if her previous owners had been into that sort of thing. But I know for a fact that they were not. Emily has a prettiness that stops people in their tracks. Whenever we have somebody new to the farm I know that after the pugs have stopped circling and dancing, had a pat, settled down and the novelty of a house full of pugs has worn off they'll eventually get round to looking more closely at each one's face and they'll soon zoom in on Emily. They always, always zoom in on Emily. Now a days I don't even have to look which one they are referring to when they ask about the pretty one. I just keep on making the cups of tea, don't even turn around, just shout over my shoulder that her name is Emily. One even referred to Emily as being Cinderella and I didn't like that at all because it would mean that her siblings were the ugly stepsisters and I wasn't having any of that kind of talk in my house and told them so. All the pugs in this house have been through some form of sadness that brought them to us, and some have been through absolute hell and they deserve understanding. And even the ones who were truly loved and well looked after before they came here, well they've suffered to, not as much as some of their siblings have suffered but their lives have been turned upside down all the same. They've still had to get used to a new home, new people, and a new routine and when one is old such things can take a bit of doing. So no negative comments no matter how flippant were going to be spoken about them. Sure, I understood how attractive Emily was, I mean she'd have stood out in a house full of young healthy pugs so I knew why she stood out here in amongst those who had been forced to live incredibly hard lives. But I didn't think she should have been the only one to receive an extra round of praise, I felt the attention should have been spread around more evenly. I remember my Mum told me once when I was quite little that everybody has something good about them and that it was our job to look for it, she said in some people it was harder to find but it was there all the same. That has always stayed with me. Sure, we'd all like to look like supermodels but those creatures make up such a small percentage of the population. The rest of us are sitting there being perfectly nice and kind and beautiful people on the inside and yet eyes are drawn elsewhere, and I wasn't going to allow the other little souls in the house to have what was special about them go unnoticed. One of my friends was wonderful though she would really look at all the pugs and saw what I saw in them and she'd rub their little ears and tell them what she'd seen, and I loved her for doing that. I think the only one on this earth who wasn't aware of Emily's beauty was Emily herself. She didn't much care what she looked like. In her eyes she was no different to any of the other pugs. No matter how many people made a fuss of her she couldn't see why she was receiving so much attention. They were not as important to her as she was to them and this was especially true at the start, back then Emily had a lot of other things on her mind and it took her a while to get those things sorted out, but I'll tell you about that a little bit later on.

Naturally Emily liked getting attention, she played up to it a lot of the time, danced about, came close, jumped up for a pat then danced off again before coming back round for another shot at it and of course the guests are always thrilled to see her coming back. Happy eyes search for her as she comes dancing through the crowd. I sit at the kitchen table smiling at my other pugs and wait for the Emily extravaganza to demise. The older pugs all go back to their beds when Emily is being adored, they've seen it all before countless times and are bored by it. I used to feel sorry for them, go over stroke their heads and whisper in their ears that it's ok because they are the most beautiful things in the world to me, but now I just smile at them from across the room, some are so old they don't want all the attention Emily receives anyway. They are beyond that, they are loved and secure in themselves and once the visitor has acknowledged them with a soft stroke and a warm hello they are happy to go back to their comfy beds and continue sleeping. And once the novelty has worn off for Emily, she too becomes disinterested and so will go and lay down and drift off to sleep. But with Emily appearances were very deceiving, her problems lay hidden, they are, or should I say were, on the inside, they were undetectable to the adoring eye. My other pugs, well, their past life battle scars are on the outside so everyone can see them, to the human eye Emily's battle scars were invisible but they were there all the same and no less significant or traumatic because you couldn't see them. Emily came from a troubled background and her mind was scarred because of it. A pair of elderly dog hoarders had her as part of their collection, she was shut away in a house, whose four walls were her entire world, the only world she knew.

One day I got a phone call from a lady in rescue that had been to visit Emily's house. She and a few other rescue organizations were working together to help re-home a large percentage of the dogs living in that home. I was only familiar with two of the rescue groups, and by familiar I mean I knew their names and had on occasion exchanged emails and phone calls, the other organizations involved I'd never had any association with at all. This particular lady had been talking with the old woman who had Emily for a few months when the phone call came through. She didn't go into any great details when we spoke, only said that there were a lot of dogs living in that house. She was pushed for time, I could hear it in her voice, she just needed a quick "Yes" or "No" answer from me so she could be on her way. And she wasn't being rude, this happens a lot in rescue, I know how hard the people running rescue groups work, they are some of the busiest people I know and so I always let them say what they have to say and let them go because there are many more phone calls to be made and many more jobs to get done. A lot of the time I get a call while somebody is on the road driving to their next pick up or drop off, so I keep my side of the conversation as short as I possibly can as way of being respectful to them and all the jobs I know they have lined up. They work all day and well into the night sometimes and get little time to themselves.

All I was told at the time was that this rescue lady had been sitting in the lounge room of the old lady's house when a little pug peeped it's head round the corner. She tried to get the pug to come to her but it quickly disappeared down the hallway again and never came back. I guess Emily was just curious to see who was visiting the house that day and once she'd had a look at their faces went back to whatever she was doing before the doorbell rang. This lady said she'd thought about me instantly and wondered if she was able to get the woman to give this pug up would I be interested in taking it in. I said yes right away and she hung up the phone. I didn't even find out if the pug was male or female, that's how quick the conversation was. There was a black pug living in that house too, but the black pug wasn't mentioned to me during the initial phone call. Only later was the black pug brought up in conversation and I said that I would take the two of them, but there was a mix up with so many dogs being taken from the house and the black pug ended up going to somebody else which was a pity really because I would have liked to have kept these two pugs together, I thought it would have helped them both tremendously to do so. Well I know Emily would have managed better if she'd had a little friend from her old home helping her figure out her new one, she wouldn't have felt so alone in it all, she would have had somebody who understood all that she was going through because they'd have been going through it all as well and could have helped each other I thought. I mean I was helping Emily but of course I couldn't comprehend everything she was feeling because I'd not lived through it the way she had. But the black pug did so they would have been an asset to one another. I hope the black pug ended up being well taken care of and its needs understood too, the way Emily's were being. A lady from one of the other rescue groups rang up one day and asked how the two pugs were settling in and I said I only have the fawn one, it was only then that she realised a mistake had been made and the black pug hadn't come to me. But all the rescue groups involved were run by fantastic and incredibly dedicated people so I've no doubt things would have worked out for the little black pug.

During this conversation I was told a little bit more about Emily's previous home, this lady had more time to talk so I sat back and listened. Someone who'd visited the house said there were at least seventy dogs living there, another one said fifty-five, I guess with so many dogs running round it would have been pretty hard to count them all. A large percentage of them, including Emily, were living inside the house, no access to outside. Some were outside permanently I was told but the house was on a normal sized suburban block with a normal sized suburban backyard, so most were kept inside to prevent them from barking and being complained about. I guess the people who lived either side of this house must have been on pretty good terms with the hoarders otherwise those dogs would have been removed from the home a lot sooner than they were. I guess they had been living next door to this elderly couple for many years and could have even been elderly themselves. Either way they must have been incredibly easy-going neighbours to be living beside that house and not protesting about the noise. Perhaps they had been living there so long that they no longer heard it, you know the way one does when living beside a freeway.

I couldn't believe what I was hearing when she said about the amount of dogs, in fact I asked her to repeat what she'd just said because I was certain I'd misheard it. Steffy was standing in the middle of the lounge room screaming her head off for a reason that I hadn't quite figured out yet and Ruby, because she knew dinner time was approaching was swaying by the oven doing her growly little woofs and because she was woofing a few of the others had decided to join in. Ruby was like a dinner bell in our house, once she started up everybody jumped to attention because they knew what her woofing meant. I was listening to the conversation but it was constantly being drowned out by my hungry little pugs. In-between the screaming and the growly woofs I thought I'd heard the wrong amount of dogs said so I stepped out onto the veranda, closed the door behind me and asked if she could please repeat the number of dogs for me again. But I'd heard right, no mistake made, Emily had somewhere between fifty-five and seventy brothers and sisters of different breeds. All small breeds of dogs I was told and only two of them pugs, but yes so very many in total. That information blew my mind. I couldn't imagine what that sight would look like. I couldn't even imagine thirty five dogs let alone fifty five or seventy, my mind couldn't begin to conjure up such an image, and that's really saying something for me because I am very visual, very artistic, I sometimes see things other people don't see so when I couldn't get a picture in my head to go with what I'd just been told that blew my mind even further. After Emily came to live with us, I'd be driving along the road and see sheep or cows grazing in a paddock and pull over and start counting them, trying to get a picture in my mind of how Emily's life had been, the most I counted were forty and that looked like a whole lot of animals visually. I once pulled up at the afternoon milking of a dairy farm up the road, there was a long line of cows, two or three abreast, all waiting to go into the milking shed and that line went on and on. It kind of gave me an idea of Emily's previous life. I imagined there being a line like this at mealtimes starting in the kitchen and stretching all the way down the hall way. But at least those cows were out in a wide open space breathing fresh air. I was told some of the outside dogs were kept in cages. Inside the house they were all running free and doing their business in the house too, imagine what that would have smelt like. I don't know the full story of how those rescue groups found out about this lady but I'm glad they got to her when they did otherwise the situation could have gotten much worse. Her husband was sick at the time, and I think perhaps that's what made her reach out for help. But she wasn't letting go of her dogs so easily, she trusted very few people, but luckily the folks running those rescue groups were some of them.

    I actually had the opportunity to talk to the lady myself and at the start she was very abrupt on the phone, seemed quite guarded, like she was used to people being nasty to her and expected that I may be the same. But over the course of this long conversation she started to warm to me and began talking about Emily, not a lot about Emily more about all her other dogs. Although she did say that Emily was special and used to sleep on her bed every night but I'm not sure how true that was. I can't recall what Emily's name was before she came to us, I'm pretty sure she had one though just can't recall it for the life of me now and neither can David. Anyway, I named her Emily after Emily Dickinson because I had a quote on the wall at the time about hope having feathers that Emily Dickinson wrote and I really loved that quote so that's how Emily became Emily. During our talk the lady said how much she was against flying dogs. She was elderly and set in her ways, she had never put a dog on a plane before and wasn't about to do so now. She herself had never been on a plane and didn't want to put a pug she loved through such an ordeal. I guess when she picked up the phone she had too many dogs barking to hear the interstate peeping, either that or because we'd been talking for over an hour, she had forgotten that I was not in the same state she was in which in fact meant Emily did have to get on a plane. At one point she asked if I lived far away from her and I said that I did and I think she was about to delve further when one of the dogs yelped because she'd stepped on its paw, when she came back to the phone after sorting that out she had forgotten what we'd been talking about and I didn't remind her. I just kept quiet while she told me about another one of her dogs, she'd told me this same story once already, but I listened again anyway. There was a lot of that going on, she was talking about one thing then kept constantly swapping to another when she became distracted. And she was being distracted a lot by what was going on inside her house.

In the end the old lady agreed to hand over Emily to one of the rescue groups and she was then put on a plane and sent down to me. But because this particular group didn't know much about me they had a lady from a rescue group here in Melbourne collecting Emily and I was to meet up with her. I think this was done for two reasons, one was in order to fully check me and David out, see what kind of people we were face to face. I have no doubt that if this lady had not liked what she'd seen or had gotten a funny feeling about us in any way that Emily would never have been handed over and nor should she have been. I would never hand a dog over to somebody I had a strange feeling about and I wouldn't care if I offended them either, gut feelings are given to us for a reason. Once a dog is in that persons care they are helpless to protect themselves, so the rescue groups need to be very careful about the people they allow to take their dogs. The other reason would have been because I may not have even showed up to collect this pug and I guess if that had been the case then Emily would have gone off with this other lady and a good home would have been found. And I agree wholeheartedly with what they did there. You get told an awful lot of lies in rescue and you learn not to trust people, trust has to be earned. People will promise you the world and it'll all just be meaningless words spewing off their tongues at an alarmingly fast rate, I've never understood how people can do this, it's certainly not how I was brought up. But the funny thing was the group who sent Emily down rang this lady while we were getting our new pug out of the crate, it was hard because you could tell they were asking her question after question about us, questions that were hard to answer while we were standing right there. But bless her, she was doing her very best to answer each one all the while smiling sweetly at us as she was doing it, clearly the people on the other end of the phone had no idea we were standing right beside her. David was giving Emily a drink of water and I was handing over the money for the flight and here this poor lady was trying to answer these questions without really saying what she truly wanted to say, she was sort of speaking in code and I felt sorry for her having to do that so I motioned to David that we should move away and let her talk to these people privately. By this time we'd been in this lady's presence for a while and I think she got a sense of the kind of people we were. You don't get eye to eye contact over the phone so lying is an easier thing to do, in person there's nothing to hide behind, everything is out in the open, little quirks and gestures of uneasiness can clearly be seen and I've no doubt this lady had been in the game long enough to know what to look for. But the conversation flowed so easily and a few laughs where had. She was sussing us out I know she was, but it didn't come across that way at all, it was all done so naturally. Eventually the lady came looking for us and when she re-joined us she seemed a lot happier and more relaxed than she had previously been. We passed the test and all reports back said that we were lovely people. She'd even told the rescue group that we'd brought water and a bowl for Emily because they are always thirsty after a flight, she said a lead, harness and some chicken was brought for her as well and that the biggest fuss was made when she came out of the crate. I think it showed that some thought had been given to this pug that was coming into our care.

I remember meeting the lady and talking to her but at that point we had not been shown Emily, then after a bit of conversation had taken place she said "Would you like to see your pug" and both David and I took off fast after her. I couldn't wait to see what Emily looked like. I remember peeping round the enclosed crate to the mesh area at the front so I could see her face. The lady said "She's a pretty one" and she certainly was. David was kneeling down in front of Emily's crate fiddling with the clasp to get her out. She was frowning looking at what he was doing and her wrinkly forehead was amazing, then she turned when she saw my face peeping round at her. She had the most stunning face, perfectly set ears, a wonderful apricot coat, I said to David "She's not fawn she's apricot" before gazing at her again, really taking her all in, that wonderful head, that perfect mask. Everything about her appearance was amazing, her fur was super soft too I was about to find out. She looked like a soft toy, a very well-made soft toy pug, really really plush. Whether she'd been living with a hoarder or not she had been very well taken care of and I mean not just fixed up by a rescue group to go to a new home taken care of, but long term taken care of, extremely well looked after and I know with hoarders that isn't always the case. I think the elderly couple must have been receiving a lot of help with their dogs because no way could they have done it all by themselves. Unless not all the dogs were as well cared for as Emily and I'd just been lucky enough to have gotten one of the good ones. The condition she was in made me smile because I really wasn't expecting that. When Emily started panting her teeth were revealed and I noticed there was a huge gap in between her bottom row of teeth. Dead centre it was. Not like she'd lost a tooth or anything it was just naturally how her teeth were. I guess that's how the hoarders had gotten hold of her in the first place, she was perfect for the show ring until the judge had a look inside her mouth, points would have been taken off for the set of teeth Emily had been born with. I thought she looked kind of cute sitting there smiling up at me with her gappy crooked little teeth. It was like she'd played a trick on me the first time we met, like she'd let me soak in the flawless vision and then all of a sudden sprang open her mouth. Like she was saying to me "Oh you think I'm prefect don't you, well get a load of these" and you were now looking at a row of teeth that where just about as crooked as you could get, all up and down they were, so uneven, like a rickety picket fence. And of course, I thought that was it as far as imperfections went, and it was until we got her home and the trauma of her past life began to unfold. I knew Emily had issues even before I found out what her old life was like because she had begun telling me about them through her actions long before I got that second phone call from the rescuer.

Emily was a troubled little girl. She was unresponsive when I spoke to her, she'd look at me blankly, didn't even put her head on one side, just stared at me from across the room all vague like and she wasn't deaf I checked, she was just dazed, shell shocked about what had just taken place in her life. She'd gone from a dark, heavy curtained over crowed house with barks and bodies, many many bodies, bodies standing, bodies sitting, bodies laying and bodies sleeping all over the place to bright wide open spaces with only a few old pugs wandering around. For the first few days she sat motionless in the house, she was aware of the sheep and horses outside the windows and of course she would be they are too big to miss, but she didn't respond, she saw them I know she did because her eyes went to them and she stared blankly at them too, the same way she did with me. She didn't go closer to the windows for a better look or anything, just saw movement out there, acknowledged it very quickly with her eyes and then went back to being unresponsive again. I tried picking her up and placing her on my knee to have a quiet time with her like I do with all our new pugs, but Emily wasn't having any of that, she madly fought me off. Clawed at my arms until they bled but it wasn't her fault. Clearly Emily wasn't used to being held, I think she thought I was going to do something terrible to her. So, no more picking Emily up for a while, I tried something else, something less scary as a form of bonding. I thought I'd give her head a little stroke and say hi each time we passed each other in the house, I thought that would be less distressing to her. But she'd duck when I tried to pat her and would run a mile whenever the fly swat came out. There are hundreds of flies on the farm every year, but I never like to use fly spray when the pugs are in the house. I don't like the idea of those little lungs breathing in the fumes. So, I swat and swat even though it takes forever to get them all, it's like playing fly tennis only I usually have a swat in each hand to make it quicker. Emily was absolutely terrified of the fly swat, which told me that this was how discipline had been dished out to her at some point in her life. And what made things worse was that Emily arrived on the farm during some very hot weather and that is the worst time for flies here, she'd run and hide under the bed or run to the other side of the house and peep round the corner before re-entering the room just to make sure the swats had gone away. I tried showing them to her, letting her have a sniff, placing the swats on the floor and walking away so she could approach them at her leisure, but nothing made any difference, the hauntings of her previous home still took up a real lot of space in her mind. She even watched on as a few of the pugs picked up a swat and carried them off to have a chew, saw that they weren't afraid of them, but she still was.

None of the others had a problem with the fly swats, Horton didn't particularly like the sound they made but he wasn't scared, Harper was oblivious, and Sarah would try and catch the fly in her mouth but only if it landed on her face or body she wasn't the type to go chasing it all around the room. Steffy couldn't hear it so it was all the same to her and Tommy was so laid back you could swat a fly off the top of his head and he wouldn't bat an eye which is a beautiful thing really that he's so calm, but of course I'd never swat a fly that was on top of somebody's head. I'd shoo them off first then try and hit them mid-air sending them tumbling to the ground, then quickly step on them before they have time to come round and fly away again. You have no idea how many times this has happened in our house, you think they are dead and then out of the corner of your eye you'll see them rise up and fly off and then of course the hunt is on again. But the funny thing was they would often come back and land on Tommy's big old head again, he was like a Venus fly trap for luring them in, for some reason they were drawn there, probably because there is so much space or because his big flat head looked like a perfect landing spot to them, like they'd be flying through the air then zero in on him. I used to say to David that it was like there was another fly on top of his head waving flags guiding them in. And I would have dearly loved to be able to massage the top of Tommy's head with a fly swat all the while rolling a fly into an early death. I think Tommy would have enjoyed that, the fly not so much, but such a thing would have lulled Tom to sleep I'm sure of it. But that's not how it works with flies is it, you can't approach them slowly, it has to be hard and fast and hitting them hard and fast would have startled and hurt Tommy and Tommy had never known cruelty in his life, he'd never been hit, I wish that was how it was for all dogs in this world but sadly it isn't. Obviously Emily had been hit. Maybe it was before she went to live with the hoarders. I don't believe the hoarders would have hit her, they wouldn't have the time to, unless a fly swat or similar object was used as a threat to keep all those dogs in order, a way of gaining control of the mob perhaps. I've never understood how anybody can hit a dog. There's really no need, dogs long to please their owners, they are in love with us, we are their world and they live to make us happy, to hear our words of praise or get a reward. They'd much rather hear your voice light with praise than low and firm with rebuke. Your voice is all you ever need use, once you've spent some time on basic training that is. Any dog that comes into your home will need you to spend a bit of time with training otherwise they have no idea what's expected of them. You wouldn't know how to behave in a new home if nobody explained the rules to you, it's no different for your dog, many people spend little to no time on training and yet expect a dog to instinctively know what to do. That's asking the impossible, dogs are smart, but they are not clairvoyants. People then have the nerve to be annoyed with the dog when it does something they don't want it to do. Basic reinforced training doesn't take long, and the rewards are well worth it, plus it can be a lovely bonding time for the two of you. Once a dog knows what is expected and has settled into their new home the two of you can then live in a harmonious state together.

    I'd never had a dog in my care like Emily before. I began reading her the way I do with every pug I welcome into my home but at times it was hard to figure out what was going on in Emily's mind. She reacted to things so differently to the way other dogs did. We would try and work out why she responded the way she did to certain situations so we could help her through them. The fear of the outdoors was where her biggest problems lay. She would stand trembling when I took the other pugs for a walk, I didn't push her to come with us, just left the door open so she could join us when she was ready. But it took her a very long time to be ready and of course it would, she was used to living her life inside a house. It saddened me that something as natural as a walk terrified her so badly. It was like she wanted to come with us, desperately wanted to be with her new family but her mind wouldn't allow her to do it and it was hard bearing witness to that because I knew what was going on inside her. Her little mind was caged, she was imprisoned. Physically she had all the room in the world to run around in but mentally she was trapped, you could see it in her eyes. She was torn, tortured and stuck because of what was going on inside her head and my heart went out to her. Her face when I walked out the door was the saddest sight to see, but I had all the other pugs to think about, I couldn't disrupt their routine it wasn't fair on them so I turned and walked out the door, but gee my heart was heavy when I did so, the entire walk was done thinking about little tormented Emily sitting in the house on her own. I did think of picking Emily up and doing the walk with her tucked under one arm, but I didn't feel that was the right thing to do. Sure, it would have gotten her used to being outside quicker but I didn't feel I had the right to force her hand and of course she didn't like being picked up so to do such a thing would be doubly wrong. No, if Emily was going to come outside she had to do it herself and only time was going to make that happen, and of course we have plenty of time here.

A fortnight on and Emily was more responsive, she'd become used to being in a new house and became queen of it in a way, it was her domain, she wasn't bossy with the other pugs at all she was beautiful with them actually, but she did make sure she was in front of them all when I was moving around the house. And she wasn't trying to be their leader I just think she was a young pug who needed to have something to occupy herself with at all times and following me around the house was it. And being so much younger than most of the others she did find it easier to make her way to the front, at times I don't think it was even intentional, it was just naturally how the pack flowed. She was always a few steps behind me watching what I was doing, if something was happening inside the house regardless of how boring, she wanted to know what it was and followed me from room to room, at first on her own and then a few weeks later when she discovered the toy box and the joys of diving head first in there she started following on with a toy in her mouth. I don't think she'd had many toys before coming to live with us but she sure did love playing them now that was clear to see. She played with them daily, and not gentle play either, more like a bull in a china shop, grabbed hold of one by the arm, leg or ear and go thundering through the house with it. She liked flinging them into the air and catching them in her mouth then dancing round and round the kitchen table with them before flinging them up into the air again. And then she'd be off either dancing in circles or thundering. She amused herself for hours doing that. Even during the night she did it, I'd wake up and hear the racket and smile because I knew Emily was enjoying herself. She'd pounce on her toys and shake them like crazy, lots of limbs came loose because Emily played so rough but she was so joyful in those moments, when she was playing it was like she forgot all about her fears and it was lovely seeing her that way, a sign of things to come I thought and that made me happy. Inside the house Emily was now more or less just a normal pug, well apart from the going to the toilet indoors but that was to be expected wasn't it and we would deal with that in time. You can't blame her for doing what she had been doing most of her life. In time she would be housetrained but you can't possibly housetrain a dog that feared going outside because where else was she going to do her business, we had to deal with her fear of the outside world first and that was going to take some doing so we just cleaned up her mess and didn't give it another thought. And because Emily was going to the toilet inside a few of the others started doing it as well, Grace had a relapse and started weeing indoors again. I think she thought if it was good enough for Emily then it was good enough for her. But I knew once Emily got sorted out in that area Grace would too, so I just cleaned up both of their messes for a while and left it at that.

It was around this same time that Emily decided that everything outside the windows was now worth keeping an eye on. She became very interested and aware of every little thing that was going on outside, sure she still didn't want to be out there herself but she liked knowing what went on and spent a lot of her time sitting staring out the windows, watching birds, watching the horses and sheep, watching flowers in pots blowing in the wind, these days most things out there fascinated her. She'd be on the couch and fly off as soon as one of her paddock siblings came into view. And she'd hit those windows so hard at times I was afraid she was going to break them. She wasn't an overly heavy pug, but she sure could make those windows bounce, I'd hear it and I'd see it. She must have entertained herself like this in her old home, and who could blame her really because it'd be pretty boring for a dog to be locked inside a house all day and night, she'd have to do something to eliminate the boredom and looking out the windows must have been it. And when she came here this house with our floor to ceiling windows, entire walls of them, well she must have been in her element. She'd see a bird fly by close to the windows and leap up trying to catch it and she could get pretty high into the air as well. She'd go from four paws flat to the floor to her entire body up in the air in no time, such a great springing action, very fit, very healthy and incredibly agile and such a thing really stood out here with all the oldies. I was actually a bit surprised by her fitness level, I didn't expect her to be half as fit as she was considering she'd lived her life inside a house but I guess she must have spent all her time running around that house, she ran round our home too and never got short of breath, I knew when she eventually did start coming on the walks with us that she'd have no trouble keep pace. She was just so athletic. And I never feared for the real oldies in the pack because although Emily was constantly thundering around the house, she always slowed down and moved very delicately round the other pugs and sometimes she would jump right over the top of them without any trouble at all. I once saw Ruby stagger to her feet and begin slowly walking to the water bowl to get a drink, at precisely the same time something outside caught Emily's eye and she flew off the couch fast. I could only watch on and hold my breath as there was no way I was going to beat Emily across the room. If I knew it was going to happen, I would have scooped Ruby up or gone and stood in front of her to protect her from getting knocked over. I stood watching on thinking that there was no way this was going to end well for Ruby but then Emily just very gracefully sprang up high and went straight over the top of her then hit the window with a bang and started going nuts at whatever was out there. And little Ruby just carried on doing her penguin walk across the room. I don't think she even realised that Emily had gone over the top of her. In fact, I'm sure she didn't because her face didn't alter and she didn't pause and look up, she just kept on doing her determined funny little walk to the water bowl, head down, powering along with that resolute look in her eye that Ruby used to have whenever she was on a mission. I think Ruby and I were just very lucky that Emily could jump so high, she could jump up and touch the doorhandle on our glass sliding doors, well when the door was closed she would anyway because it was more or less just like a window then. But if the door was open she wouldn't go anywhere near it, always kept herself a few steps back, like she was worried if she got too close one of her siblings may accidently knock her out the door and she wasn't taking any chances. She always made sure to keep herself safe, like she'd be enjoying all that was going on but always well aware of how close she was to all three doors at all times and I thought that was a very sad way for a little pug to live.

It made me wonder what had made Emily so fearful of being outdoors. I wondered if this was just an individual thing or if all the other dogs living in that house were as terrified as she was. My mind kept going over things wondering if she was actually bred in that house and never allowed outside or if she'd come to live there as a one or two year old and been held captive for so long that she couldn't ever remember being outside. I wondered what brought her into the lives of those people in the first place. I also tried to figure out what kind of set up her previous owners had because it'd be pretty hard to keep so many dogs inside. I mean as soon as the door opened you'd imagine all of them flying through it, running for their lives just to be able to have a sniff at a flower or wee on a bit of grass, even just to feel the wind blowing across their faces or the sunshine on their backs. It'd almost be like a jail break, those dogs would be pushing past their owner's legs trying to get out. In a normal situation you'd have a doggy door and the dogs could come and go as they pleased and for all I know this may well be what they had and that it was just Emily who refused to use the doggy door. If so, then something must have terrified her at some point and I had no idea what that was. I wished she could have told me, that way I could help her through it, help her heal and start really enjoying the benefits of living life on a farm. I figured she would let me know what it was in time, when she once again came across what had caused the crippling fear her actions would reveal everything she was feeling. Then again, she may never encounter it here, farm life is very different to suburban life, she could well go for the rest of her days and never see the likes of it again and for Emily that would be a good thing. I guess I would just have to wait and see.

In the meantime Emily was as happy as a lark with her life inside our house, sure I didn't like that she was still living exactly as she had in her previous home, but I had to let go of that for now and be proud of the progress she had made. And she had improved in little areas. I did think at one time of trying to give Emily her meals outside as a way of teaching her to be out there, like put the bowl closer and closer to the door each day until one day I actually put it on the doormat outside. Emily really did like her food and I figured if I had the door open while she was eating and just sneakily move the bowl slowly closer over the course of a few weeks, so slowly she wouldn't even know I was doing it, that I would soon have her main problem solved. But I decided against it because her fear of the outdoors was so great that I think she would have gone hungry rather than have to venture out there, so I'd still have a terrified dog on my hands and one that was now starving as well and what was there to be gained from that. Besides Emily had done nothing wrong, why should she be punished for something what wasn't her fault, something she had no control over. If Emily had it in her to go bounding outside and running around like a maniac, she would have been doing it already I've no doubt about that. All dogs like walks, they go nuts for them and the fact that Emily was terrified told me how much trauma she had suffered and for such things there are no quick fixes, no magic pills. Whether it's a human being or an animal that has suffered trauma, the road to recovery is the same, they heal when they heal and sometimes they never fully heal but are able to get to a place where a happier life can be lived. So Emily's tummy got filled each day and I felt good doing that. I liked that she was taking to our way of eating with such ease. Emily liked being in the kitchen when I was making dinner, forever watching me with those incredibly beautiful soft amber eyes of hers. She'd sit behind me when I was doing the dishes, always with her face looking towards the back door. The back door is the main door we use here on the farm, and she could see a lot from there, that's why it was so popular with Emily. She'd still not go anywhere near it, but her little apricot body would sit a few feet behind me whenever I was at the sink, I think it was because she knew I was going to be there awhile, so it gave her time to look out at things and have me standing there for security as she did so. She'd turn her head when she heard me muttering about our possessed sink because she thought I was talking to her. Well it wasn't the sink that was possessed it was actually the plug itself, it always used to let the water out in spring and we could never figure out why that was. I would leave hard to clean pots and pans soaking in warm soapy water and come along a few hours later to give them another scrub and find them siting in an empty sink, just a few bubbles lingering on the handles. We used to say that plug was possessed by the spirit of the great water waster. We came here in springtime and I can't remember if it happened that year or not, too much else going on with settling in and unpacking. But by the second spring the man we bought the house off had died and it used to make me think that perhaps he had something to do with it. He was always nice to me when he was alive but now he'd passed on maybe he wasn't a hundred percent happy that we were living in his home instead of him. Or maybe it was just his way of letting me know he was still around. But I thought doing it by using a sink plug was pretty weird and that maybe he could have found another way, a way of letting me know he was around with something that was perhaps a little bit less wasteful. Still, it sure beat him sneaking up behind me and tapping me on the shoulder. I thought about that one day while I was refilling the sink for the second time and suddenly the sink emptying itself didn't annoy me half as much as it used to.

Emily would also sit on the end of the couch watching on as I lit the fire. I have a real knack for being able to get a fire going in no time, that's from an empty Coonara with not a single twig in it to a roaring fire that resembles the pits of hell. Roaring and raging with the unlatched door banging, then I'll chuck a few more logs in and close the door fast and that's it, warm house, warm pugs, warm heart. I'm not sure if me being the fire lighting legend that I am is due to having years of practice or because I want to get the pugs nice and warm as quickly as possible. Either way I reckon I could give a boy scout a run for his money. When we first came to live on the farm I used to worry about how I was going to keep my old pugs warm in this house. We had no heater other than the log fire, I knew I wouldn't be able to flick a switch or turn a knob and have the house toasty warm in no time like I was used to doing in suburbia, I knew I had to get a fire going all by myself and not just get it going but keep it going day and night. Old dogs don't do well with cold. Our first night here I couldn't believe how cold it was. And because there was a mix up with the bank, on Johns side not ours, we couldn't get inside the house for a few hours and time was ticking away and we were all sitting in the shed just waiting for a phone call confirming the money had been transferred into his account. It was hard for the removal guys as they wanted to unload and be on their way and I felt bad that they were left sitting in their truck waiting. I felt bad for little old Ruby too because she kept going up the back ramp and swaying near the door wanting to be let inside. I think she remembered the warmth from the day we came down to look at the place and she desperately wanted some of that. But John wouldn't open the door for us until he knew the sale had gone through. And of course, by the time we actually gained access it was too late and too dark to find some wood and light the fire. So we all gathered in the bedroom with our small coil heater, closed the door to keep the heat in and put the pugs on the bed with us. Ruby was fine she had her little old head peeping out of the top of our blankets, she slept really well all night long resting her head on David's arm. We couldn't let that old arthritic body of hers get cold. Grace slept up on my pillow and Sarah and Harper made a nest on the side of the bed nearest the heater and that's how we all spent our first night here. The rest of the house was icy cold and it really hit you in the face when you nipped out to retrieve something from one of the boxes, hit you even harder when you took the pugs out for a nighttime wee. The next day we gathered some wood and got the fire going and we only needed to do it for a few weeks because the temperatures started to rise after that. But in remembering how cold it could get here in winter I started gathering sticks and branches whenever I was out walking the pugs and I'd drop them off in the shed to dry out before going back into the house. It was a good thing to do for two reasons, one because we had plenty of things to burn come winter and two it kept the paddocks clean and free of anything that the pugs could catch their eyes on. I still do the same thing today whenever I'm taking the pugs for a walk, do it all year round, if I spot a branch I'll race ahead and pick it up before anybody has the chance to walk into it. I'm always protective of the pugs eyes, it'd really hurt if they accidently walked into a fallen branch, so I make sure that doesn't happen. By the next winter we had replaced John's tiny Coonara with one three times its size because that's what was needed to keep us all warm. I've no idea why he put such a small log fire in a house such as this, in a house with so many floor to ceiling windows you need something far bigger to do the job properly. I guess he was just cheaping out.

My battle with getting a fire to actually light and then keep ticking over caused some issues our first winter here, when you have no idea about fires you just think that a bit of newspaper, a handful of twigs and a few logs on top of that and away you go. Well away it didn't go, time and time again that fire kept going out. I was a fire lighting failure back then. I had absolutely no idea about layering or about different types of wood. I didn't know what kind burnt longer and hotter than all the other types. I remember one day carrying this enormous log in from the shed. In my mind that log was going to keep us all warm for the afternoon and early evening. I heaved it up onto my shoulder and marched into the house trailing a pile of pugs behind me, Emily was watching from the middle of the lounge room and went and jumped on the couch as soon as I walked in the door. I don't know if she thought I was going to try and put her outside but with the size of that log I kind of had my hands full, still she was wary so backed away and went and sat in her safe place watching as I put the log in the fire. Well, tried to put the log in the fire anyway but it was too big to fit in, I had the fire really roaring because by this time I'd learnt I had to do that in order to keep the huge logs ticking over. At first I thought I just hadn't lifted the log up quite high enough, it was heavy so took some effort for me to put in. I thought it had caught on something, maybe a stick that hadn't fully burnt down yet so I half took it out and tried reloading it, but it still wouldn't fit in no matter how hard I shoved, so I tried moving it around a bit to see if it would fit in on another angle. No two branches are exactly the same, they are all unique and in some ways it can be like a jigsaw puzzle putting the logs in, especially when it's

my eye in case she came back. I knew in time she wouldn't be so boisterous, but that wasn't going to happen today or tomorrow or even next week, so I had to be always ready to brace myself for when Emily came charging at me. Some days she would accidently scratch my arms, neck and face as well, such was her frenzy and such was her strength that she would draw blood. Some day's one hug was enough to suffice, other days she returned time and time again. But being so overzealous she did tend to exhaust herself pretty quickly and eventually go back to her safe spot and fall asleep and whenever I heard her snoring I'd think to myself "Well thank god for that" and then checked where I was bleeding from in between dishing out hugs to the other pugs. Sometimes I didn't know if she'd bitten me or scratched me, either way it wasn't too bad, I've had worse, so when the oldies had all been well and truly hugged I would go off and tend to my wounds. I could handle the hugging and I was happy she'd had another breakthrough, but I had to warn people coming to the house not to hug Emily until she had settled down somewhat. And everybody wanted to hug Emily because she was so beautiful, and some had been waiting many months to actually be able to hold her in their arms. But they'd see my scratches and know to hold off, well all but one of them did, and that lady ended up getting bitten by Emily and it wasn't Emily who was at fault. I don't know if it was an excitable nip or if she was terrified of somebody who she wasn't used to hugging her, I think it was the latter though. Again, it wasn't too much of a bite and the lady had been well warned, the bite came up in a bruise but there was no blood drawn and that lady never tried to hug Emily again. And nor should she, like you talk to the people who enter your house about the new dogs in your care, but they think they know better and that's when things go wrong. I remem-

going to be a very cold night and you want the fire to last. David can be crouched down in front picking up different sized logs to fill every available space. And you never quit until there's no more room to put anything else in. You can be boiling by the time you move away but you persevere because you want to keep your old blessings warm all through the night and it can be quite a feat loading that fire because pugs being the curious little creatures that they are want to be up front seeing what's going on and you have to keep moving them back for their own safety, so it's you, the pugs and a basket full of logs and sticks all gathering round and then a pug will grab a stick and run off with it and have a little chew, but they never think to bring it back when the novelty wears off so you then have to go picking up the sticks that at times can be scattered all throughout the house.

Well I tried hard with this huge log but it still wouldn't fit in and all this took a bit of time so when I finally gave up the battle and dragged it out one end had already caught fire. Sarah was standing closest to me so I put the fire out fast so she wouldn't burn her face and then of course the log started smoking, and I was trying to pick it up but it now seemed a lot heavier than it had been in the first place. So I'm struggling with the smoldering monster and all the while the house is quickly filling up with smoke and Emily was watching all this going on, still on the couch but her beautiful eyes never once left me. I kept looking over at her and talking to her and she acknowledged me but she never moved position. After a few tries I eventually managed to pick that log up again and I knew I had to get it out of the house as fast as possible. So there I am tripping over pugs trying to get out the door and I make it onto the deck, glance down to make sure no pugs are in my path and then I run and sling that smoking log off the edge of the veranda and out into the front paddock to cool off. Emily with her amber eyes was viewing all this with much curiosity, I could see her though the window, she was now teetering on the arm of the couch to get a better look, she'd seen me rushing by and was all bug eyed with excitement. That beautiful face of hers turning towards me then looking out into the paddock trying to see the log, she jumped up onto the back of the couch, saw what she was searching for then quickly jumped back down again. I bet she was thinking that her old home was pretty nuts but watching me and my antics was something else entirely. I'm just glad she couldn't talk because many things happened during the day that due to not wanting to look like an idiot I failed to tell my husband about, and I'd imagine on my most foolish days that Emily would have been rushing at David telling him all that had gone on as soon as he got home from work. And I wouldn't want that, the less he knew about my stupidity the better.

So the log has been dealt with now but I'm left with a house full of lingering smoke. Instantly I go rushing round ushering all the pugs outside because I didn't want them breathing it in, but of course Emily wouldn't go out, so I left her where she was and went around opening all the doors and windows, having large sliding glass doors going off the lounge room and kitchen area was great because you open them up wide and it's almost like taking out an entire wall. I pulled the fly screens across so the pugs couldn't get back inside the house and they are all there lined up, little faces pressing against the lower part of the screen, but smoke rises so it was blowing out of the house over the top of their heads, a fact I was very happy about. I put the ceiling fans on as well to get the smoke moving faster and in no time at all the house was cleared so back inside come all the pugs and they are so overjoyed about that that they go dancing round the lounge to prove it, but of course now the house is freezing cold so I had to get a fire going again. This time two smaller logs were chosen instead of one big one, which is best for keeping a fire going and I just kept adding more and more logs throughout the afternoon. That incident taught me that there are no shortcuts when it comes to log fires. Log fires need constant tending to and watching, it's almost like having an extra pug in a way, you always have to be keeping an eye on how they are doing and seeing if they need your help. But they are worth it because they are beautiful to look at and I like the sound of them too, the crackling is something I love listening to at nighttime when David and all the pugs are fast asleep. And of course the warmth you get from a log fire is amazing. Towels can take three days to dry with a normal heater but with a log fire they'll be dry overnight, and we go through so many towels here with the oldies so that's a good thing, nobody is a looser when you have a log fire in the house. And it's pretty nice seeing all the pugs sleeping in front of those beautiful dancing flames when it's bucketing down outside.

The pugs are smart though a lot of them will stay in their beds until I've got the fire roaring, some will be beside me, but most don't come near until they hear the roar of the flames, the level of warmth has to be worth the effort of them physically moving. Until that noise is penetrating they know it's probably warmer to stay where they are for the time being. But once the fan is on, once there's a heat source, they rise up and come gathering around. I love watching them there all huddled together, they look like a litter of young pups only they are all different shapes and sizes and most of them are wearing colourful knitted coats. They resemble a basket full of Easter eggs. One day they were all huddled up together like that and I was standing above looking down lovingly at my precious little bundles and thinking about how blessed I was, then out of the corner of my eye I saw something moving inside the fire, the fire wasn't exactly in full roar yet but it was getting there fast, a few flickering flames were bopping about behind the glass and I had been aware of them, but this movement was slightly different to that of the flames. So I bent down for a closer look and there was this tiny little lizard peeping out of a hole in one of the logs I'd just thrown in. I couldn't get that door open fast enough, the log was blackening but not totally on fire yet so I grabbed the end nearest the door, the end where the little lizard was staring out from and raced outside with it. I was hoping the lizard would stay put throughout all of this because if he jumped I could have stepped on him as I ran and not even realised I'd done it and I also didn't want him falling and breaking his little neck and I didn't want one of the pugs spotting him and pouncing on him either. I could have just put that log outside the back door, it would have been easier and faster but I wanted to get it back inside the shed, put it down as close to the spot where I'd just picked it up from in case the little fella had family there. The log was warm and I guess I could have put it back in amongst the pile of wood but I figured that this would be the one time in history that a slightly warm darkened bit of redgum had been able to ignite a cold stack of wood and set an entire shed on fire. Would have kind of defeated the reason for rescuing him in the first place wouldn't it. He was such a cute little thing though, a skink lizard he was, and I was so glad I'd seen him. If I'd walked off as soon as I'd put that log in and not paused to marvel at my sleeping pugs, he would have been burnt alive. Also, if I'd stood staring out the window into the green paddocks like I tend to do a lot, well I wouldn't have seen him either. I guess he must have been sleeping and felt the rising heat and on realising that it was a lot hotter than the heat of the sun decided he'd come out and see what was going on. I mean I would never have known I'd killed a skink so wouldn't have that on my conscience but it's nice to know that a little soul didn't die that day. From then on I always moved the logs around in the shed first and walk away, just to give anything living in there the chance to scurry out and off. Then I'll go back half an hour later and bring them inside for the fire. I make a lot of noise and movement when I'm carrying those logs inside. And sometimes I'll prop the logs with the most holes beside the heater for a few moments just to give somebody a second chance and I stand there watching on and if a spider crawls out I jump on it because I don't want it biting the pugs. I just say to it "Sorry mate, you can't win them all" and stomp stomp stomp until they are dead. Normally I don't like killing innocent things and I do allow some spiders to live in the house, the ones that are known for eating other spiders for example, the ones that are not harmful to the pugs. But when you are bringing something in from the shed the rules change because there are all sorts of nasties living out there and the safety of the pugs comes first. It was the same one day when I was carrying in a bit of wood and looked down to see the biggest huntsman spider sitting there looking up at me. I am not afraid of a lot of things in life, but a huntsman spider can have me screaming like a little girl in two seconds flat. It's because of an incident in my childhood and I've been terrified of them ever since. So here I am carrying this log in and was just about to walk up the back ramp when I saw the spider and my heart went ballistic. And I was looking around to see if there was an area where I could toss that log but with so many pugs around me I knew I didn't have a clear enough space, so I just quickly brought my other arm round, made a fist and flattened him, then carried on walking into the house. As I stepped inside the back door I thought to myself "Well that's another thing you've conquered in your life Andrea". I guess nothing, not even my crippling fear of huntsman spiders was going to make me endanger my pugs.

I reckon it was a good four or five months before Emily decided that she'd like to try this hugging thing for herself, and I can clearly remember the day she asked to be hugged for two reasons. One was because she'd had another breakthrough which was great and two because of how rough she was. After the first attempt at hugging Emily during the first week of arrival I hadn't approached her again. I figured she had enough on her plate without me hassling her with something else so decided to let the hugging thing go and that in time she would let me know if she was going to be a hugger or not. After my experiences with Steffy I knew that some dogs just didn't want to be hugged and that was ok, if I was now going to have two dogs in the house who didn't like hugs so be it, that was going to have to be how it was because I believe they all have a right to be who they are and accepted for it. Their overall happiness is all that is important, nobody should be forced to do something they are not comfortable with. Emily was always sitting next to Steffy and because Steffy didn't like hugs but loved tummy rubs I'd make time each day to give her some of what she adored. Whenever I had a spare moment, I'd go over and sit next to Steffy, rub her tummy and hug whoever else I'd brought up onto the couch at the time. Emily would be on the other side of Steffy watching what I was doing, soft amber eyes noting what was going on but never once joining in. She felt protected I think having Steffy in-between us, the end of the couch was her safety zone. And because I wanted her to feel like she had a safe place I never reached my hand over Steffy to touch Emily. Sure, I could have done so quite easily but then Emily would have felt like her spot wasn't safe anymore and I didn't want that. Emily's eyes were on us but she never once moved closer to get involved, she did lean forward to see what I was doing with the pugs on the other side of me, saw they were being hugged but she didn't seem to want any part of it. And I wondered if she even knew what we were doing. Steffy didn't ever want to be on my knee, but she did love being sat next to and stroked but Emily didn't even want me doing that. She was happy to watch or not watch and just go to sleep depending on how she was feeling that day. As I sat with Steffy who generally within the first five minutes of me sitting down would be flipped over getting her belly rubbed and screaming with joy about it, I would study Emily's sleeping face, I used to wonder if she missed the dogs she once lived with and how often she thought about them. I'd never witnessed her looking round for all those other dogs, but they had to cross her mind from time to time didn't they. Our pug family was pretty big to some people but to Emily it would have been miniscule compared to her previous home.

    One day as I was studying her sleeping face Emily woke up, I was miles away and didn't notice at first that she had woken up. I used to look at her face and then gaze out the window totally lost in my thoughts. Steffy was stretched out on her back, I had Ruby on my knee and Sarah, Harper and Grace were fast asleep on the other side of me. Tommy was on his special chair beside the couch and was snoring away contently. I was deep in thought, totally lost in my own little world and when I glanced down again at my bundle of blessings I noticed Emily's beautiful eyes were open and she was staring right at me. "Oh you've just woken up" I said to her, which is always a silly thing to say I think because of course she had just woken up, why else would her eyes be open. Me talking to Emily caused her to bolt upright. She was now sitting facing me and engaging. I made space near Grace and moved Ruby over, Emily looked at my knee, I saw her eyes go to it, she saw that it was now vacant. She sat thinking about things for a few moments and then all of a sudden leapt over the top of Steffy and landed splat in the middle of my lap. From there she didn't quite know what to do with herself, I guess she'd been watching me with the other pugs and decided that day she wanted in on the whole snuggling experience. I didn't envelope her for a few moments because I wondered if she'd made a mistake and was jumping on me on her way down to the floor, did she just want a drink of water and was using me as a steppingstone. But she didn't jump down she sat there looking up at me, so I put my arms around her and she got so carried away that she flew at my face hard. I thought she'd broken my nose, there was a lot of blood. And it wasn't her fault, she was being rough because she didn't know how else to be, I knew that once being hugged became second nature to her that she would soon settle down which is exactly what she did.

I don't know what changed her mind, what made that particular day any different to any other, but she decided from now on she would like to hug me. But she was such a rough hugger, it seemed the tomboy in her really came to the surface when she wanted a hug, for weeks I had to be careful of not getting head-butted in the face.

She went from not allowing me to put my arms around her to trying to smash my chops in due to the excitement of it all. There were no baby steps with Emily and hugging, she went from one extreme to the other. That first hug caught me off guard. It didn't dawn on me that she didn't know how to hug nicely, that she didn't know anything about tenderness. But I knew what to expect from then on so kept my nose well out of the way whenever Emily came over for a hug. In one way Emily's hugs were beautiful in another way it was like being attacked by a lioness. She really hurt me that first day, but I couldn't let on what she had done because I knew it had taken an awful lot for her to come over to me like she did. So I just hugged her roughly back, I wasn't going to be able to get her to settle down and be gentle on our very first hug so I hugged her the way she was hugging me because that's about all I could do. But I was also sneakily trying to keep her from causing more pain, not enough so she would feel rejected because I didn't want to do that to her, just enough to lessen the impact of her. I tried to dodge her blows and run my hands over her all at the same time. And I also had to try and keep her from accidently banging into one of the other pugs who like me were now sitting there wondering what on earth had hit them. Our hugging sessions were normally gentle, slow and soft, but this was like having a hot piece of coal in your hands and juggling it to stop it from burning you.

 I couldn't have the older pugs upset and I couldn't have Emily upset either, so I was trying to work in with them all and keep everybody happy. But gee I was glad once Emily had her fill and went charging back over to the other side of Steffy, it gave me time to catch my breath, recover and then carry on snuggling one of the calmer pugs but I was always watching Emily out of the corner of

ber Grace got very sick one day after I'd had a few ladies over for lunch. I had politely asked them not to feed any of the pugs as we all sat down at the table but one of them had to have done at one point because a few hours later Grace began vomiting up what I'd served those ladies. I always say things for a reason, and it does annoy me when people are disrespectful and refuse to listen because more often than not it's my pugs that pay the price.

Emily was now doing really well with most things in her new home, but she was still terrified of being outdoors and I was kind of hoping that by this point she would have been coming with us on the walks. But she was no different in that area than she was when she'd first come to live with us and that saddened me a lot. The months were wearing on and I still had a pug that was afraid to go outside. So twice a day I would leave her behind and off we would all go and have a wonderful time out there, I think if she knew how much fun walking around the farm was she would have been more inclined to come along because Emily sure did like having fun. But there was no way I could let her know how much fun it was without forcing her out the door and I was not going to ever do that to her. I'd look for her when coming over the hill on the way back to the house, but I could never see her until I stepped inside because she didn't sit by the door waiting for us she sat a fair bit away from it as open doorways still terrified her. This went on for months and months but over time she moved a little closer to the door, not much just a little bit, but I could now see her when I stepped foot on the ramp that led up to the house. I'd see that little face leaning forward sneakily watching for our return. She wasn't ready to move her body closer to the door yet so she'd lean as far as she possibly could do without toppling over trying to see as many of us as she could without physically moving her entire body. Her mind was still chained but she was at least interested in what we were doing which I thought was a good start, and she was especially interested in when we were coming back. She'd get giddy when we all filed through the door and start happily dancing in amongst us all. Never barked, never said a word, but she sure did dance. Danced and danced all around the room and swerved in and out between her siblings then off she went circling the room again. And even though she was excited she was graceful when she danced, she reminded me of a little fairy flittering around. She was thrilled to have us all back inside the house again and it was a lovely thing seeing her so happy. Especially after the way her face had been when we'd all walked out the door. She really did love her new family, her love for us was strong I could see that, but it was not quite strong enough yet to make her forget her past.

 I was almost at the point of accepting that maybe Emily was never going to be able to live life as a normal dog, never going to become the dog she deserved to be when one day I came over the hill and saw her standing at the back door, sure her face looked worried but she was at least looking out the door now and that was a beautiful thing to witness. I've had dogs with physical disabilities come flying down that ramp the first hour they arrived and yet here was this perfectly able bodied pug too afraid to put even one paw out the door. Not even confident enough to sit out on the back door mat.

When Emily saw us approaching she would get so excited her entire body would shake. Her ears altered, her entire face softened, and she'd start doing the whole excitable wiggly bottom thing. She was so pleased that we hadn't left her, so pleased we were coming back. At times she would be so concentrating on us that she'd have wiggle bottomed herself a few steps outside the back door before she realised what had happened and I thought great this is it, this is the day she's going to run towards us then walk the short distance back to the house in amongst her pack. But it was not to be because once she realised what she'd done, her eyes would change, fear returned to them and she'd shoot back inside as fast as she could go then stand in the lounge room with her entire body trembling, trembling out of fear now, all excitement gone. And I'd come inside and talk to her to try and calm her down, on those days she didn't dance in amongst us all, on those days dancing was the furthest thing from her mind. She sat underneath the kitchen table and shook, and it took one of the other pugs barking at something by the window for Emily to stop shaking and start concentrating on something else. One day I felt particularly sorry for Emily, she was sitting under the kitchen table minding her own business and we'd just taken in a Chihuahua, we all came in the back door after our walk and then all of a sudden Henrietta the ferret faced Chihuahua came flying in behind us and went straight over to Emily and bit her, bit her hard enough to draw blood and Emily had done nothing to provoke the attack. She was just sitting there with her fears and at first I thought perhaps Henrietta sensed that fear and out of nastiness decided to have a go and of course Emily being the little nonaggressive sweetheart that she was did nothing to defend herself. She could have easily had old ferret face on the floor in a death hold if she'd wanted to because she was so much bigger and heavier than Henrietta was, but she just sat there and let herself get bitten. It was the saddest thing to see. Henrietta was given a time out until she calmed down and I tended to Emily's wound. It was the only time this happened, I didn't see it take place, yes, I saw Henrietta run in and heard Emily yelp but because I was facing the opposite direction I can't say exactly what went on. Henrietta had very little vison so perhaps she wasn't being nasty like I first thought, perhaps it was something as innocent as her running inside the house and simply bumping into Emily and in fright getting confused and lashing out. There are all sorts of reasons why things like this happen and it's not always a case of you having a nasty dog. Yes, Chihuahua's have very different personalities to pugs and can be quite vicious at times but it was a one off incident and it happened during the first few weeks Henrietta was living with us, while she was still getting used to being in a new home, so you have to take that into consideration.

I remember when we were picking up Henrietta from the airport. She was in a carrier and I had been talking to a friend who had a lot of experience with taking in Chihuahua's and she was telling me how some of them are so vicious that the rescuers have to pick them up wearing oven mitts. I had this funny vision running through my head when she was telling me but really it wasn't a very funny situation at all. It would have been a bit scary and intimidating for the handler, imagine having this little thing going nuts and having to protect yourself from its bites by wearing padding on your hands and arms. She said sometimes they strike out due to fear, sometimes it's previous life issues and what the poor little things have been subjected to and sometimes it's just the personality of the dog and that more often than not once they are in your arms they'll soon settle down and you can then ditch the mitts. In knowing this I had fully intended to take some oven mitts with us on that trip. But I was busy setting the pugs up for us being gone awhile, giving them a long walk to empty their bladders, putting extra water bowls and blankets down that sort of thing. And with rushing around so much I left without the mitts, and I hadn't yet told David about how some Chihuahua's could be. I thought about doing it as we were driving along but we were talking about so many other things. Well, that and I had forgotten the mitts hadn't I so didn't want to be frowned upon again. We were very late leaving as it was and it was all because of me and Dave wasn't too happy, I didn't want to be frowned upon for something else as well, so I let that one go. But when we reached our destination, I did something I'm not very proud of, I chickened out and let my poor unsuspecting husband get Henrietta out of the carrier and stood there silently watching on all the while praying like mad that we hadn't been sent down one that was vicious and nasty. And maybe I am just trying to defend myself here, but I did think it wise that somebody who didn't know how Chihuahua's could be was the one lifting her out, if I was doing it she may have been able to sense some uneasiness and that could have made her worse. But David having no idea what could potentially happen confidently opened up the carrier and gently lifted her into his arms and she didn't respond in any way at all, she wasn't nasty and she wasn't overjoyed, no tail wagging but no teeth baring either which I thought was a good thing. I finished signing the paperwork and breathed a sigh of relief that it had all gone so smoothly. On the way home I did tell Dave about the oven mitt thing, I sat there with my new ferret faced daughter on my knee and told him the entire story and you should have seen the look he gave me, and that look was quickly followed by a few choice words. He wasn't impressed with me for a while after that, sure we laugh about it now, but back then he thought I was a bit of an asshole for doing that to him and I can't disagree there either because I know very well that I was.

One day something glorious happened with Emily, she was sitting at the top of the ramp when we came over the hill and she wasn't shaking and she had no fear in her eyes, this time her eyes were sparkling when she saw us and although her body didn't run towards us it did start dancing all around the deck and once we got to the top of the ramp she began dancing in amongst us and then danced herself back inside the house with us all. She was so happy and so much freer than I had ever seen her. It was like she knew she had done something very special that day and was proud of herself for doing it. I had to step back outside again to collect one of the lingering pugs and I was hoping Emily would come outside with me to do that, but she didn't, she kept on dancing round the lounge room instead. And that was fine, she was happy, that was all that mattered but it did make me wonder if this would be a onetime thing, I hoped it wasn't going to be but in the back of my mind I was wondering if she was thinking to herself that she'd been outside now, and it wasn't all that different to how things are inside. And in a way she would have been right in her thinking because the deck and the house aren't really all that different to one another but a walk, well a walk is where the real fun can be had, but she had to be willing to take those extra steps to experience it. The next day we all walked out the door and Emily sat on the couch watching us go, I glanced back but she made no effort to come with us, wasn't even interested in politely walking us all the to the door. And she didn't have a toy to occupy herself with because that had fallen to the floor a little while ago and she didn't bother jumping down and picking it up like she would normally do so I figured she'd lost interest in playing with it and knowing I would soon be taking the pugs for their walk I thought the loss of interest was a good thing. I was hoping it may make her want to come and join us. I knew if she was squeaking a toy then the toy would win, but it made no difference, Emily was staying put. So out the door, down the ramp and into the paddock we all went and much of that walk was spent thinking about Emily. I was desperate to know where she stood as far as a taste of the outside world went but I couldn't rush the pugs and ruin their walk, they loved sniffing, so I strolled along at a leisurely pace watching them enjoying themselves. But when we started heading home, I found myself striding ahead with all the pugs clambering to keep up with me, I stopped once or twice to let them catch up then off I'd go again. As I neared the house, I was overjoyed to see Emily once again sitting on the back doormat waiting for us. I think perhaps she didn't come out at the same time we did because she was still afraid of being pushed or having me close the door behind her, I think she felt safer creeping out when there was nobody else in sight. It was lovely to see her body dancing but this time her eyes looked like they were dancing too. She even danced halfway down the ramp to meet us. It was only a few small steps as far as distance went but it was a huge step as far as progress went and Emily had taken it all by herself and that thrilled me no end. I started praising her softy, only softly because even though I could have roared and cheered and been loud due to my excitement I didn't think that was the right thing to do. So a whole lot of soft praise was given in an enthusiastic but low voice, and I held out my arms to her and Emily came to me and I stroked her velvety soft ears and told her what a good brave wonderful little girl she was. Emily got a treat, and her siblings got a treat too and even though nobody knew what the treats were for they ate them quickly and looked around for more. After that Emily was always sitting at the top of the ramp when we returned from our walks. Now both the house and the decking area were her safe places and I thought that was great because she could get used to all the outside noises while she was out there and if something scared her for some reason, she only had to take a few small steps or one big bounding leap and she'd be back inside the house again. This was the best way for her to get used to everything around the farm, sounds, smells, sights, everything and yet feel perfectly safe while she was doing it, she was building up her confidence every time she went out there. Then one day she was further down the ramp as we came over the hill, and then a few weeks later she began waiting for us at the bottom of the ramp. One afternoon I was carrying Grace back home and put her down when Emily and the house came into view. I held out my arms wide and called out her name and Emily went from sitting down to standing up but didn't come towards me, so I called her again when I got to the gate and this time she came to me, but she didn't walk upright while doing it, instead she kept her body close to the ground and crawled along, like a person would do when crawling underneath a fence. Although she was moving much faster than a human being would be able to move so covered the distance between us in no time. I think being close to the ground made her feel more secure. When she reached me she stood upright and danced around my feet all wriggling and giddy with excitement, lots of body shaking being done but no fear there. After that I'd call her as I was further and further away from the house and she came to me each time, still crawling along the ground though and only standing upright once she reached my side but she didn't go back to crawling when we all walked to the house, she kept herself upright for that so I guess being in amongst her pack gave her some security and I was glad that they could do that for her. Then one day she was actually sitting in the middle of the paddock waiting for us as we came through the clearing in the trees, and I opened my arms wide and she flew into them. No crawling done this time she just stood up and ran at me. Clearly her eyes had been fixated on that clearing because she knew quite soon her family would be coming through there. Seeing that beautiful apricot body sitting on the lush green grass was an amazing thing to see. One of the pugs started doing little woofs at Emily as we approached, as if to say "What are you doing out here, don't you belong inside the house". I guess it wasn't only me who'd noticed that Emily didn't come on the walks with us, I hadn't thought about it at the time because my mind was only on Emily, but it seemed that the other pugs had given some thought to Emily's behaviour too. As they shuffled down the ramp I guess their minds occasionally wondered why the new pug was staying behind. I doubt they would have thought about it as long as I did though because the first sniff at something interesting and their minds would be on that, whereas my mind was always drifting back to Emily because I was worrying about her. When you think about it our farm with its wide open spaces must have been absolutely terrifying for a dog that had spent all its time locked inside a house. And the noises we enjoy, the noises that we think are so soft and relaxing must have been deafening to her, like everything was on high volume. Dogs have so much better hearing than we do, I bet even the birds chirping must have been crashing sounds to her. And the cows over the road even more frightening and we have a lot of tractors round here, imagine what those engines sounded like to Emily. Even our horses calling out to each other would have been magnified and terrifying because she wasn't used to hearing them. No wonder she was too scared to venture out. It'd be like a deaf person who had been deaf their entire life suddenly being able to hear then being made to stand in the middle of a busy city street. How absolutely petrifying would that be for them, they'd be begging to be made deaf again I'm sure, well I know I would be anyway. I had a lot of understanding for Emily and all she was going through. Her first week here even our house would have seemed enormous to Emily, the reality is it's only small but without another sixty dogs filling it, it would have made the place appear far bigger than it is because there would have been more room to move around.

I think it took great courage for Emily to do what she did after the closed up life she'd lived. Once she conquered her fears and gained self-confidence her true personality came through and she revealed to us she was a bit of a tomboy. Supermodel looks but rough and tough and ready to tackle anything, she became super interested in life and started hitting it full on regardless of the consequences. She was like a toddler getting into everything and making a mess as she went along. Emily became a very mischievous little pug. If there was trouble happening anywhere in the house or around the farm you could bet your life Emily would be in the thick of it and nine and a half times out of ten she will have started it. She didn't just sneak off and do things by herself either, she'd get everyone else in on the act, she was a bit of a ringleader. It was like she was always on the lookout for something new to get involved in then informed all her buddies what she'd found so they could have fun too. And by this time Steffy was well settled in, she no longer thought what anybody did was wrong, when she first came here she thought everything they were doing was the wrong thing to do and drew my attention to it by screaming the house down. But these days she was more at home so no matter what Emily was doing or how big a mess she made Steffy stood silently to one side watching her do it. To be honest I think Steffy was besotted with Emily, they were both the same age so were more agile than all the other pugs. They were the only two in the house that could get up on the couch by themselves, so they spent a lot of time sleeping up there side by side, the others being older all had to be lifted up. But Emily and Steffy ran across the room, flew through the air and landed on the couch with a thud then side stepped one another until they were comfortable. I had a few cushions on the couch at that time and Emily would grab hold of one of them and run through the house, then she'd drop it and pounce on it and sometimes run back and get another one and do that same thing with that. And that was fine I'd go pick them up once the cushion game was finished. And most days the cushion game was a quiet one but other days it got pretty rough because Emily would start shaking the cushions violently, at times hitting her siblings in the face and head while she was doing it, and they'd go toppling over and Emily would hear them fall and stop and look at them having no idea they were down because of her. I had to be very careful with her doing that with Ruby and Grace. Ruby could be sent to the ground so easily and Grace really got annoyed at being smacked in the face and would go and tell Emily off and in doing so would end up getting whacked again. Tommy and Harper never went near Emily when she had a cushion, they had little interest in what she was doing and Sarah, well Sarah could put a stop to that game faster than I could. I think even though Emily was in a mad crazy shaking fit she could still sense this looming disconcerting presence and would put the cushion down and slink away without making eye contact with Sarah. I think Emily was so young and so wanting to expel some of that built up energy and the cushion shaking game was her way of doing it. I knew once she began coming with us on the walks that she would be well sorted out in that area but until then she needed something to do and so when I saw the cushions taking a beating I'd go and pick Ruby and Grace up and move them away and then call Sarah to me so Emily could have a bit of fun. The cushions were old and ratty looking anyway so Emily was doing no harm there, if anything she was doing both me and the cushions a favour. Sometimes Emily would shake her toys as violently as she shook the cushions so for a few months all the long-limbed toys were removed from the toy box. I mean those things have quite a reach on them, the monkey's arms were almost twice the length of their bodies and Emily being so engrossed in the game would swing them round and round without care.

There'd be days when Emily would be getting into mischief non-stop. I'd hear a crash and think to myself "What's Emily up to now" I didn't have to think twice about who it was I knew it was always Emily, so I'd set off in the direction of the sound and I'd walk into the room and there she'd be smiling up at me with her gappy teeth and beautiful face. And I couldn't get annoyed with her because I felt she deserved some happiness, even if that happiness took me half an hour to clean up. I figured once she'd had a go at everything the novelty would wear off and it kind of did, in time she settled down a bit. But there were times when I'd accidently leave a box of cereal sitting on the kitchen table and go out to groom the horses without giving it a second thought. And Emily was a jumper, she could easily jump up on the kitchen chairs and from there would be able to reach her paw up and fling the box of cereal onto the floor. The box was then torn to shreds and the contents quickly eaten, she shared it with the others, but I have a feeling that she'd only let them have a go once she'd fished all the yogurt clusters out. What she was doing was harmless really, all just ways of expelling energy that she wouldn't have stored up if she was able to come outside with us for a walk, and also if there was no box left on the kitchen table there'd be no mess on the kitchen floor, how could I blame her for doing something that is natural to a dog, the fault there was mine so I'd put the grooming brushes away, sweep the kitchen floor and try to remember to put the cereal box back in the cupboard in future. A bit of spilled cereal is hardly worth getting upset about is it, it's just part of life with a houseful of dogs and especially part of life with a dog who is having problems in another area of their life. I do get upset when I hear about people scolding dogs for doing something without taking the time to really think about why it is that they are doing it. If you look at the behaviour and think about the dog and try and see it from their point of view it all becomes a whole lot clearer, and a lot of problems can be solved fairly easily this way. Once Emily started walking with her siblings she quietened down a lot in the house and I always knew that would be the case because now she had something to do in order to get all that energy out of her. She used to run full out across the paddock and circle round and round, she was having an absolute ball out there and then she'd come back into the house and have a rest. Emily now led the pack on most of our walks, she was like a race horse that everybody had counted out coming up from behind to win the race. When she first started joining us, she would always hang back, hang way back, like she didn't want to have anybody else behind her, nobody that could possibly block her path, get in the way of her getting back to the house as quickly as possible. She needed to have that as a form of security for herself and nobody much cared that she was hanging back or would sit down and wait until they were all a good distance away before slowly creeping closer again. To be honest I don't think anybody but Steffy really noticed, the others were far too busy walking and sniffing and entertaining themselves. Emily wasn't on their minds as much as having a good time was. Steffy noticed because that was her thing, she took it upon herself to make note of what was going on with all her siblings at all times. She was concerned about everybody in the pack and when one had this much fear inside of them well, Steffy would have quickly picked up on that. Steffy was a nurturer and a very caring little soul, just an all-round lovely kindhearted pug, the concern Steffy showed for her family I've not ever seen anything quite like it before or since and I'm not sure if I ever will. Steffy is special and has a gift, she is selfless, and it was beautiful to see her looking after everyone. I think some appreciated her help more than others but that's just how it goes sometimes, it's the same with human beings, some are grateful for any help they receive in life while others simply expect it. Steffy was the pug who bonded with Emily the fastest, but that was nothing new, a lot of the time Steffy seemed to bond with a new pug before anybody else did, it was just in her nature to do that. Also, I think that Steffy was able to sense everything that her new sister was feeling. Being deaf she took everything in with her eyes. Where the other pugs would have simply glanced over Emily, Steffy lingered, and a lot can be revealed when somebody is this observant. I know that Emily felt good when Steffy was around her, I could tell by watching the two of them together. Steffy tried to help Emily along a bit. She didn't stay in the house with her when we went walking because Steffy really did love her walks and looking out for her older siblings. I don't think she was going to stay in the house with one pug when she could be outside helping so many others. And helping others was always on top of Steffy's list. She loved her elderly siblings and had been looking out for them for quite a while before Emily entered the house and I don't think she was ever going to let them down in any shape or form, her caring heart wouldn't allow her to do it. But she did start doing something that I thought was really lovely and because I was concentrating on other things it took me a few days to pick up on it. Steffy started breaking away from the pack when we got close to the house, she enjoyed her walk with us and kept her regular pace but as soon as we neared the house she took off at high speed and at first I thought she may have needed a drink and ran ahead to the water bowl. When we come in from our walks there can sometimes be a mad rush to have a drink that's why I always make sure to freshen the water before leaving the house because if I pause to wait for somebody who is having an extra long sniff some of the pugs will beat me back inside and I want them to be able to have cool fresh clean drinking water waiting. Then when me and the lingering sniffer finally walk in the house the first thing I do is freshen the water once again so they too can have a nice clean fresh drink. I don't like built up slobber murkying the water, that's not nice for anybody to drink. To me it's like being in a family of seven kids and being the last one to bathe in bath water that the rest of your siblings have bathed in, oh I know you wouldn't be drinking that bath water but it still wouldn't be nice would it, you'd be trying to make sure to be the first kid in or if not the first at least be in the top three because anything after that would just be plain nasty. Anyway, Steffy wasn't running ahead for a drink because her chin was never wet when I came in, what she was actually doing was racing ahead to check on Emily. I guess she must have had the new family member on her mind as much as I did. I'd see her running up the back ramp as quickly as she could go. Then a few moments later her little head would peep out the back door as if to say "She's fine, we're all good in here" it was like she'd done a sweep of the place, found Emily, made note that she was ok and was telling us about it. She did this for quite a few weeks and once I realised what she was doing I used to look forward to seeing it each day and tried to position myself in the paddock so that I could see both the back door as well as the pugs that were walking with me. Some days it worked out and I'd see Steffy's little face pop out the back door and other days the pugs would be taking their time so we didn't break through the trees quite fast enough, and of course I couldn't rush them, so I missed seeing it and was always a little sad about that.

Normally Steffy was silent when she popped her head out the door but one day she stuck her out and started screaming like crazy, such was her distress that I left the pugs to make their own way back to the house and quickly ran inside. And as I was running so many thoughts where dashing through my mind, was Emily ok or had she hit the windows too hard this time and was laying in a pool of blood and broken glass, had Emily had a seizure, was Emily dead. Although all my thoughts were on Emily, I did first check Steffy over to make sure she was ok, she was still standing by the back door when I ran in so it was easy to do that, but she was fine so I turned my attention to Emily. I still had Steffy in my arms and was lowering her to the ground while glancing around the room seeing where Emily was. I noticed that she was on the couch, normally she was under or near the kitchen table but this time she was on the other side of the room. But she wasn't facing outwards, instead she was sitting with her back to the edge of couch, she looked like a naughty school kid who'd been made to go sit in the corner as form of punishment. She was also doing something else that I thought was strange, she was vaguely staring into space all weird like. I called her name, but she didn't respond and that was fine because she was still having days where she wouldn't. I felt a bit sick actually because I thought from the way she was behaving that she'd completely shut down, like mentally had a breakdown, that the loss of her old home, the flight down here and then having to get used to a new place had all been too much for her little system to cope with so she'd zoned out as way of protecting herself from that which she could no longer deal with. And from the way Steffy was screaming I felt that she had sensed it too. Emily hadn't even been this disengaging the first week she came here, she would at least turn and face me then, but now it was like she didn't even want to look at any of us. It made me wonder what had changed and why the change had happened so quickly. She'd been fine when I walked out the door, so this started me thinking that something had to of taken place while we were gone. Had Emily perhaps tried to follow us on the walk, gotten a few feet from the house before becoming completely gripped with fear and then slithered along the ground making her way to the back door and had that experience caused this rapid regression and was she ever going to be ok again. I thought it best to approach Emily slowly, no quick movements, but I also didn't want to startle her, I had to let her know I was coming. I wasn't even sure what I was going to do once I reached her because I'd not dealt with anything like this before. In my mind I was thinking that I'd get to her and she'd just sink down and pass away. Because she was facing slightly more towards one direction than the other, I decided the best thing to do was approach her from the side so that if her eyes were responding she would at least see me coming. Doing that meant I would have to walk through the kitchen, enter at one end of the island bench and exit out the other, because she was up on the couch Emily would still be able to see me if I did this, at no time would I be concealed from her view. But before I moved towards her I popped my head out the back door to see where the pugs I'd left behind were. Some were coming up the back ramp, but Ruby was still in the paddock doing her little penguin walk, but she wasn't walking towards the house she was going in the opposite direction. I glanced back at Emily and her situation hadn't changed but Ruby was getting further and further away so I dashed outside to grab her and Ruby being Ruby quickened her step when she saw me coming. I scooped her up in my arms and power walked towards the house. Steffy was no longer screaming when I stepped inside the door this time so I put Ruby in front of the water bowl and set off to see where things stood with Emily. As I walked through the kitchen I started singing to let Emily know I was there, she was used to me singing because I'd been doing it since she first arrived and she neither liked it nor disliked it, she just knew that such sounds always came from her new Mummy. As I walked toward her I noticed there was a bird sitting on top of the couch and that was what Emily was staring at. I hadn't even noticed the bird the first time I came in, I guess with being distracted by Steffy's screaming and the urgency in her voice I'd been on the lookout for something bad. It was hard with Steffy because her screams were hard to decipher at times, she was screaming because there was a bird in the house, but I'd picked up on it as her trying to draw my attention to something being wrong. And I guess to Steffy a bird being inside the house was wrong, or maybe she was trying to get me to help the bird find its way outside again, that it was the bird she knew needed my help not Emily. Either way with Steffy no longer screaming there was a lot more relaxed atmosphere in the house. I stood still and watched Emily. She was totally mesmerized by this bird, couldn't take her eyes off it, even all her siblings clambering in the door didn't distract her from her new little friend. Certainly, she was behaving a lot differently to how I thought she'd behave. If I had to pick a reaction to Emily encountering a bird in the house it wouldn't have been this one. Lunging at it yes, chasing it round the house maybe, but sitting still and staring at it like she was, well I would never have picked that. It was like she was thinking to herself "I've seen you many times flying by the windows and now you are in here sharing the couch with me, well fancy that"

The bird was a blackbird and of course it would be because I've been feeding blackbirds by the back door for a long time now. Not a cluster or anything just one or two at a time and when those two die off or go and set up home somewhere else I start thinking to myself that'll be it for me as far as feeding blackbirds go and then a week or so later another one will pop up and after it's gotten used to the routine of feeding it's mate it will start getting in on the act as well which is nice. I like helping them out especially on very cold days or when its pouring with rain. They wait for me each morning and come back many times throughout the day. I guess on this particular morning I had forgotten to feed them so this one decided to come in and help itself and on encountering Emily wasn't fazed at all. The blackbirds don't fear us. Most have been born in our hayshed so are used to the pugs, very used to me and David as well because they've been peering down at us all from the first day they hatched. We get so many nests in the hayshed, and it always thrills my heart when I see them being built because I know babies will be coming soon. And it thrills me even more when I see the female sitting on those eggs, from then on I'm forever watching and waiting for the tiny yellow beaks to finally appear and when I see those baby beaks stuck up in the air chirping for food, I start counting how many babies the nest has been blessed with. I feel like those babies are mine, my reasonability because they've been born on my farm. I close the shed door of a night so they are protected from predators. I feed the parents good quality food so they in turn can go nourish those babies, make them grow up big and strong. It's no surprise to me when I walk into the house and find a blackbird sitting in there somewhere. It's normally that year's babies that end up doing it because their parents tried the same thing last year when they were just as young and quickly realised it wasn't the right thing to do. But then a new family will be born, and they see their parents hanging around the back door without any fear. And I guess they are new to the world so say to themselves "I think I'll have a peep at what's in here" and then they don't know how to get outside again because their little bird brains haven't thought that far ahead. And their parents are outside more than likely thinking to themselves "Well you got yourself into this mess you can get yourself out of it". And they always do, after much fluttering they always fly through the door again, sometimes on their own, other times with my help. The light fittings are favourite spots for them to sit on, as are the top row of kitchen cabinets. I found one sitting on a kitchen chair once and he was a defiant little thing, he was looking at us all filing inside after our morning walk like "Took you long enough, now what have you got for me to eat" I never ever feed them when they are inside the house though because I don't want to encourage them to keep coming in. I always feed them on the deck but when the door is open that wide I guess it's too tempting for them not to want to come and see what the inside of the house looks like.

    I glanced over at Emily, and she was still sitting there looking at the blackbird, but more looking at it now like it actually belonged on the top of our couch. I suppose it had been sitting there so long she'd actually gotten used to it. This bird wasn't that far away from her face and Emily being the jumper that she was could have very easily had that little thing by the tail, but she didn't even try and attempt it. And as for the bird it must have sensed he was safe because he wasn't for moving. The other pugs were all standing around my feet and I knew this could get award, the blackbird was only a young one and I didn't want him or her freaking out now that all of us were inside. He seemed ok and calm when it was just him and Emily but now he was outnumbered and the look in his eye told me he'd just figured that one out. I didn't want him flying into the big glass windows and breaking his neck. In his haste to get outside he could have mistaken the windows for the wide open door, there wasn't much different in them, not to me and definitely not to him. I had to think fast before the pugs started heading to their beds, their beds were close to the couch, and I thought if the bird saw them all descending he may think it was him they were interested in not their comfy beds. I stood still for a few moments so the last of the pugs could have a drink and then slowly guided them all out onto the front deck and once they'd settled in the sun I came back inside to deal with the blackbird. Grace was the last one to file out the door and she was taking so long to come out that I did for half a second consider leaving her inside. She was a calm pug after all but then I quickly remembered that chasing birds was her thing and that having one inside the house would have been like Christmas morning to Gracie. Grace loved chasing anything with feathers, seagulls when we were walking along the river where at times the only things that made her walk and not constantly ask to be carried. The only birds she didn't try and chase were the pelicans when we lived on the lake, they were too much for her to take on, so huge against her small frame, and they'd swoop from across the other side of the lake to our back door and land right in front of us. The way they flew at us with that massive wingspan they looked like a jumbo jet about to touch down. It was imposing for me, imagine what it would have looked like to little 5.5kg Gracie. Still, she amused herself barking at them from her safe point behind the windows. They normally came in pairs and stood a few feet apart and she took turns barking at both of them. The pelicans for their part didn't even bat an eyelid at her. They were probably talking to one another in their pelican tongue saying "Is it just me or does that little dog look like an alien to you"

I closed the door to the front deck behind me and it was ok to do that, I know my pugs, I know once they've been fed and walked they generally settle down to sleep pretty fast. I knew none of them would come looking for me for a little while, so I had time to get the blackbird safely outside. Emily was still sitting on the couch with the blackbird, only this time she was facing out, she had watched me guiding the pugs outside and no doubt was wondering what was coming next. I thought her moving about so close to the bird would have been enough to send him flying across the room, but it wasn't, he just sat there above her head, and he too was staring at me wondering what was coming next. So I said to him "What is coming next dude is that you are going back outside where you belong". I moved closer to him, but he wasn't scared, more excited than anything because I think he thought I was going to bring him some food. I didn't want to wave my arms around and set him off in a panic, but he wasn't for moving so I walked around the lounge room and came at him from a different angle. When he saw me getting closer he took off and went and stood on the rug in front of the fire. I thought it would be a quick hop skip and jump from there and he'd be out the door in no time, but he still didn't move, not even when I got close to him, he seemed to not really care that I was there, so this time I moved my hands around a little bit but he just stood there looking up at me. Emily wasn't moving either, she was happily on the couch watching the scene unfolding in front of her. So I grabbed the corner of the rug and started dragging it and the blackbird across the room to the back door. I thought once he sensed the door was open, felt the breeze, smelt and heard the outdoors that he would simply fly off into the distance and all would be well. But he didn't do that, instead he flew to the couch again, flew over Emily's head to the exact spot he'd just come from. So I put the rug back in front of the fire and walked the same path of the lounge room I'd just walked and once again he flew down and stood on the rug. So again, I dragged him and the rug to the door and again he just sat there happily letting me.

I got to the back door and looked over at Emily. She was still sitting there watching what was going on. I think she thought this was just what we did here. Give young blackbirds magic carpet rides. To Emily everything here was very different from her old home, how was she to know what was and wasn't how her new Mummy spent her days. I tried getting behind the blackbird but he started jumping backwards on the rug and I didn't want him flying back to the couch again, so I stood still and called Emily to me. At this point she wasn't very good at coming when called, some days she'd respond other days she wouldn't. At first she just sat there staring at me like "What new Mummy, what are you saying to me, are you asking if I want a ride on the rug too". It was hard for Emily because if she did realise I was calling her she may have thought I was going to try and take her outside, I was standing very close to the back door after all. But I wouldn't have done that to her, if I hadn't done it already, I wasn't about to do it now. I guess Emily must have realised this because on the fourth or fifth call she did exactly what I wanted her to do. She jumped down from the couch and came bounding over to me and that was enough to make the blackbird fly out the back door. So the rug was put back, Emily was given a treat and the glass sliding door that led to the front deck was reopened. I then went around with a damp cloth cleaning up all the bird poo and you have no idea how much one little bird can do in such a short amount of time.

For a very long time Emily was happy enough to come on the walks with her family but she wouldn't come with us through the tree line because she couldn't see the house if she did and she needed to be able to see the house at all times for reassurance. But little by little she let go of that fear as well. Curiosity got the better of her and one day she just flew through the gap in the trees and ran around madly discovering the joys of the back paddock. She didn't take it slow either, no crawling along the ground, no timidly creeping in all quiet and shy, instead she came thundering through the gap then did lap after lap, checking out the fence lines, racing from one fence to the other doing incredible speeds and once again jumping over the top of her elderly sisters if they happened to be in her way. Steffy took off after her a few times but then was contented enough to simply watch on as Emily exerted herself. She reminded me of a horse competing in the Grand National only she looked far happier doing it. The one thing Emily didn't jump over and I so wish she had of done were puddles, instead she would run straight through them and seemed to love doing it, she didn't seek them out but if she came across them she'd run though each one making a splash. Even on cold days she'd run through them, she didn't seem to feel the cold, me and the rest of the pugs would go round them, but not Emily she loved getting wet and she loved getting dirty. Mud and horse poo were her two favourite things to roll in. Sheep poo she couldn't have cared less about, she didn't seem to notice that, perhaps it was because it was so small, and she was always running too fast to see it. Emily was given so many baths once she started going outside and she'd wrestle with me whenever I was trying to lift her into the laundry sink, so I too became smudged in mud and horse poo. I think she was making up for all that time she's spent locked inside a house, so I gave her free rein and let her do whatever she wanted to do, even if two baths needed to be given on the same day which did happen a couple of times, so be it, she was enjoying herself and that was what I chose to concentrate on. I'm amazed I didn't wash all the apricot out of her fur the first year she was here. I said to David once that I think she'll be a fawn pug soon if she keeps this up and we laughed about it and in the end I just used conditioner on her on the days she wasn't too dirty and a very mild shampoo when she did need a full wash. I was always aware of not drying her coat out. If it was only her paws that were dirty, I'd fill the sink up with just enough water to cover them and stand her in the warm soap suds for a few moments then lift her out and wipe her paws with a hand towel. And if it was only a little bit of splattered mud on her legs and tummy just being wiped down with a damp cloth was enough to clean her up, but horse poo well that was a different story all together, especially if it was fresh. That definitely had to be fully washed out otherwise she would have jumped on the couch and dirtied that as well and she could get herself up onto our bed and I didn't want her running all across the bedding when she was in that state. Although the couch was in more danger of being messed up than the bed was because although Emily could get on our bed with ease, she very rarely did which made me think that perhaps she had never spent the night on a bed in her life. The old hoarder told me that Emily had always slept on their bed with them, but I don't think she did, if she had of she would have sailed through the air each night when we got into bed but she never even thought about doing it. They always tell you what their old lives where like by their actions and if Emily was used to sleeping on the bed with her owners she would have said so. I think it was just the old lady's way of saying she had a lot closer relationship with her dogs than she actually did, I mean she was probably telling everybody she spoke to the exact same story, which would mean that around fifty dogs would have been sleeping on her bed and no way could that have been the case. The most dogs we've ever had sleeping on the bed with us at the one time was nine and we know what that was like, very little room for us, but they were old, and they were needy and we got very long years out of those dogs. David made a special partition and attached it to our bed to give everybody more room but as those of you who sleep with dogs know, you can give them as much room as you like and it makes no difference at all they are always going to want and come lay right beside you or right on top of you as is sometimes the case. They want to be as close to those they love as they can possibly get and there is absolutely nothing wrong with that. I mean you sleep all squashed up and pray for more room sometimes but then you lose a few of them and you'd give anything to be laying there in that squashed up position once again. Although maybe I am reading the old lady wrong, perhaps she was saying to everyone that the dog they were getting slept on the bed so that the people who were adopting them would take the best care of them, have them living as true members of their family and not just be chucked outside to live and I certainly can't blame her for doing that.

One thing with Emily that became evident as soon as she entered the house was that she liked being up high, couch, coffee table, kitchen chairs, kitchen table too sometimes but she always got told off for that, she liked jumping up and sitting on all these things, so I'd have to keep a close eye on her because jumping up is one thing but jumping down is quite another because they can really hurt themselves. Emily could jump higher than any pug I've ever shared my life with. At feeding time she would be jumping up at the glass sliding door, so excited was she about her dinner coming out. I had to put her outside while I loaded up the bowls because she could jump so high, she could reach the kitchen countertop. And she didn't have to take a run and jump at it either she merely sprang up into the air any time she liked, sprang high enough to come level with the handle on the doors, that's as high as she got, but for a small breed of dog that's incredibly high and no pug I'd ever lived with had reached the handles before but then again most of the pugs I live with are elderly and so such things are beyond them. And even if they could do it and I know they can't due to their bodies, but even if they could they wouldn't because with age comes sense and intelligence, they know that bowl is going to be put down in front of them soon so why put all that energy into exerting themselves when they can have a little woof and dance then be standing there ready to eat when the time comes. Younger dogs are quite different though and Emily would see me walking toward the door and boing, boing, boing she'd go jumping up in excitement. She was like a cartoon character only she was real and very talented in what she could make her body do. I thought she was pretty clever for being able to reach those heights and I thought I was pretty clever too because I'd be balancing four and sometimes five bowls in my arms without dropping them. I looked like a waitress at a busy restaurant and for a clumsy sod like me that was a pretty impressive accomplishment. But I'd have to watch my step for sure because as I was carrying those bowls out Emily was going boing, boing, boing beside me and all the older pugs would be dancing around my feet.

I did worry about the impact all this jumping was having on Emily's body though, yes she was young and agile now but what about when she got older, all that high jumping was going to catch up to her one day I knew that and so I'd try as best I could to discourage her from jumping up. It was her hind legs that worried me the most, they were taking the full impact of her body every time she hit the ground and of course Emily wasn't concerned about any of it, she was having a ball. You could see it on her face, but I saw things differently. I guess being used to older dogs I know how their bodies are when they reach double figures. And hind legs are a bit of a common problem area for older dogs, that's where a lot of weakness shows up, those back legs do take a lot of wear and tear over the span of a dogs life. Not just with jumping but the way they sit, those back legs take the weight of their entire bodies and if they've been sitting on cold flooring a lot of the time, which sadly some of the dogs we take in have, well that has a bad effect on them too. I see the impact their past lives have on my pugs. Their bodies tell the tale of how they've lived before coming to me and there is discomfort there, I can see it. Swollen arthritic joints are no fun at all. They are painful and make moving around hard. I didn't want this for Emily, sure I have a lot of dogs that come to me with arthritis but I have no control over how they got it, with Emily it was different, I had a chance of preventing her from painful golden years of life, well if not preventing then at least lessening it and so I tried as best I could to help her look after herself. And that can be hard because she was young and unthinking. It's the same with young children and teenagers, you try and tell them how life is going to be, but they think you are over fussing and tend not to believe a word you say. I remember the high heels I used to wear when I was a teenager and how my grandmother would try and warn me about how I'd be later on in life, she was there already and so was speaking from experience. She didn't want me suffering the same fate she did but of course I took no notice of her because all I cared about was how wonderful my heels were and how long and lovely my legs looked in them.

Although Steffy and Emily were the same age they weren't cut from the same cloth, they had two very different personalities dwelling within, so I didn't have to worry about Steffy quite as much as Emily. Emily was silly and careless. But Steffy was sensible. Yes she too jumped up on the couch and back down again but Steffy sort of leant into her jump down, almost like a diver leans into the dive and the couch is not all that high so she cut off some of the distance to the ground by doing that whereas Emily just flew through the air, she jumped level with the couch, sprang from it with no thought to how she was going to land. Her mind was only on that she was jumping off the couch for whereas Steffy's mind seemed to be on both getting off the couch carefully and then once she'd done that she'd trot off after Emily seeing what all the fuss was about. I tried hard to stop Emily from being too silly because I loved her and also Emily's mind had been traumatized, I certainly didn't want her body suffering trauma as well. It did make it easier though that Steffy had a whole lot of maturity and common sense built into her because it meant I would only have to be on the lookout for one pug. I only had to try and help Emily. If I saw they were about to jump off the couch I would race over and lift Emily to the ground which no doubt spoilt some of her fun, and I'd lift Steffy down sometimes too but more often than not Steffy had already lowered herself to the ground by the time I turned round to help her. Steffy would follow on watching everything Emily did, but she didn't try and copy her, no pounding hard on the windows for Steffy she was too levelheaded for that, she was contented to watch on while Emily acted the goat. And there were times when Emily hit the window so hard I thought any moment now I'm going to hear the sound of breaking glass. All throughout the day she'd do this and at feeding time too and it wasn't because she was fighting to get inside the house because by this stage being outside no longer worried her, she more just wanted her food, and I wasn't getting it to her quickly enough. Steffy often went out and stood beside Emily while she was out there, but she stayed low down. Although sometimes when Emily started jumping up Steffy would scream her loudest scream, it was her way of letting go of some of the excitement that was building up inside her. Emily never bothered at all about how loud Steffy was screaming, never looked over at her in astonishment the way some of the other pugs did, I guess Steffy filled the gap in the difference in noise levels between Emily's old house and her new one. I think Steffy went out there to keep Emily company but then would pick up on her excitement and start going nuts. They were a funny little pair, seeing them together used to make me laugh, here was one bouncing up and down and there was the other one screaming her head off. It was like they had their own comedy act going and preformed it often.

I did like the closeness between Steffy and Emily, they had a friendship and I thought that was good for both of them. Once Emily settled in she proved to be more dominant than Steffy was, but it didn't cause any issues between the two of them. Not even when Emily went and joined Steffy on the couch. The end spot was the golden spot and once Emily jumped up it didn't take her long to realise this. But the end spot was Steffy's special spot and had been for quite some time. When Emily decided to steal it Steffy didn't seem to mind, there was no squabble or anything Emily just stepped over Steffy and sat on the arm of the couch and when Steffy moved over an inch Emily slid down beside her and they both went to sleep. After a few days of doing this Steffy just naturally left a space on the end of the couch for Emily and that's how it was from then on. I guess in Steffy's mind leaving a space saved her from having to keep moving over all the time and because she wasn't territorial she let go of the prime position and didn't seem all that concerned about it. Emily liked sitting there because she had full view of the front paddock, full view of the driveway as well and the back door could also be seen clearly from that spot to. I think that's why Steffy had chosen it to begin with because it allowed her to be able to keep an eye on her siblings at all times, Emily couldn't have cared less about the others I think she just liked it because this was her home now and she wanted to know everything that went on around it. And they both lay pretty close together so Steffy could still see quite a bit, not the great view Emily had but enough of a view to still be able to look out for her siblings. And she'd often get down and go after them when she saw them shuffling along. Once Emily got rid of her fear, she would shoot out the door all the time too, no pausing didn't have to give what she was doing a second thought, she just flew through the doorway and off she went. I think the term "Hitting the ground running" is the most perfect way to describe Emily because that's exactly what she ended up doing. Never for her siblings the way Steffy did, it was always purely for herself and her own entertainment. Everything that went on outside those windows was seen and she'd fly off the couch, hit the floor with a thump and fly through the open door then go thundering down the front paddock to have a closer look at whatever it was that caught her eye on that particular day. And she wasn't one of those pugs that needed to always be by your side either, sure she always knew where I was, but she didn't need to be near me all the time to feel secure. Not anymore she didn't anyway because our entire farm was Emily's secure place now and she spent her days running out of the house then back in again once she'd had a good look around. While she was gone, I'd take the opportunity to grab the flyswats and play a bit of fly tennis, I'd be swinging at them like crazy until that little apricot body came shooting back inside. Then I'd quickly put the swats away and Emily and I would deal with the blowflies together. She was brilliant at catching them and the bigger they were the happier she was and because she could move really fast, she'd get them time and time again and that amazed me almost as much as it did the blowflies. She'd wait until they came bouncing along the lower part of the windows then snap at them faster than you could blink your eye. But she never ate them as some pugs do, I'm living with one here at the moment that eats them, but no not Emily, she'd spit them out as soon as she hit the ground and then go running off searching for more. She was a great asset to me in that area. The sound of blowflies drives me insane, when I hear them I go completely off my head until they've been dealt with, I hear that all too familiar buzzing and imagine they've just been sitting on a big pile of horse poo and are now flying through my home about to land on a nice clean surface and start rubbing their legs, dropping their filth. Sometimes I'd use a dishtowel and try and flick them as they flew by, Emily had no issues with dishtowels so I could flick one about anytime I liked. But it didn't work as well as a flyswat did, my aim was good, but they could feel something with that much weight coming towards them and turn and fly off in the other direction which of course drove me even more insane. But then one day Emily sprang forward and caught a big blowfly I had been chasing round for half an hour. And I was so impressed that she got it. I wish she'd gotten it when it first flew inside the house but she got it eventually and that was the main thing so much praise was given. She really liked the blowfly game. She would hear them the same time I did and go after them in almost the same mad fashion as I went after them, she'd be at one end of the room catching them in her mouth and I'd be at the other end dish towel in hand. Or sometimes I'd go grab a tissue instead and wait for Emily to work her magic then scoop the flies up as soon as she spat them out, being in her mouth seemed to stun them which gave me time to pounce. We became "The Blowfly Busters" me and Emily, we made a really good team. The only ones who weren't team players in this game were the blowflies, but nobody gave much thought to them. I think blowflies are incredibly cunning and very adapting, it's like every few years a new breed of superhero flies pops up, they are stronger and noisier and smarter than the ones you are used to dealing with so new tactics have to be put in place. You whack them and whack them, and they still won't die, they come flying back at you with a vengeance like they never felt a thing. It's at this point that you remember you have a can of fly spray hidden underneath the laundry sink, and you are almost at the point of getting it out, but you don't because you never want chemicals getting into those precious little lungs. Once the blowfly game was over Emily would go straight back to the couch. If Emily had been gone a while Steffy would have sometimes reclaimed her spot, but it was always freely given back to Emily on her return. Steffy didn't mind playing second fiddle and Emily was never mean in taking back that which she now considered hers. If Steffy was in a deep sleep Emily would simply sit on the arm of the couch waiting patiently for her sister to wake up and when she did a little bit of shuffling around was done and they'd be set for the afternoon.

That prime seat allowed Emily to see whenever we had a visitor, she saw the body approaching the house long before anybody else did so Emily became our greeting pug. She was the first one to make it out there to meet people and saw it as her job to see them off when it was time to leave. The rest of us would stand on the deck in a bunch, me waving, the blind pugs standing close to my legs and the sighted pugs trotting to the end of the deck, but that was as far as they'd go. That was enough for them, and we'd all watch Emily escorting the guests off the premises. She'd walk them to the gate and once it was closed and they were on the other side Emily would come galloping back up to the house. It didn't surprise me that Emily made such a good guard dog. She had perfect vision and the most excellent hearing so such a thing would have come naturally to her. She would hear and see a lot of things the other pugs missed. She knew everything that went on around our farm and there wasn't anything that happened on any of the neighbouring properties that she wasn't aware of, she took it upon herself to know everything that the neighbours were up to at all times of the day and night. She became quite the stalker actually and a very good one at that. I suppose even when they were doing something boring it was of the utmost interest to Emily. Being locked up in that house she would have missed out on a lot, but she was sure making up for it now. Emily had never been much of a barker, a few little woofs every now and then was about all you'd get out of her no matter how exciting the scene in front of her was. I thought the longer she was here and the more relaxed she got that her voice would eventually become bigger, but it didn't she was just a little soft spoken girl. And because she was so quiet lot of the time the people next door had no idea they were being watched. But there was always a set of perfect amber eyes noting everything that went on from her little hidey spot underneath our row of trees. Their comings and goings were always keenly observed. If Emily could talk she'd have a few good stories to tell I'm sure of that.

Having such a good guard dog in the house was comforting to me, especially when David was away on business which he quite often was when we first moved here. When he wasn't around the days were long and the nights even longer, so I used to try and really wear myself out during the day. I knew I would sleep well if I was exhausted and of course that would then be another lonely night I'd gotten through and one day closer to him coming home. I'd tackle any job that needed doing and not come back inside the house for hours on end. If the weather was nice the door was always left open for the pugs to come and go as they pleased. At the start they were all out there with me but then one by one they sought the comfort of their soft beds and would lay quite happily watching me through the windows. As long as I was in sight they were ok. But if I moved on, they would one by one come wandering out to see where I was, then back inside again for comfort once they knew what was going on. I used to make a bit of extra noise so they knew I was still close by and didn't have to keep getting up and checking on me all the time, they were old and I wanted them to rest so this worked out pretty well. One day I came inside and was so exhausted, I'd gone out after breakfast and it was now two thirty in the afternoon, so I decided to finish up for the day and close the door behind me, and because David wasn't here I locked it too. I didn't really need to lock it but when Dave wasn't around doing so gave me a little bit more peace of mind. I decided to plonk down and have a moment on the couch with the pugs, so I gathered some of them up and sat down for a little while. Well, it was only meant to be for a while but you know what it's like once you sit down, if you keep going you can get a lot more done but you sit and you find it almost impossible to get moving again. And besides I was now covered in sleeping pugs and didn't want to disturb them. I figured I may as well stay put so swung my legs around and was now laying down. I wasn't in the most comfortable of positions though because I had to work my way round the pugs when I lay down, it looked like I'd been thrown up in the air and landed all uncoordinated. My back wasn't how a back should be when laying down and it was letting me know it wasn't happy, my limbs were all bent on odd angels to accommodate the pugs. If I'd known I was going to end up laying down I would have done so in the first place then lifted the pugs up and they would have positioned themselves around me instead of me trying to position myself in around them. One arm was above my head to give a pug more room, the other arm was hanging over the couch touching the ground and I was stroking the pug who was sitting beside the couch, one leg was side on with the knee brought up and the other one had the knee bent so I didn't squash the pug sleeping underneath it. I knew I'd pay dearly for how I was laying but in that moment I didn't care. I was almost falling asleep when all of a sudden Emily started woofing, it wasn't her usual softly spoken woof either she was more determined in her effort which made me take more notice of it, she'd heard a sound and alerted me to it like a good guard dog would do. So I started massaging the back of her neck to quieten her, I wanted to hear what she'd heard, and I wasn't going to be able to do that if she was woofing. It sounded to me like somebody was trying to break into either the house or the shed and I was too exhausted to go investigate, I knew I'd really over done it that day with the extra chores because I couldn't have cared less which one it was. I just thought to myself "Oh well I guess I'll find out soon enough" and carried on massaging Emily's neck. I figured by the time I'd untangled myself from all these pugs we'd have already been broken into anyway so I may as well stay put. And also, how threatening would a half bent over woman be to potential robbers, the way my body was feeling I figured I'd resemble the hunchback of Notre Dame for at least a good five to ten minutes before being able to fully straighten up, they'd see me staggering towards them in my contorted state and probably burst out laughing. I heard the noise again, to be honest I was kind of hoping it was the house they were breaking into and when they got inside on seeing me laying there all slumped and pathetic like that, they would take pity and go make me a cup of tea. And if I sunk a bit further into the seat and made myself look even more pitiful than I already did perhaps that cup of tea would be accompanied with a biscuit or two. Of course, I'd have to show them where we kept our biscuit tin and that would have been done with a lazy wave of a worn out finger. When I did finally go see what the noise was, I found that one of the horses had made their way into the shed and roughly shoved things aside to get to the food bin. He had then lifted the lid and was happily helping himself to a rather big feed. "Horse proof my ass" I thought to myself as I lead him out of the shed and went to sweep up the mess. You never leave spilled feed on the floor ever, because that leads to mice and rats, and mice and rats lead to snakes so even though I was tired I made sure the shed floor was spotless before going back inside.

The next day I didn't push myself too hard with the jobs, no reason to really because Dave was due home the following morning. It had been a long two weeks, long for me and even longer for the pugs. The longest he was ever away was three weeks and that was hard on everybody, I really thought we were going to lose Ruby that time. She had me here, but she really missed her Dad and I thought she had reasoned it round in her little mind that perhaps he'd left us forever. Not left as in died because she would have witnessed my reaction to that and could clearly see that I wasn't self-destructing, perhaps left as in we'd gotten a divorce and I'd gained custody of the pugs, which by the way would be the one thing I would be fighting for. But twenty-one days is a very long time for a little pug to be missing somebody and not know if she is ever going to see him again. And these two had a very special bond so it must have been like agony for Ruby not having David here. Ruby was ok for the first week, she had gotten used to him going away for seven days at a time because that's what most of his trips ended up being, but then the following year they started sending him overseas for longer. It was mainly two weeks at a time with the occasional three weeker thrown in when they were really busy. I remember once when he was going away during winter, he lit the fire on the morning he was leaving and it was still going when he walked back through the door fourteen days later. I never let it go out, it was too cold for that, I kept shoving more and more wood in to keep the pugs and myself toasty warm. I had that fire blazing away twenty-four hours a day and I'd lay in bed of a night time watching the dancing glow on the bedroom wall.

The three week trip was what really bothered Ruby. In the middle of the second week she started going downhill, she wasn't interested in going for a walk and only got off the bed for her meals, she was lethargic, depressed almost, rarely lifted her head. She just seemed to give up, I actually thought she was dying. Ruby always slept on our bed of a night, but I started putting her on there during the day, on David's side so she could smell him and get comfort from that. I got the t-shirt he wore the day before he left out of the washing basket and spread that out across his pillow and put Ruby next to it, it was the closest thing I could think of to having David there with her. I lay down on the bed beside her, stroked her head, looked directly into her eyes and told her that Daddy wouldn't be home for ten more days, I asked her if she could hold on till then. I also told her that if she couldn't do it that it was ok, Daddy and I would understand. David adored Ruby, he made a beeline for her when he came through the door of a night and on the weekends, they were inseparable. I knew David would want to see her one more time and be able to say a final goodbye. He was ringing everyday checking on me and the pugs, although most of our conversations were about the pugs with him quickly asking how I was before hanging up. I lay there with Ruby telling her everything what was going on. I told her why Dad had gone away and explained to her what he was actually doing over there, I lay there talking and stroking, telling her everything I could think of, but she just didn't seem to want to listen to me. I didn't know if she even heard a word I was saying, certainly from her body language she wasn't hearing me anyway. I wasn't just talking about David and his trip away I told her about the farm and my dreams for it, my worries for the sheep that had a sore leg, I told her about the hay and how it wasn't too good this season, and that next seasons would be better because we'd had more rain. Basically, I was talking and talking about anything and everything just so she could hear the sound of my voice. In the end she fell asleep, so I got up and went outside to feed the livestock. I went into the back paddock and called David in Singapore, with the time difference he didn't pick up so I left him a message telling him that I didn't think Ruby would be here when he got home. I didn't want her to hear me saying this so I leant against a tree and made the phone call from there so I could talk freely about my fears. It was hard for David being so far away and he couldn't rush back, his company had sent him over there to do a job and he couldn't leave until that job was finished. I hung up, fed the livestock and started wandering back up to the house thinking about how David was going to feel when he got that message.

I had left the back door open so the pugs could come outside for a wee if they wanted to. I was gone about an hour and as I got nearer to the house, I could see a few pugs standing on the veranda. I came through the gate and as I locked it behind me I could hear the sound of Ruby barking, her bark was very distinct, I knew it was her right away so raced inside to see what was going on. I walked into the bedroom and she was standing in the middle of the bed swaying and barking, she always barked when she was up high and wanted to be lifted down, some pugs you can't leave on the bed unattended because they'll jump off to come find you as soon as they wake up and there's fear of them breaking their legs doing that so very few of my pugs can be trusted to be left on the bed by themselves, but Ruby was good in that she would always call out for me to help her. Steps are good for pugs getting on and off the bed by themselves, but Ruby due to how her body was now could no longer handle steps, she would have fallen. Seeing her swaying made me smile. Her eyes looked brighter than they had been when I'd left her. She always swayed whenever she was either happy or hungry and looking at her face, I could tell it was both. The next day Ruby was even better than the day before and each day after that she brightened a little bit more. On the day David was due to fly in Ruby was terribly excited, it was the best she had been, she was up before the others, this in itself was unusual because she was a pug that liked sleeping in. She was a ball of energy that day and kept doing her little penguin shuffle to the back door looking out then shuffling back to her bed again when that which she wanted to see wasn't there. It was as if she knew today was the day Dad was coming home and she was looking for him. It was like she'd understood every word I had said when laying beside her. David's plane was delayed, he now wouldn't be getting back to the farm till after dark, but that didn't bother Ruby she kept her vigil up all the same. He kept ringing for updates on his little girl and every call I was able to let him know how well she was doing. When David finally came up the driveway Ruby beat the others to the back door, she shouldered everyone else out of the way to make sure she was the first one he saw as soon as he stepped inside. He put his luggage down and scooped her up and she squealed with excitement. He kept Ruby in his arms but squatted down so he could greet the other pugs and she carried on squealing with excitement as he did so. Each pug came dancing round for multiple pats and all the while Ruby was there with her little mouth open and her eyes sparkling away like crazy, it was like this had been the moment she'd been waiting so long for, and she was absolutely bursting with joy. After that every time David was going away he'd put the pugs on his knee and explain to them how long he would be gone for. All the pugs were told what was going on, but the ones who seemed to be more troubled by the event got a little bit longer on Dad's knee. Ruby was by far the worst but Grace could get out of sorts as well sometimes, so she had a special little bit of extra talking to. Sarah, Harper, Steffy, Tommy and Emily all had time up with Dad, not all of them needed it but all of them got it regardless and Ruby was up there the longest, he told her the number of days and nights he'd be gone and the date he was going to come home on. After that she was a lot happier when he was away on business and always terribly excited on the day he was due home. I am not saying that Ruby could read the dates on the calendar or anything like that, she was probably picking up on my excitement level and taking her lead from me, she knew when I started acting differently that Dad would soon be walking back through the door again. It was the same when he was leaving, she'd see the suitcase being dragged out of the cupboard, sat on the bed watching clothing being folded and loaded in, and then she'd sit on his knee being softly spoken to, little cloudy eyes gazing up at his face as he spoke, all these things told her what was about to take place. The one she loved was leaving for a little while, but he would be back, he always came back. And then when something special was being taken out of the freezer and set on the bench to defrost, well those little cloudy eyes of hers were taking all of those signals in too. She knew if it wasn't something quick and easy for dinner like it had been for the last week or so then his face would soon be reappearing. So, the vigil once again started up, the path to the back door was shuffled along a good many times throughout the day. And when it was him out there making a noise and not one of the sheep or horses well the elation level went through the roof. He was home, finally home, a special meal was prepared, and everybody joined in on it. I think all the dogs loved the first few days Dave was home the most because he would quite often be jetlagged and all the pugs loved being up on the bed with him while he slept, they'd scramble over the top of one another to try and be the closest ones to him. I'd creep into the bedroom making sure everybody was ok and there'd they'd all be, wrapped around each other in the deepest slumber. And when the much needed sleep was finally caught up on, that was it, life for everybody returned to normal and we were all really glad about that.

Emily shared our lives for a wonderful seven years. She was eleven years old when she passed away. She had very little loss of vison and no loss of hearing and she didn't show any signs of having arthritis either and her face showed very little grey, a bit underneath her chin but that was about all. She was a pug that more or less stayed young looking and beautiful her entire life. Emily was lovely with the oldies and a great little playmate for Horton. She kept him well amused and in doing so kept herself well amused also. And as I came to the end of this chapter I started thinking about Emily's final days and I got really panicky because I couldn't remember when she'd died. I remember her not wanting to eat and us taking her to see the vet. But for the life of me I couldn't recall any dates. I was trying really hard to work it out yet the date, nor the month or even the year would come to me, nothing, nothing at all came to mind and that bothered me. All that was going through my head was

"Can't remember, can't remember", "I've forgotten, forgotten, forgotten" and I felt really bad about that. It was very strange too because I always remember those days clearly, they always stand out in my mind because they hurt my heart so much and yet I just could not remember. David was sitting across the room from me at the time, I was writing at the kitchen table that day and he was sitting on the couch covered in pugs with his work computer on his lap. I stopped typing, looked up and asked him about Emily in case he could recall. But he said "That's your thing, that's what you are good at" and he was right, its normally him who is asking me this question but not this time and this made me panic all the more. I kept thinking "Why, why can I not remember", how could I possibly forget the day I lost a daughter. What kind of mother does that, like I could remember that she was at the vet on a drip when we got the call to say she had passed away and we were kind of expecting it because the vet did say she only had a small chance of coming good and that if she was going to come good it would happen within the next twenty four hours so when the call came early and it was the vets voice on the line we knew exactly why he was ringing. I remember collecting Emily's body, carrying her to the car and riding home with her on my knee. I couldn't see her because they had wrapped her up in a garment and put her in a bag that would disintegrate when she was put in the ground. So I just nursed her on my knee and thought about the life she'd lived with us as David drove home. We buried Emily together not long after returning to the farm and I know where she is buried but I can't recall anything much about burying her. I only have a slight vision in my head now of that white cloth bag being covered over with dirt as David filled Emily's grave in. The rest of it I just do not recall at all. I do however remember telling my Mum that I'd lost one of my pugs and she remembered Emily dancing around her feet when she'd visited the farm.

And then it came to me precisely when I'd lost Emily and exactly why I had so much trouble recalling it. I believe thinking about telling Mum is what triggered the memory. Emily died in August 2014. It was early August I believe either the 4th or the 5th but I am just guessing here because I cannot be one hundred percent sure. But yes, it was definitely in the first week sometime I'm certain of that. My mother-in-law died the same month and the same year as Emily did, she died on the 19th of August 2014 and then nine days later on the 28th of August 2014 my wonderful Mother died too. David and I were walking the pugs round the farm the day after his mother's funeral, we were talking about his mum, and I was having a little cry as we ambled along. The pugs were scattered about contently sniffing but David and I were in deep conversation. We came inside and I started getting the pugs dinner ready, we always feed them before we eat ourselves because let's face it nobody is going to be able to eat in peace with a pile of hungry pugs at their feet. I had just finished lining the bowls up along the countertop when the phone rang. Because I was busy in the kitchen David went to answer it. I could hear murmuring in the background, but I wasn't really paying too much attention to who he was talking to because I was happily watching the pugs dance in circles around my feet. I was looking down and talking to them as I always do when getting their food ready. I'll be saying things like "Who's a hungry hungry hippo then, who is a hungry hungry little hippo" and no I am not being mean and no I do not think they are hippopotamuses it's just that we have a kid's game here in Australia called Hungry Hungry Hippos and it's a term I picked up from that and use quite often at dinner time. I say it in a highly excitable voice too and the pugs go nuts when hearing it because they know food will soon be coming their way. Sometimes it can take a while to get their dinner ready and all their medication dished out, but I find if I am talking to them as I'm getting things organised it helps keep their minds off their rumbling tummies and more on what Mummy is saying. Sometimes I'll sing to them while making their dinner but that night I wasn't singing. When David walked back into the room, he motioned for me to sit down. And from the look on his face I realised that I should do what he said right away but I had no idea why, and I didn't even have time to contemplate why before the phone was handed over to me. I put it to my ear and heard my dad's voice and that was it, life as I knew it was over. And there are those few tiny moments of disbelief, like you can't take it in, or you don't want to take it in, like the words you are actually hearing cannot be right. There's been a mistake made somewhere, they've gotten it wrong somehow, the nurses at the nursing home have made a huge mistake it's not your mum who's just died its somebody else's, but then your dad's voice sounds very different to how you have ever heard it sound before. And it's his voice that you believe, it's his voice that lets you know it's the truth, not his words because you are still rejecting them, but his voice tells you that she is really gone. And then time stands still for a little while, again mere moments but you just stare at nothing in front of you with a blank look on your face and all the while your mind is roaring. Rejecting it, accepting it, challenging it, letting what you've just been told sink in. In the matter of a few seconds, I went from happily talking to the pugs to having my entire world altered, saddened and lessened. And I sat there with all my pugs gathered around the chair and I sobbed and sobbed and sobbed.

I don't know how long I sat there like that for but another phone call made me get up, it was my mobile this time, not the house phone, my sister's name flashed up as the ringing went on. I paused for half a second gathering my thoughts and then answered. She was asking if I thought she should visit Mum tonight or come straight home and go see her the next day. I knew she had just finished work and was in the car traveling. I knew I couldn't tell her something like this over the phone, not while they were driving, so I kept my voice neutral, trying as best I could to not give anything away, it was a really bad night weather wise and therefore a bad line and I was grateful for that. I said that I thought she should come home and then hung up. She didn't ask any questions, I suppose she thought I was thinking about the conditions on the road. I was glad it didn't have to be a long conversation because there was no way known I could have pulled that off. It was a misty night, cold, fog descending. I remember telling her to drive safely before putting my mobile phone back down on the kitchen bench. I was glad she had rung me to double check, imagine if she'd just gone to the nursing home and found out from a stranger that Mum had died or worse still walked into Mums room expecting to see her smiling face and found her gone. Me and my youngest sister are very close, she and her partner live with us here on the farm. I knew it would have been quicker if she had met me at the nursing home. But how could I tell her not to go in to see Mum but to wait until I got there. She would have known something was up. I wanted to protect her from having to deal with that on her own, so I stayed put and waited for their car to come up the driveway. It was a long wait, her usual hour long drive, but it seemed that night she was taking twice as long to get here. I fed the pugs in a daze, pausing every so often to sob. I felt sorry for the pugs because they had no idea what was going on. I felt sorry for David too because he was dealing with his own mother's death and now he was trying to help me cope with mine. I really wanted to drop everything and rush to Mum right away, but I knew I had to talk to my sister first. Best that we be together at a time like this, best for her to hear the news from me and then be given the option of going together to see our mother for one last time. For all I knew she may have not wanted to come, I didn't know what her reaction would be, people deal with death differently and she had every right to do whatever she wanted to do, and I would be fine with it. I'd be ok with telling her and then going to say goodbye to Mum on my own. I was on autopilot, I was standing silently doing the dishes when I saw headlights in the driveway. I left the pugs in the house with David and walked outside. It was dark so my sister couldn't see my face until we stepped inside the hay shed. She thought I was going out to feed the horses and sheep so followed me in. I think she was coming to talk to me like she so often did while I was mixing up their food. She walked in smiling, being her normal happy self. She was just about to go and sit on the bales of hay and tell me about her day like she normally did, but instead she paused and turned towards me. And as instantly as my world had changed an hour or so earlier her world was changing now and she, like me, didn't want to believe what she was hearing.

One phone call can forever change your life, one sentence spoken can take you from elation to despair. One moment it's you and your family doing your normal everyday things and in a matter of seconds everything changes. Your life is different now. Having this momentous person gone, taken so quickly, rocks you, it affects your life in every single way. It's like the ground disappears from underneath your feet and you are falling, falling, falling. That's why I couldn't recall Emily's date of death, how could I possibly recall anything that happened around that time. My Mum wasn't here anymore, that was forefront in my mind, that's all I could concentrate on. With Mum's loss a part of me became sadder, lesser and emptier and I've never quite gone back to being the same again. It was like the wall of a damn had broken and it cannot be fixed and the severity of it is enormous. I'd felt the same way in 2011 but because I'd felt that depth of pain before I handled this differently, the pain of loss was no different, that still shatters your world and everything in it, but because I'd gone through it once I knew what to expect this time. I knew it was going to hurt like hell for a very long time, that I would be angry at the unfairness of it all for some time, that I was going to miss every single little thing about her for the rest of my days, but I also knew that in time there would come a day where I would be able to look back and smile, be grateful and feel blessed for having not only had her for my mother but that I'd been lucky enough to have known her at all. But that was some distance away yet so for now you just deal with getting yourself through the day and the day after that, and it was like a tsunami a lot of the time and then I'd have these moments where I felt completely numb, like this wasn't even happening to me, that I was merely looking on at somebody else's life, I was kind of disconnected to what was going on. And I think your brain does that to allow you to have a rest, emotional exhaustion takes a lot out of you and so I believe your brain puts you on pause so you don't self-destruct. So you go numb for a little while, it's the body's way of protecting itself. But then all too soon I'd be experiencing everything up close again and being completely consumed by it. And you'll also have times where you are looking at the world around you wondering how people can go about their everyday lives when she is no longer here. Don't they know that the world has now changed, don't they know life is never again going to be like it was, but of course they don't know that, so they go about their days complaining about stupid little things that really don't matter, still getting irritated about being caught up in heavy traffic or grumbling about the rain. And you want to shake them or yell at them or do something to make them see how ridiculous you think they are. You want to make them see that none of this stuff matters in the long run. But you don't say anything because you don't have the energy to, you just sit quietly by watching it all and in a way it distracts you from your other thoughts for a little while at least.

It takes a long time to work out who you are without your mother, I felt that my world wasn't sitting right anymore and because of that I wasn't sitting right anymore. It's a strange feeling and it took a while for me to sort everything out in my mind. To have somebody who was always there for you gone disturbs the balance of your life. And it wasn't like you relied on her for everything because you are a grown woman living your own life, but to know that she's no longer there to talk to and laugh with and tell all your troubles to and be fully accepted and understood, well that's a lot to lose all at once. I always knew mum was special and I always knew she'd leave a huge void, but you don't fully understand how it's going to be until you actually lose her. And of course, she is the person you would normally go to for guidance at times like this and the fact that you can't only echoes just how great this loss is. But I do think I am very fortunate because once the initial grieving period eased and I didn't feel quite so lost and broken, I started to live in the way I am living now and think I will be living in for the rest of my life until I see Mum again. You see as much as I know she is no longer here I do not feel like she has completely left me. I feel her love enveloping me every single day, all these years later I can still feel it intensely and I think that is a real credit to her. I also feel a huge amount of everything Mum was and everything she stood for, in me and with me and part of me. I was asked by a friend to join a group called Motherless Daughters and I didn't do it because I don't feel like I am motherless I really don't. My Mum is still hugely influential in my life, and I feel like she is always going to be. She gave me so much and taught me so much and I am still benefiting from that guidance and knowledge and love to this day. Of course I wish I could still talk to her personally, tell her that I love her, kiss her face once again and especially to say a huge "Thank you" but I won't be able to do that for quite a while and so I carry on with my days with what Mum gave me, the gifts she left me with and they are enough, well ok to be honest some days they are not anywhere near enough because I want her back, but most days they are enough to see me though and will continue to see me through until I'm standing next to her again.

The night before Mum's funeral I literally thought I was dying myself, my heart hurt so much, there was such an unbelievable amount of pain in that area. I remember we were sitting there watching television together, me David and all the pugs, just trying to bring some form of normality back to our little family. I could do no more for the funeral because it had all been arranged now so I was just sitting there hoping I'd gotten it right because I wanted it to be perfect for Mum, this would be the last thing I would be able to do on this earth for her and I wanted it to be right. I was sitting there quietly stroking one of the pugs, I can't for the life of me remember which pug it was, but I know I had a few of them sleeping around me and David had the rest of them near him and I felt this enormous pressure in my chest and I thought "Well, this is it" the pressure was so great that I didn't think it could be anything else but "It", "The big It", and I didn't tell David because he looked so contented sitting there with so many pugs around him. I didn't want to steal his joy because it had been a hard week for him as well, and he was actually watching the television show and laughing, it was a comedy show and his mind was on that and nothing else and I thought it was doing him good to have a break from how things had been over the last few days. He deserved it. I couldn't spoil that for him, so I didn't tell him what was going on in my body. I figured I'd just quietly pass away, just gently fade out and that would be it. But I didn't die, I got myself through it and carried on living and I believe that's what I was meant to do, what Mum would want for me. I think she would have been very disappointed seeing my face up there so soon. I mean she would have loved seeing me, she always did, but she would know my life had been cut short and I know she wouldn't want that for me. What I think happened that night was that everything just caught up with me, it was the only time I'd sat still since Dad rang to tell me Mum had died, after that call it was all about organising the funeral, but now there was nothing else to do, I could sit still and not have my mind occupied with arrangements. And really that was the worst thing I could have done because it allowed me to start thinking about everything and I started wondering how on earth I was going to cope seeing that coffin with yellow roses on it knowing that my wonderful Mother was in there. That's what set my heart off racing, the television show couldn't distract me from what I knew I was going to be faced with in the morning and everything I was feeling hit me in the chest like a really hard blow. What I was experiencing was probably a major anxiety attack and who could blame my body for having such a reaction. I think that was the fast body reaction I had to losing my mother the slower body reaction came over the next few months when I began losing my hair. I didn't go completely bald thank goodness, but I did lose it in chunks, I was almost afraid to brush my hair because I knew what I was going to see on the brush and for a while there I had to wear my hair in a different style to compensate. But it did grow back, it took some time, but it did grow back and that was a relief because I've heard of cases where people have lost their hair due to shock or stress and it never grew back at all. Human hair is incredibly strong, and I wanted to turn a negative into a positive so I pulled the strands of hair off my hairbrush and went and carefully hung them across the branches of trees. I did this because I knew the birds around here would love to add it to their nests. It was coming up to spring so it was the perfect time for me to lose my hair really, I mean if I was going to lose it then I'm glad it happened at that time of year because it meant somebody else could benefit from it. For years I've been walking round the farm and seen nests that had been blown out of trees, no dead chicks nearby, just these beautifully structured nests that a heck of a lot of work had been put into. I'd occasionally pick them up and study the craftsmanship, what highly skilled creatures birds are, I'd see strands of my long blonde hair woven in there and thick black strands of horse hair too. Mane and tail hair all entwined with mud and twigs and leaves. After I saw that they were using my hair I began leaving it around for them during springtime, I do it every year, even now I still do it, but that year I was able to give them a whole lot more then I normally do.

And then there was Emily, if I thought I was going to lose a pug that year then my mind would not have rested on Emily because we had so many other pugs in the house that were older and in lesser health than she was. Emily dying wouldn't have crossed my mind, there would have been at least three or four names before hers. Losing a pug at eleven years old is always upsetting because that's still very young to me, it may seem old to some people, well old enough anyway, but it's too young for me. I've lost a couple of pugs at this age, and it always seems unfair. I am able to get a real lot of the pugs we take into the mid-teens and sometimes even higher than that, and the mid-teens I'm always happy with and the high teens I am absolutely ecstatic about. But I do know Emily had a whole lot of happiness here, she felt loved, truly loved and I have much peace about that, I know she adored living on a farm and everything that farm life entailed. And when I think about Emily, I never picture her sitting inside the house shaking, it's only in going back to it for this chapter that I'm remembering it at all. No, when I think about Emily my mind always sees her running flat out in the front paddock, her special paddock, happy and fearless and so carefree. And that's a beautiful image to have of her isn't it, just a stunning little pug running full length with that beautiful apricot coat of hers standing out perfectly against the lush greenness of the grass.

CHAPTER TWO

Tommy

I remember being extremely excited when David and I were driving to the airport to pick Tommy and his little friend up. It was an afternoon flight and I remember talking a lot which I tend to do when I'm deliriously happy. I think my husband may have tuned out long ago but that didn't deter me from my idle chatter, I was more thinking out loud if anything so a response from him wasn't really necessary. I had no idea what either one of them looked like as no photos had been sent. All I knew was that we were getting a bonded pair, a male and a female, a black and a fawn. Both elderly and of course that made me even happier because that's what we'd bought our little farm for. Grace Farm was about to open its doors to an old bonded pair that were down on their luck and I could barely sit still in my seat. Their names were Quick and Vegemite at the time and I thought to myself "Oh I don't think I can live with that" I just couldn't imagine myself calling out those names when out and about on the farm. I tried it once to see how it fit and it didn't. I'd gone out onto the veranda and shouted "Quick, Quick, Vegemite, Veg-eee-mite" as I leant over the edge of the decking, and it didn't roll off my tongue well, to be honest I felt like a bit of a twit saying either one of those names and knew that I wouldn't be able to keep on doing it every day. And besides calling a dog Quick was pretty dumb I thought because he wouldn't know if you were merely saying his name or if you wanted him to walk faster because a storm was brewing and you didn't want him getting wet. Although I don't think that would be such an issue with Tommy because he was always going to go at his own pace regardless of what you said to him, you see Tommy is a saunterer and saunterers don't tend to quicken their step for anyone. I just assumed the old lady's favourite drink was Quick and her favourite spread Vegemite. I could maybe have lived with the name Milo if that had been her favourite milk flavouring but clearly it was not. And I had to wonder if the names were chosen because she thought they were cute or if she had lived with her new dog for a few days and out of desperation had chosen the names at dinner time rather than go one more day with a nameless dog. And Tommy entered her life first so maybe she thought when Lilly came along that she would give her a food name too. I guess these names told me a little bit about their previous owner, like if she'd called them Pizza and KFC then I would have known she was into take aways. Quick and Vegemite conjured up images of an old lady with not much of an appetite, like all she could manage to make for herself some days was a small glass of milk with a teaspoon of flavouring dropped in and stirred with a fragile hand and a single slice of toast with a smearing of butter and vegemite scrapped over it. And in a way this made me sad and in a way it pleased me because milk is a substantial drink and Vegemite is full of all the B vitamins or as the ad calls it "A paste containing a great big dollop of niacin, riboflavin and thiamine, with 50 percent of the recommended daily intake of folate. You'll also get a good dose of calcium, magnesium, potassium, iron and selenium" so if the lady was living on these two things, then they weren't the worse two things she could have chosen, at least they would have been doing her some good. I wondered if she was a thick or thin spreader when it came to Vegemite. David likes the stuff more than I do so he spreads it thicker than me and he'll only have it on toast whereas if I'm going to have it it'll more than likely be in a sandwich with cheese. I think with Vegemite you either love it or hate it, it's just one of those things. I could very easily go the rest of my life and never eat it again and it wouldn't bother me one little bit, I wouldn't even realise that I'd not had it whereas some people will eat it every day. I used to have it on crackers when I was a little kid. Butter and vegemite spread between two crackers and then I'd sit there and squeeze them together until Vegemite worms appeared through the holes in the crackers. Ok if I'm being honest, I still do that today as an adult. I can't remember the last time I had Vegemite, let alone Vegemite on crackers but I guarantee when I did, I would be squeezing out those Vegemite worms before eating them that's for sure because it's no fun at all if you don't.

I don't always change the names when the pugs come to us from a loving home and these two did, but Vegemite, I mean come on that really had to go. So, I set about thinking of two new names and because I hadn't seen any photos I decided to wait until I met them before deciding. And I thought we were going have two pugs that would stay nameless for a while, and I didn't really like doing that but I felt it best to live with them a bit first and see what came to mind once their personalities were revealed. And it can take a few weeks for them to fully come through. And yes that was the case with Tommy, but his little friend got her name very quickly after meeting her. With Tommy I was sitting on the couch with him, and he was on his back getting his belly rubbed. Now Tommy was a huge, huge pug, massive chest span, very big and strong but a real softy on the inside. To date Tommy is the biggest pug I have ever shared my life with. I've got a beautiful boy living here with me now that comes close to Tommy, and he could well be the same size for all I know and for that reason I wish I had made a mark on the wall where Tommy's head came to so I could go and see how Brian measured up. But I didn't think to do it at the time so I'll never fully know who is the biggest out of the two of them, there wouldn't be much difference between them, but I do think Tommy is slightly bigger and David says the same thing. But then again Tommy always walked proud and tall whereas Brian tends to hold his head lower, not in a sad whimpering kind of way, it's just his natural way of walking, the way he's no doubt been walking around since he was a young pup.

One day in the second week of Tommy's arrival I was massaging that big chest and tummy as he lay beside me on the couch. I hadn't been sitting with him or anything just wandered past and decided to have a bit of quality time with my new son and as I gazed down at him smiling the name "Old Tommy" shot into my head. So, I told him his new name but he didn't open his eyes, to be honest I don't think he was even listening to me, he was on his back chilling and he was happy, in that moment in time I doubted very much that he cared about having a new name as long as my hand was stroking him that's all Tommy cared about. If I stopped stroking he would have instantly opened up his eyes, began pawing at my arm, perhaps even sat up level with me, I could have told him his new name face to face if he had, but he was so contented that I just kept on patting him and thought to myself there's plenty of time for me to inform him that he will now be known as "Thomas Comer". Although I used to pronounce it the way English people spoke in years gone by as a nod to my English heritage, as a nod to how my Grandad used to talk, he wasn't "Old Tommy" as much as he was "Owde Tommy" and everyone who ever met him would try and get it right and it was pretty comical hearing my Australian friends with their Aussie dialects talking that way. They spent more time laughing than they did saying my new boys name and Tommy would just stand there looking up at them like he couldn't understand what was so funny.

It wasn't hard to tell Tommy apart from the other pugs when out and about on the farm. Whether scattered or walking in a bunch there was never any difficulty spotting Owde Tommy, he never blended in, never got lost in the crowd, even from across the paddock you could pick him out from the pack because he was always head and shoulders above his sisters. And he had a way of moving that was all his own, quite different from any of the other pugs. I mean all my pugs walk a bit differently to each other, it's one of the ways I can tell the fawns apart when they are on the other side of the farm. When they are sniffing around the base of the trees, I can always tell who is who by their unique movements and the way they hold their tails, although sometimes it can take a few moments to recognise one or two of the girls as a few of them have bodies and tails that are quite similar. But not Tommy, there was never any mistaking him and his lovely way of moving. It was fantastic watching him walk, he sort of glided round the property and always had this wide grin on his face when doing so. Out in the paddocks, down the long driveway, floating up the back ramp and sauntering into the lounge room, always always with the happiest of happy looks on his big squishy face. I thought he should be accompanied by a Disney tune, like that's what you should have always been able to hear playing as Tommy went sauntering by. It just seemed very fitting to me, then again perhaps he actually did have a Disney tune playing inside his head, perhaps that's why he was never without his joyful sway or his wide faced grin. Sometimes I'd see him coming along and start humming a happy tune as he went by.

Due to his size Tommy could have very easily made a good guard dog, but he didn't have that kind of spirit dwelling within. He was far too laid back for that. Tommy would rather act the fool than be all fierce and in your face. He left the guard dog thing to Emily, she seemed to have it under control. He saw her bouncing around all over the place keeping a keen eye on things and I think he decided she was doing a good enough job so she may as well carry on doing it leaving him to spend his days strolling about enjoying himself in the stress free manner that was completely Tommy. If somebody started barking at something he may sometimes have a bit of a look at what was going on, he just didn't feel he needed to be the first one to notice it that's all. Emily was a lot smaller than he was, but she was born to be a guard dog whereas Thomas was definitely not. He wasn't a scaredy cat though, don't get me wrong, Owde Tommy certainly was a big soft docile boy, but he wasn't fearful at all. If we got robbed, he wouldn't have gone and hid under our bed shaking or anything like that. I think he would have more than likely helped the burglars load up their truck in that very obliging way of his. Or if not that than he'd have gone and put the kettle on and organised a tray of refreshments and offered them to the robbers with that big beaming face of his. His way of thanking them for all the hard work they had just done.

Tom, Tommy, Thomas, Owde Tommy, The Colonel, we've used all these names for him, and he responds to every single one of them. Before Thomas came into my life, I had only ever rescued female pugs. To me it was the females who needed my help the most, due to greed I know a lot of them are over bred by breeders, some to the point of death. That's what made me have a soft spot for little old ladies. Made me really and truly want to devote my life to caring for them, it's not that I had anything against male dogs it was just that for a very long time I felt it in my heart that I should concentrate solely on helping the females. And I will always go where my heart leads me. Even today I feel for any female dog that is used for constant breeding, those bodies pushing out litter after litter just breaks my heart. I want to scoop them up and spend my days looking after them, spoiling them and giving them a beautiful life. But Tommy was part of a pair and I feel very strongly about splitting pairs up. Tommy and his little friend had lived together all their lives and there was no way I was ever going to allow them to be parted. And with Tommy I really lucked out because he was the most wonderful old dog. Tom opened up my world to the joys of male pugs. I think elderly fawn males are just about the easiest pugs to settle in and the most beautiful souls to share your life with, over the years I've seen it time and time again. A few days before I was to collect Tommy from the airport a lady I knew was telling me how great old male pugs were and of course I'd never had one here at the farm so I kind of didn't believe her. I was sold on elderly females and at that point in time nobody was ever going to be able to alter my mind. But then I met Tommy and instantly my thoughts changed, I mean how could they not, Tommy was such a magnificent natured soul, so placid and calm, huge in body but so very gentle in every single way, very kind, incredibly easy going, just an all-round happy boy. And he was so beautiful towards all his elderly sisters, some would boss him around and he just let them do it. A few where less than half his size but they'd tell him off for something and he'd do exactly what he was told, how could I not fall madly in love with him. This lady also said to me that once I took in an elderly male that I probably wouldn't ever want a female again, but I couldn't ever see such a thing happening and it never has. Today both females and males are equally as precious to me.

When taking in Tommy and Lilly I only knew that they were old and that one was black and one was fawn, I didn't even know if it was the male who was black or the female. Going to the airport to pick them up was exciting because I didn't know what two faces were going to be there to greet me. Come to think of it it does seem kind of fair doesn't it, because Tommy and Lilly had no idea what two faces were going to be waiting for them when they got off the plane. I think Tommy couldn't have cared less who was there to pick him up or who he was going home with, but Lilly was different, she got concerned about things. Word had got around that not only did I love keeping pug pairs together, but I had a special place in my heart for elderly pugs so that's why I was contacted about Tommy and Lilly in the first place. On the drive to the airport I felt like a kid on Christmas morning and was behaving pretty much the same way. The airport is over an hour's drive away and we couldn't get there fast enough as far as I was concerned, when we finally pulled up, I shot out of the car and raced towards the place we were collecting the pugs from. I had a map of the airport in my hand and was going from that. But we had parked in the wrong area and it was a long walk, and of course we would have done something wrong on this trip because we had absolutely no idea what we were doing. We didn't know what rules applied when picking up dogs, so we parked in the normal parking area and it cost a bit to do that, but that's all we knew to do. We didn't know that you bypass the largest parking area altogether, shoot off in the other direction, not have to pay for parking and avoid the main part of the airport and people in the process. It's all very easy once you've done it a few times, they keep the animals well away from where all the people are. If the plane is on time and unloaded quickly you can be in and out in no time at all.

Show them proof of identity and be on your way home with your precious cargo while tired looking people on the other side of the airport are lined up in long queues with long faces.

The plane Tommy and Lilly were on was late and that made me panic a little bit, now a days I don't panic at all, we just sit there chatting until we see the crates being wheeled through the door and then charge at the cages until we spot a pugs face. But I didn't know what the deal was back then, after years of flying pugs in the one thing you get to know is that planes are like new born babies, they rarely arrive on time. They come when they are good and ready to and our job is to simply wait around for them to arrive, and getting impatient does you no good, they don't arrive any faster just because you are excited to meet them. And with planes if they are ever on schedule that'll be the one and only time you yourself are running late. But this airport pick up thing was alien to me, so the wait was torture. And it was a very long wait as well, it seemed our plane had been held up for almost an hour before taking off, these days we check landing times on the internet before heading down the driveway so we can be there at the right time. It's no use rushing off when a plane is late, we may as well stay home and give the pugs an extra walk around the farm then set off and arrive at the airport the same time the plane does, but back then such a thing didn't even cross our minds. Although come to think of it, that information probably wasn't available to the public back then, so we sat there freezing watching plane after plane land and still no sign of our pugs. I said to David that it's almost like our plane has gone to the wrong airport. We watched the sky turn dark and now we were only able to see lights in the sky and lights on the tarmac. Back then you could see everything coming and going through a high mesh fence and freeze you ass off in the process, things are very different now, now you have a nice warm waiting room to sit in and a vending machine. These days we are spoilt, almost treated like royalty. I mean the wait is no shorter but at least you can be more comfortable while doing it. In all the years we've been flying in pugs the collection area at the airport has changed three times with each new collection office being flashier than the previous one. They seem to always be making improvements, but we really wish they would start flying animals in to the airport closest to us, but that airport is so small we don't think such a thing will ever happen which is a real pity as it's only twenty minutes from the farm and that would make a big difference to us and to the dogs as well I think. But our local airport is only used for joy flights and for people who have more nerve than me and want to parachute out of a plane.

And as for that map I had clenched firmly in my fist when I leapt from the car. Well, it did me absolutely no good at all because they'd gone and changed everything around. The animals were no longer being collected from the office it showed on the map, in fact they weren't even being collected from any of the offices nearby either, they were now coming in at a completely different part of the airport, but I didn't know it at the time so I stood outside the darkened office with my utterly useless map in my hand because I didn't know what else to do. This was where we had been told to collect our pugs from, but the office looked like it wasn't being used anymore, not for dogs and not for people either, from the little I could see it looked more like a storage room than a collection office. Our very first airport pick up on our own was fast turning into a complete disaster and I was beside myself, I wished the lady who'd helped us when picking up Emily was here to help us now, she'd have known what to do for sure. All I wanted to do was get my two pugs and get out of there. But we had no idea where the pugs were, and it seemed nobody we asked knew where they were either. I pressed my face to the window of the little dark office in the hope that I could perhaps see a back room with a light on, but there was none. I had hoped the person in charge was merely on a tea break and had locked the door to stop people from disturbing him while he ate. I was in total panic mode by now but David being the easy going person he is took it all in his stride and went off to find out where we could collect the two pugs from. Before he took off he turned and asked if I was coming with him but I said no because I thought at least one of us should stay put in case the person who was meant to be running this office decided to return. This was where we had been told our pugs would be brought to after being unloaded from the plane. I thought somebody should be here waiting just in case. I mean for all I knew this office was being run by only one guy and he could well have gone off to collect some more dogs. I thought Tommy and Lilly may even be sitting in the darkened office and all of a sudden a light would flicker on and I'd see their two little faces staring at me. Perhaps they had been staring at me all along, watching every time I walked to the door or window for another peep in. Maybe they had even been woofing at me, the glass was pretty thick, if they'd only been doing little woofs I wouldn't have been able to hear them due to all the outside noise. I pictured them sitting in their crate elbowing each other and making smart ass comments about me whenever I came back to have another peep through the glass. They would probably be saying something like, "Get a load of this twit, clearly her first airport pick up, obviously a novice she's a nervous wreck" and the other one would chime in with "If the idiot couldn't see inside the first time she looked in why on earth would she think she'd be able to see in the nineteenth time she looked in" I bet they were secretly hoping that I wasn't the person here to pick them up. I bet they were looking behind me to see if anybody better was heading their way.

I was peering through the office window for the umpteenth time when I heard some rather loud whistling behind me. I turned round fast and saw my husband waving at me from the other end of the terminal so I scrunched up my useless map, shoved it in my coat pocket and bolted as fast as I could in his direction. Being a tall man, he stood out from the others, I could see him clearly above all their heads, there were about a hundred people standing between me and David and I wondered if any of them thought he was rude whistling for his wife like she was a dog. We were talking about it on the way home and started laughing because David said "Now you mention it a few people did give me some nasty looks" He thought it was due to the fact that he was whistling loudly in a public place, and I guess it may have been that too, but I more think it was due to the fact that he'd dog whistled for his wife and I bet they thought very little of me for actually answering to such a call. Apparently David had called my name a few times but with the noise of busses and taxis pulling in and out the sound had been lost so he thought he'd do something else to get my attention. And a loud whistle stood out amongst all the other noises. I heard it clearly and instantly knew who it was, I ran past all those people without really looking at them, I could see their heads turning in my direction but didn't make eye contact with any of them because my mind was on other things. To me they were just obstacles between me and my husband and I wanted to get to him as fast as possible because I figured he'd found out where our new pugs were. And I was right, David had gone into the main part of the airport and after standing in line a nice gentleman had given him directions to where we needed to be.

But because we had parked in the wrong parking lot we had to bring Tommy and Lilly back past all those people queuing up for transport and they seemed pretty annoyed that we were bringing dogs into the people area, maybe they thought their expensive luggage was going to get urinated on. But Tommy never once cocked his leg, he just took off walking beside David and Lilly and I followed on close behind. She was only little, but boy could she move, her little legs were going like crazy, she wasn't letting David and Tommy out of her sight and neither was I. When we got to the car the pugs had a drink and a handful of chicken each and then we headed home to the farm. Lilly sat on my knee and Tommy lay sprawled out on the back seat. He'd had a big day so slept most of the way home, not little Lilly though, she was wide awake and alert, she kept trying to sit on David's knee while he was driving, I had a feeling she may have done this a lot with her previous owner. It seemed to upset her terribly that I wouldn't let her to it, so once we were out of the city traffic and on the quiet country roads near home Lilly's wish was granted and she put her paws on the steering wheel like she was driving. She seemed very content doing that, it seemed to be her thing, there was hardly any other cars on the road at that time of night, so we just drove along slowly and let our new little daughter enjoy herself.

It was so late by the time Tommy and Lilly were unloaded from the plane and I wasn't happy about that because I always like to show new pugs around the farm in daylight. I like to have them here a for a few hours before it goes dark so that they get a chance to have a look around the place, have a walk and a sniff and get an idea of where they have landed. In the dark the farm is a totally different place, as all farms are. Unless there's a full moon it's just total darkness out there in the paddocks, the pugs have no idea of what our farm looks like. By the time we got Tommy and Lilly home it was 9.30 at night, all we had time to do was take them to the hay shed so they could unload their bladders and then give them something to eat. I remember we bought roast chicken especially for the new arrivals and for the other pugs too as a way of celebrating having two new family members. The other pugs were all waiting by the back door when we walked in, the poor little things had been on their own for a very long time. I was well aware of how long we'd been gone for and so were they, they gave us looks as if to say "Where the heck have you been all this time". If they'd been wearing watches they would have been standing on their hind legs, tapping their little wrists and shaking their heads. The way they were looking at us now they were well aware we'd missed curfew, and nobody was impressed with that. They didn't pay much attention to their new siblings at first because there were more pressing matters to attend to. In a group they all raced out to the shed and had a wee, poor little things had been holding on for such a long time. There were a few puddles in the house, but most had been holding it in until we got home and let them outside. Tommy and Lilly saw where the others were heading, one stood under the porch light watching them go while the other one took off after them. Lilly got a bit confused and started heading the wrong way, she started doing her fast walk down the driveway so David raced out to help her so she didn't get lost in the dark. After a good sniffing of the shed had been had by one and all, they came inside and ate their roast chicken together. And that was it as far as Tommy was concerned, he was home. Lilly took a bit longer to settle like all us ladies tend to do. With men you feed them and it's like "Ok thanks, now show me to the nearest bed" and that's about it, they are asleep before you know it, but little old ladies tend to need a bit more than that for them to feel fully settled. Up until that point Tommy was by far the easiest pug I have ever settled in. He just walked through the door, ate almost his entire body weight in chicken, then jumped up on the couch and settled down to sleep. He was fed, he was warm, he was happy and that was pretty much how it was for Owde Tommy for the rest of his life here.

When I first met Tommy I thought he was a crossbreed because he was so huge, not fat at all just tall, real tall, but he was definitely all pug there was no other breed in him. I think he just came from a long line of really big pugs. He was very athletic looking, 11 kg of pure muscle, he had this huge goofy head too and I thought he was brilliant. His face made me smile. I quickly fell head over heels in love with him. I patted his great big old head and said to him "Our vet is going to love you". We'd had a conversation the week before with our vet and he was saying that he hardly ever saw any athletic looking pugs and then here was Tommy, yes he was old but he sure was a fine physical specimen of a pug. He reminded me of an old man who'd played sports all their life, like a retired professional athlete or something. I think having only females before he came I was used to much smaller pugs. But Tommy is big even amongst other male pugs, we measured him with a few of our friends males and he towered over the top of them. When he first arrived, I used to worry about him with Ruby, she was so unsteady on her feet but he never once knocked her over, always guided his big strong body around hers and kept her upright, even when he was running past her in the narrow hallway he never set her off balance. He actually never sent anybody flying, not even by accident, he just breezed past the lot of them doing his smiling face as he went. Yes he was huge, but Owde Tommy was smooth and would glide around with so much ease, he was great at maneuvering his body carefully around the smaller pugs and I guess that was because he'd had plenty of practice at it living with little Lilly. It was the same when Horton joined the family, he never knocked his little paraplegic brother over either. Horton may have toppled a time or two on the odd occasion he was playing with Tommy, but it was not Tommy who caused it, it was little Horton playing a bit too roughly and overbalance in the excitement of it all. And Tommy seemed concerned about that, went from laying down to standing up in no time, then stood over his baby brother as if checking him out. But Horton was fine, he'd still be in full play mode and start chomping on one of Tommy's legs as he stood there watching him.

When he came to live on the farm with us Tommy was nine years old and only had four or five teeth left in his head, but oh that smile. When I bent down to greet him at the airport he came up at me fast, all huge faced and smiling, much like a scene from jaws, minus the teeth. Lilly didn't jump up at me she just sat there quietly watching all that was going on. With Tommy being so big and Lilly being so small I did think it was wrong for the two of them to have been put in the same crate together. She was less than half the size he was, and you get a lot of jostling about when you are up in the air, the constant moving of the crate, the loading and unloading. Airport staff are on tight schedules, they don't always have the time to be as careful as they should be. There would have been many times when he would have been sent off his feet, falling on top of her, she would have no doubt done the same thing to him a few times as well, but she wouldn't have had quite the same impact, he wouldn't have been able to feel her the same way she would have felt him. She would have been squashed between her brother and the walls of the crate and I didn't think that was fair on her. She was far too little a pug for that, she should have been protected. I had paid for the flight down, if they'd told me they intended sending them down in the one crate and had told me the size differences in the two of them I would certainly have said "No, don't do that, use two" and I wouldn't have minded at all paying for an extra crate. But they didn't inform me of their plans so there was nothing I could do, and I thought that was really wrong of them. These days it wouldn't be a problem. These days they will not allow two dogs to travel in the same crate together who are over the age of six months. I guess that's due to fighting and I agree with that as dogs on flights could start lashing out due to fear.

Getting to know Tommy was a really lovely experience for me. I thought he was the most placid pug I'd ever come across, so laid back, very different to the females, nothing fazed him. He had a serine personality, almost hippy like, it took a heck of a lot to get Tommy upset. He just took life as it came, met the sheep and the horses with minimum fuss. Tommy was mellow, calm and all round cheerful. In a way he reminds me a lot of my husband, both huge males and both if born with a fiercer personality dwelling within would be scary, intimidating and threatening, you'd run a mile when you saw them. But because they are not that way at all you can't help but be drawn to them. Tommy oozed happiness and his big goofy grin was contagious, he was like one of those people with faces that always look like they're smiling even when they're not. And he smiles wide, like a contented frog. Imagine a frog on opium and you've got our boy Thomas. And due to his lack of teeth his gums would kind of fold in sometimes, at those times he used to remind me of a pensioner who'd taken their teeth out for the night. Also, you'd think because he didn't have many teeth that he would have had trouble eating, but he didn't, he put the few teeth he had left to very good use. I never once had to mush up Tommy's food like I had to do with some of the other pugs. Tommy had an amazingly strong jaw, I think that helped him a lot, he'd clamp down on something and it was like it was held in a vice. Once he had a hold of something you'd never be able get it off him. Tommy loved his food and would chomp down until it was all gone. Not a slow eater but not a gulper either, just enjoyed all his meals and he kept up with others who had a lot more teeth than he did, then stood there with a clean bowl until I went over and stoked his head. He wouldn't move off until I picked up his bowl, I suppose until that point he was ever hopeful of some more food coming his way. But don't worry Tommy never once went hungry, I saw to that, I fed him accordingly, took in his size and the amount of exercise he was doing. I didn't want this old boy getting too thin, it wouldn't have looked good on him so he did have more food in his bowl than some of his sisters had in theirs but there was never any fear of Tommy becoming fat, he was far too active for that.

I'd walk by Tommy as he was laying sprawled out on the couch and couldn't help but stop and bury my face in him. I'd blow raspberries on his tummy, and he wouldn't even move just lay there all floppy limbed with his long legs dangling down over the side of the couch. And I'd massage him as well sometimes, not that he needed it because he was already so relaxed, but the massages made him even more so to the point that you've have to stop him from sliding onto the floor headfirst. Sort of protect him from himself because he didn't care that he was heading downwards, he was getting his tummy massaged, that was all he had on his mind at the time. But I didn't want that big old head of his coming to any harm, so I'd slide him backwards and keep massaging him as I went. Took a bit of skill doing that too because of his size, but he was so soft and so loose limbed that he'd easily go wherever you moved him to, never stiffened up, which was good because that would have made him even harder to move. Just a big gangly pug he was and relaxed to the point of appearing like he'd been sedated. Tommy's tranquil personality was very much reflected in the way he walked, and I wasn't the only one who noticed it. One of my friends turned to me after watching him come across the paddock and said "He walks like such a dude doesn't he" and I couldn't help laughing because that really was exactly how Tommy did walk, it was the perfect way to describe him. Some called it a saunter, others a swing, some said it was more of a sway and they were all right in their descriptions. And the funny thing was that he ran exactly the same way as he walked, exact same movement only slightly faster. I used to watch them all from a distance, if I got a phone call when I was walking them I'd stop, lean against a fencepost and enjoy the show in front of me as I was having a conversation. There would be little Ruby doing her penguin walk and Grace her sweet little trot, Sarah would be stomping, Harper ambling, Steffy close by my side and Emily racing about all over the place like a maniac. And there swaying in and out in-between the lot of them would be Tommy. He always moves about the farm like he doesn't have one single care in the world, and I honestly believe he doesn't. He goes off walking about the place froggy smiling at everyone and everything he encounters along the way. From day one he's been like this, he woke up that very first morning, looked through the windows at the sheep and horses in the paddocks, didn't bark, just looked as if to say "Hello there. I didn't see any of you last night" then he turned around and followed the rest of us outside for our morning walk like he'd been doing such a thing for years. He wasn't timid either, didn't stay with the pack for security like some of them do until they know the layout of the land, no Owde Tommy went on ahead and had a good sniff at all the new things he came across, he familiarized himself with it all and lifted his leg and christened everything too, he seemed to be really enjoying his new home.

After a few weeks of Tommy living on the farm he came to the conclusion that the sheep and horses were very different to how he was and I don't mean just a different type of animal, he grew to know they looked at things differently to how he did. I think he realised they didn't see the world quite as blissfully either. The ewe's especially can be off hand at times and after a few tried to head-butt him through the fence he tended to stay clear of the fence line from then on because I think they were harshing his mellow. For the ewes part I believe Tommy worried them due to his size, they were used to pugs of course they were but Tom's large frame was noted by the sheep because in the wild it pays to make note of such things. It keeps you and your young alive. They didn't know he was placid when he first came but as soon as they found out what kind of personality Tommy had dwelling within the head butting ceased. When he's in a playful mood he'll chase the sheep away, they'll be grazing by the gate that leads into the back paddock and Tommy will come out of the house, be walking down the back ramp all peaceful like, spot them and then run at them screaming like a little girl. But it's a pleasant and even funny sounding scream, nothing at all like the way Steffy screams, and for that I was incredibly grateful because I think I would have packed my suitcase for sure if I had two in the house who screamed like Steffy did. And with Tommy being so huge, well you don't want a chest that big bellowing out a Steffy sounding scream. Tommy will occasionally scare a visitor with his scream, or should I say warrior cry, because I think that's exactly what he's doing, summoning up his inner warrior to help scare the sheep away. And he scares visitors at times as well because it just comes out of nowhere, no warning of what he is about to do. One moment everything is quiet and peaceful the next moment the person standing nearest to Tommy shoots out of their skin. But he'll have seen something that we haven't, and no doubt thinks it deserves being explored and his warrior cry helps him do it I guess. He's not frightening at all, but from the look on his face you can tell that he thinks he is and that's the funniest thing of all. Tommy is just a beautiful gentle giant enjoying the journey he is on and not letting too much about life steal his joy. And once again that's exactly the same way my husband is. And it too is one of the reasons I love him.

When Tommy has had a good look at what sparked his interest he will then come sauntering back to join the pack. But if he's been gone a while we'll have moved on because it can get a bit boring standing around waiting for one who refuses to be rushed by life, but that's fine he never has any trouble finding us. When he does start heading our way he likes a really big deal to be made of him. He knows I'm always there watching for his return because that's just what I do whenever somebody wanders off. It's easier to keep an eye on everyone if we all stay together but when you've got one who likes to linger then you have to let them do what brings them joy. Also, Tommy had great vision and hearing, so I didn't worry about him too much and because he was tall he'd be able to look across the paddock and see where we were in no time. He'd start heading towards us and I'd see him coming so I'd stop and open my arms wide, and he'd slightly pick up his speed and come running into them, then it's a quick snuggle and we're on our way again. He gets really disappointed if I don't make a fuss, he loves that I get involved in this little game of his. There will be times when I'm distracted with one of the other pugs, so he'll drop back and have a sniff at a tree or something and wait until I'm ready to receive him. Out of the corner of my eye I can see that huge frame of his in the distance and I'll put down the pug I've just tended to, turn, open my arms wide and he gets so excited when he sees me doing this. Sometimes this funny little game of his is played out two or three times every walk and every time I act like it's the first time he's done it. And he acts the exact same way so it's all good, I don't feel like such a fool then. The times I do feel like a bit of a fool is when I'm standing there wide armed waiting for what seems like an eternity and he being who he is does not feel the need to rush, yes he'll be making his way towards me, he's not rude enough to stop and sniff when he can see my arms are open but he will be doing that slow laid back saunter of his and the paddock is pretty big so it can take him a while to reach us. This used to really annoy Sarah at times because she'd want us to be on our way. Some days she was so aggravated by Tommy's behaviour that she'd run at him when he got close and he'd look at her as if he had no clue why she was so upset, he'd veer around her and carry on sauntering towards me and Sarah would be on his tail huffing, puffing and stomping, totally unimpressed. If she could have thought of a way to put an end to Tommy's game I'm sure she would have done it. Sometimes Tommy would see her coming and give her a wide sweep and of course that would annoy her all the more, it really added fuel to her fire, and she'd take off after him and I'd have to run towards Tom and sweep him up before Sarah got there. No, she would never have bitten him, but she would have shouldered him all the way back to the house in that bossy little manner of hers and Tommy being the docile soul that he is would have let her do it. And I couldn't have that.

I'll let you in on a secret, which by the way isn't much of a secret because it's too obvious to be one, but Owde Tommy, bless him, is not the most intelligent of dogs. And I just have to pause here and point out that this is not at all like my husband. For the sake of my marriage, I thought I'd best clarify. I am Tom's mother and I love him with all my heart, it's not hard to do, but even through the haze of love I know what he is and if a mother can admit to such a thing with a clear conscience then it gives you some idea of the situation at hand. Tommy would stand and stare at things some days and you didn't know if he fully understood what was going on, there was no dementia there, of that fact I am 100% sure of. I have lived with dogs that had dementia and Tommy showed no signs of that at all thank goodness. It was more that he had this very vague look on his face at times. So I was left with wondering if he was unintelligent, lazy or whether he just didn't give a hoot. Perhaps it's the latter. Maybe everyday things were so unimportant to Tommy that he didn't think they're worth concentrating on. Like the sliding glass doors for instance, there are three off the lounge room leading to the outside world. I always leave one of them half open when the weather is nice so the pugs can come and go as they please. But Tommy just doesn't get it, he'll stand at one of the unopened doors staring in until I go get him and I always have to go get him otherwise he'll stand there frog smiling at me through the glass all day long. His sisters would go to the closed door, see it was shut, then trot around to the door that was open and run inside, and I was always hoping that Tommy would see what they were doing and follow them, but he never did. He even gets confused with the door that is half open. He will stand at the closed part of the door looking in totally oblivious to the fact that if he just moved over a few inches he'd be able to walk inside. And Tommy is a wanderer, so we seem to be playing this game all day long. He has no trouble finding his way out of the house but then goes off and is happy and when he finally comes back he will always go to the wrong door. Tommy spends a lot of his time walking around the boundary fences checking on things, looking at what is happening on our side of the fence and looking at what's happening on the other side of the fence. The front of the property is his favourite place to pause because he likes to watch the cows over the road, the sound of them mooing lures him over, it did on the first day he arrived here and it has done every day since. I think he just likes to hear the sound they make, perhaps it's soothing to him, either way it draws him in and if he's going to linger on anything it'll be the cows over the road for sure. If you lose him you always know where to find him, you just head to the front of the property and there he'll be standing watching the cows with this amazingly contented look on his face. The sides of our property where the neighbours are, that is not so interesting to him so he'll saunter on by and that's ok because Emily will be there keeping an eye on things.

Tommy would saunter right by Emily who was set up underneath the trees in her special stalking position, sometimes he'd pause to look at what she was doing but never for very long before being on his way. It was like he couldn't understand why she was watching boring people when there was a heard of perfectly good cows to gaze at, and the sitting down on the job probably had him baffled too because Tommy was a boy who was born to walk. I guess for Emily's part she was probably thinking why saunter round and round like an idiot when you can sit and be fully entertained by the goings on in front of you. Sometimes Tommy will only go around the property once, other times he'll walk round and round three or more times and when he very first came I used to stand on the veranda watching him, making sure he was ok, that he could find his way back to the house, but I needn't have worried because he always did. It used to concern me that he may have had a goldfish kind of memory. Had he simply forgotten that he'd already been around once or was it just something he liked doing, was his old back garden so small that he was now taking full advantage of his new one and enjoying every aspect of it. In time I came to realise that it was just Tommy's thing and that he really was so very happy being out there patrolling the place, when David was home he used to stand on the deck watching Tommy too, he said he was like a colonel, like he'd been specially employed to patrol the farm. So whenever Tommy was out there one of us would say shall we go and watch "The Colonel" and we'd both fly out the door, our eyes searching the paddock for him until he was spotted and then we'd both stand watching him meandering around. One lap, two laps, three laps and sometime even four and we'd stand there watching him going round and round, sometimes giving running commentaries on what we thought he was thinking about at the time. He'd come by the front of the veranda and look up on seeing us there and his tail would give a little wag as he sauntered on by. Just a quick indication that he'd seen us, that he loved us, but he still wanted to continue on with his laps. We'd talk about his happy smiling frog face and I said to David once that it's almost like Tommy's got a joke going on inside his head, a private joke perhaps, and one day I said to Dave do you think that joke could be at our expense and he turned to me and said "From the way Tommy just looked at us now I don't doubt it at all" so I got to thinking that maybe at night when David and I had fallen asleep Tommy was amusing his sisters with whispered jokes about his new Mum and Dad and they were all laughing their little old heads off at us well into the night while we slept blissfully unaware that we were being made fun off. Did he also do the same thing on the rare occasions we left them in the house on their own, did he have his sisters in fits of giggles until our car came back up the driveway. I imagined Steffy and Emily on the couch and Ruby, Grace, Sarah and Harper laying in comfy beds on the floor and Tommy holding fort from his chair. And the more Tommy mocked the more the little old darlings sniggered. If he was doing this then good on him, we laugh at the pugs and their antics all the time, why should the table not be turned on us once in a while.

Tommy's last lap of the farm was the most comical one to watch, he had a certain way of doing things, like a ritual that must be undertaken before he would come inside. We have a long row of trees down our driveway and as he was making his way back to the house for the very last time he would stop and cock his leg on each and every one of those trees and you'd think he'd run out of wee but he never did, I think he was just putting a tiny drop on each one, a way of marking his territory. But he only ever did this on his last lap, on all the other laps he'd simply saunter past the trees as if he didn't even know they were there. The marking signalled that he was done with today's burst of laps, so whenever we'd see him weeing we knew he was ready to come back into the house and one of us would shoot out the door and guide him inside. Then he'd have a big drink and settle down and go to sleep. As I write this I have a clear vision of Tommy weeing on tree after tree running through my head, I wish I had taken a video of him doing it because it was such a funny thing to watch, just this big smiling pug pausing and lifting his leg time after time as he came up the driveway. Rain, hail or shine Tommy patrolled our property, nothing would put him off and he wouldn't come inside when it started to rain, he seemed to like being out there walking in the rain and I understand this because I like doing that too. If it was already spitting when he let me know that he wanted to go out I'd put a waterproof coat on him and off he would trot. On days where he had already gone out before the rain started I would wait by the back door with our biggest thickest towel and envelope him in it as soon as he came into view. Tommy liked getting a rub down, some pugs make a game out of it, others will fight you on it but not Tommy he lapped it up. Sometimes it'd take two towels to dry him off and I'd go and put another log on the fire then encourage him to come over and sit in front so the warm air was blowing over him. It was like getting an enormous blow-dry. I never liked him getting too wet though, so the level of rain was always judged, I mean he was an old dog after all, but he was happy being out there so a lot of the time I was guided by him, I let him do what he wanted to do. You can't stop dogs from being dogs can you. Tommy would go out for a saunter many times throughout the day and there was even the odd occasion when he'd find his way back inside on his own, he'd come flying through the door with a shocked look on his face like he totally surprised himself that he found his way in. To be honest I think these were just flukes, but he was praised for it all the same. He was looking at you like he wanted to be praised so a whole lot of clapping and cheering was done. And if a friend happened to be sitting with me at the kitchen table, well their cups of tea were put down too and they joined in on the praise, which by the way delighted Tommy no end. Then the next time they were here they'd see me getting up to help Tommy inside, so a discussion was had about that. I came to the understanding that perhaps Tommy just picks and chooses what he keeps in his mind and what he lets go of. It just seems at times that he let go of an awful lot of stuff. But it's ok he doesn't have to be an intellectual, I'm certainly not and yet I am loved deeply all the same and so is Thomas and besides he has a right to be exactly who he is, and he sure makes up for it in other ways. There aren't going to be any prizes for intelligence in Tommy's future, but I wouldn't trade him for the world, not everyone is born a scholar and besides it would be boring if all my pugs were exactly the same. I love all their little differences and personality traits.

One day Tommy did surprise me though, that day I was the dopey one and he was the faster more intelligent being. I was going into the back paddock to check on the horses and sheep, I hadn't seen one of the older sheep for a while and was worried she may have hurt herself and was laying down by a tree perhaps with some sort of injury, she wasn't, she was fine, as I got halfway down the paddock I could see her up and about grazing happily with the others. So I turned around fast and nearly tripped over Tommy in the process. I had no idea he'd come into the paddock with me and was following close behind. He was so quiet and must have been slowly sauntering along and me being lost in my thoughts as I so often am, hadn't realised he was there. He scared the heck out of me but boy was he proud of himself for finding his way in, stood there looking up at me doing his big frogy grin like he'd just performed a magic trick and should be applauded for it. I quickly picked him up and hugged him to my chest as I carried him from the paddock, the horses must have seen me because I heard galloping hoofs coming up behind and the sheep were no doubt following the horses because I could hear them baaing out to me. Tommy heard them too because he started peering over my shoulder doing his warrior cry, I think he wanted at them, but I couldn't put him down because they were far too big for him to play with. I'm just glad I spotted him when I did and had the time to scoop him up before the horses noticed we were there. I couldn't have my laid back placid darling being trampled underfoot. To Tommy it was all fun, he had no idea how much pain could be inflicted if somebody stepped on him. I think he was terribly disappointed that I wouldn't put him on the ground, maybe that's the reason he had followed me in there in the first place, perhaps he'd been spying his chance of getting into that back paddock for a very long time and when it finally happened he must have been beside himself and then I went and ruined it all by picking him up. I'm glad he was a saunterer though because if he had been the type of pug that ran flat out he would have taken off fast in the direction of the sheep and horses while I was securing the gate and I'd have had no chance of catching him. And if he startled the ewes they would have had a go at him for sure as they were already wary of him and if he got in-between the horses legs they wouldn't have been too happy about that, such things can be unnerving to them. The entire situation could have gotten out of control fast with poor placid Tommy being the looser in all of this and he didn't deserve that. I actually thought he was pretty smart to have done what he did, he must have walked in the paddock after me and stood quietly behind while I was latching the gate, he must have known to keep out of my eye view and him knowing to do that really did surprise me. And after putting all that effort in to being sneaky I felt a bit sorry for him not being able to have a play especially when he'd come so close to claiming his prize. Clearly he wanted to interact with his paddock siblings so once he was on the safe side of the fence I went into the shed and grabbed some food. I knew I would be able to make the horses run if I had a treat for them and if they ran so would the sheep and I thought seeing us all running along like that would be incredibly thrilling to Tommy and it was. He got in on the act right away and started running along with us on his side of the fence. I'd run to one end of the paddock, pause, dish out a few treats then turn and off we'd all go running again and Tommy was beside himself with excitement. I'd be running, the horses trotting, the sheep ambling together in a group and there on the other side of the fence running right beside us was Owde Tommy doing his warrior cry and having the time of his life. He'd not seen us doing this before, sure he'd seen the horses and sheep running together many times, but me being in there running along with them well that was new to him, and I think the sound of his warrior cry added to the excitement of it all. Tommy kept pace with us and the look on his face told me everything he was feeling. After that he was quite happy to go back inside the house and have a rest. He'd done something different that day, he'd had a bit more interaction with his paddock siblings and he was thrilled about it. It did wear him out though because Tommy was moving faster than he'd ever moved before, it didn't make him breathless, but it was more than he was used to doing. And again, I allowed myself to be guided by my dog. I heard his warrior cry lessening and realised that he'd done enough for one day. But the next day Tommy was out there asking to play again so again I filled my pockets with treats and again I ran with the sheep and horse and again Tommy did his warrior cry as he ran along with us. After that whenever he was feeling particularly boisterous he'd go stand near the gate that led to the back paddock until I noticed him there and then off we'd all go for a run and a bit of fun. A few of the other pugs watched us but never joined in, I did think Emily would have done but she just stood in amongst her siblings looking at us all like she thought we were mad and in a way I guess we were because we did this in the rain a couple of times until the novelty wore off.

I think the thing I noticed most about having a male dog in the house was the peeing thing, well the cocking the leg and peeing thing anyway. Male dogs pee a lot higher that females do, and Tommy was christening everything in sight, and it went on for so long I thought it was never going to end and that the side of our couch wasn't going to make it. With little girls you just get puddles but with boys they aim high, and you have it running down the side of the walls, the windows and the couches and it smells differently too. And I was at the end of my tether with trying to get him to stop doing it, I called a friend in rescue and asked her what she did in situations like this, she had plenty of experience with males so her advice was golden, well I thought it would be golden anyway and the end to my problem, but it was not. She suggested putting candles near the side of the couch, she asked me if he was doing it all over the house or just one spot, he had been doing it all over the house for over a week but then decided he liked peeing on the side of our couch the best. So, she said well put a candle near the side of the couch and you'll have no more trouble. And I thought to myself well he is peeing a real lot so I think more than one candle will be needed here and I didn't muck about buying puny ones either, the ones I got were almost as thick as fence posts and I lined the four of them up in a row and went off quite pleased with myself. A little while later I walked back by the couch and there were my four thick candles completely covered in pee, the ribbon tied around them was dripping wet, it seemed when I left the room Tommy had jumped off the couch and gone to town on the candles. Emptied his full bladder on them, I guess he was pleased to have something new to pee on. So I called her back for more advice. She said don't use certain cleaning agents as some of them have ammonia in them and they will make the situation worse. I was already aware of this, but she did tell me about the cleaner she used so I went out and bought what she suggested and started using that and it helped a little bit but not much, then just when I was about to give up on ever being able to housetrain Tommy he suddenly stopped marking his territory. It was about a fortnight after the candles had been chucked in the bin. And I don't know why he stopped but he just did, and I was grateful for it. I never get annoyed over the weeing thing, sure it's hard, the smell, the extra cleaning, especially when you have so much to do in a day with all the other dogs, but you have to look at it from their point of view, how would you feel if you lost your entire family and had to begin anew. You look at it like that and a bit of accidental weeing isn't such a big deal. Once Tommy stopped peeing on the side of the couch he decided that he liked to sit on the back of it or on the back of whatever chair you were sitting in at the time. And it was handy actually because it meant you could fit more pugs on the chair with you without somebody getting squashed. Once Tommy is comfortable he'll just lay there happily and go to sleep, of course if you get up for anything you have to reposition him because by the time you come back he'll have slid down and taken over the warm spot you left behind. But Thomas sure did like to climb so now I had two climbers in the house that I needed to keep my eye on, I've found it's usually the black pugs that are the biggest climbers, even from puppies they are I've been told, if you get a mixed litter you'll find it's the black pugs who are the first ones to scramble out of the whelping box and go off on discovery missions and although they are little they still have an amazing ability to climb. A few breeders have told me that, so I guess fawns and blacks are different from day one. Tommy would get up as high as he could on things and you'd walk into a room and find him fast asleep in the middle of the dining room table, it always worried me that he was going to fall off when he started dreaming because he was such a violent dreamer and could have easily moved his body closer to the edge without even realizing he had done it. By the time he realised what he'd done it would be too late he'd already have fallen to the ground. So, I'd gently take him down and put him in one of the dog beds on the floor so he'd be safe from harm and a lot of the time he wouldn't even fully wake up when I did this, he was such a deep sleeper. And I'd stand watching him for a while before moving off. Sometimes he was still, other times his legs, head and body would start jerking around all over the place. And his jowls flapped about like bellows. It was like he was putting on a show for you, he wasn't, he was just sleeping the way he'd always done, but Dave and I gathered round and watched never the less. Owde Tommy slept on our bed at night and would try and steal our pillows, I had a feeling he used to sleep on his previous owners pillow every night because you'd put him in the middle of the bed and by the time you brushed your teeth he'd be sprawled out on your pillow and there'd be no room for your head. Tommy was a real treat to sleep with in winter, it was like sleeping with one of the sheep, he was so big and had a double thick coat, so he was wonderful to snuggle up to on very cold nights. Only thing was you'd often not get much sleep because he'd kick you in the back whenever he was dreaming. It was like he was constantly dreaming about running in a marathon and the way his legs were moving you could tell that he really wanted to win. I'd either sigh or laugh depending on how tired I was at the time, and I'd think to myself that yes Tommy truly was an athletic pug.

Regardless of the way he slept Tommy was never short on having people who wanted to snuggle up to him. After we lost Horton and Amber entered the house she decided that she'd like to sleep with Tom. She was the smallest pug in the family, and he was the largest pug in the family and they often slept side by side. He'd be on the couch but she was far too little to be able to get up there by herself, so she'd go stand near to where Tommy was and wait for me to notice her, which I eventually did and up she'd go. She didn't have a lot of vision so she'd sniff him out and stand and wait and sometimes give a little bark so I would know she was there wanting to be helped up. And due to her lack of vision I would position her behind him so he'd keep her safe because once Tommy was down and in that deep a sleep he wasn't for getting up and moving, he slept like a log. So, you'd have big sprawled out Tommy and tiny little Amber peeping her head out from behind him, but she'd settle down fast, usually with her chin resting on his back and I'd see her eyes close and know it was safe to walk away for a little while. I was never too far away, just bobbing about the house doing a few chores and constantly coming back and forth checking on how everybody was doing. When Amber first arrived she was nine years old and had just enough vision to know where the edge of the couch was and she was a sensible little girl, I watched her for quite a while, I'd seen her slowly feeling her way around and stopping when she realised she'd reached the edge. I knew she was not going to be one of these vision impaired pugs that would quickly walk off the edge of the couch with no thought given, some blind dogs will do that, in fact a lot of blind dogs will do that, so I never have those ones up on the couch unless I am there with them. You can't afford to have them falling off and hurting themselves, that's not fair. You have to know your dogs, know their different personalities and once you do you work in with them. I spend a lot of time observing any new pug I take in and when they have special needs it's even more important to spend time watching them, finding out who they are and knowing their capabilities and once you know them you are set, easy really. But as they age things about them will change so you have to be continually reassessing the situation, constantly making sure to keep them safe from harm. As their guardian you have to be always watching, watching, watching, forever making mental notes of what you see with each dog and then working within those guidelines, it's your job to do this and it's a very important job. Amber is now sixteen years old and doesn't have any vision so no being left on the couch for her unless I am right there by her side, even if I get up for a few moments I will put her down on the floor. Yes she objects greatly and lets me know she's not happy about it in her little granny way, but I do it anyway, sure she still isn't the type of pug to wander around aimlessly but at her age a fall could well be the end of her. Or the start of the end of her anyway, old dogs are like old people, both can be going along wonderfully and then an incident will occur and that will be enough to send them into a downward spiral. So I risk being told off in that groaning growly coughing spluttering way that is uniquely Amber because I know how terrible I am going to feel if she came to harm because I wasn't looking after her properly.

I thought it was kind of special that out of all our pugs Amber chose Thomas to be her friend. I can understand it though, with her lack of vision she was using her other senses a lot and she had picked up on the fact that Tommy was a beautiful souled boy, just a big snugly teddy bear really. I think that's what she loved about him. If she's not with me than she's with Thomas. She got to know my routine well, knew when I was at my busiest and if Tommy was not on the couch but laying somewhere on the floor Amber would trot off to find him. She'd sniff him out and prop herself up on him while he was peacefully sleeping away and because she was so little half the time I don't think he even realised she was there. But she didn't care she'd lean against his stomach and bob about as he took in his huge snoring breaths. They used to remind me of a cork floating out at sea, his tummy was the ocean and Amber's teeny tiny little head the cork, the two of them were quite lovely to watch actually and I spent a bit of time doing that as I went about the house. Tommy had this funny way of hanging half out of the dog beds. I used to think it was due to his size, that he couldn't fully fit into the beds the other pugs could and yes that was part of it, but I think he just liked sleeping that way because he could have fitted more of himself in the beds if he tried. I'd come along and find him there, back end in the bed and from the middle of his tummy up he was sprawled out on the floor, just sleeping away peacefully and seemed quite comfortable doing so.

Even though Tommy was huge David and I decided very early on that we would always treat him like we do our regular sized pugs, we had a discussion about it on the way home from the airport. As Tommy lay sprawled out sleeping on the back seat up front quiet mutterings were going on between his new Mum and Dad. We both decided that he would always be picked up and hugged and carried around whenever he asked to be, even if it meant that our arms would be aching by the end of it. We didn't want him to feel left out, rejected, that he was in any way different, if we picked up one of our other pugs for a big hug we picked Owde Tommy up for one as well. We'd hold him, snuggle him, carry him round the house and sit him on our knee even if he's half hanging off. In our house they are all treated equally and each one is given the same amount of love and attention. It's vital to us that we do that. Tommy liked to be upside down a lot, he used to sleep that way for hours out on the veranda in the sun, for me it'd be so uncomfortable, but he seemed to like it. And it wasn't unusual to see my husband striding around the house with Tommy cradled in his arms. He was so trusting laying on his back like that, his big head would be hanging there looking all around, seeing the world from his upside down view. You'd have to be really careful coming through doorways with him though, so he didn't knock his head. You'd also have to fully support his neck as you carried him because that was very important, really carrying Tommy around wasn't the easiest thing to do but because he loved it so much we kept on doing it. And eventually you'd put him down thinking he'd had enough for one day but he very quickly let you know that he hadn't, that he wanted more, so up he would come again until you just couldn't physically hold him any longer, then you'd walk over to the couch and lower him once again just to give your arms and lower back a bit of a rest. Lilly didn't want to be carried around at all, she never asked to be picked up, it was just our big goofy new son who wanted to be carried so we took turns of doing it and he spent a lot of time being passed from one person to the other. And he never minded that, he'd be there upside down and smiling going from David to me then back again, never wanting down, never stopping smiling, just lay there all floppy limbed and relaxed, so very trusting of us he was, and we felt blessed that Tommy was feeling so happy and contented in his new home. It's things like this that really warm your heart.

One thing that was crystal clear from the very start about Tommy and Lilly was that they were both incredibly well loved in their previous life, adored, cherished and wanted that was so obvious, you can tell the ones that have lived with love and the ones who've gone without. But Tommy and Lilly were in no way lacking in that area. I found out that they were owned by an elderly lady who had dementia and went into a nursing home. Apparently she forgot to feed them from time to time but it wasn't just them because she forgot to feed herself as well. Her family had made a promise to her that when she went into the home they would take care of her pugs. I'm not sure what happened but those two pugs went into rescue not long after the old lady entered the nursing home. And if the daughter didn't want them then I think it was for the best. If it was my Mum's dogs I would have loved them dearly with all my heart for the rest of their lives because it would have been an extension of loving my Mum, and not only that it would have given her peace of mind as well, but everybody is different aren't they and at least the daughter didn't leave them in the back yard unloved and uncared for, after living with a lifetime of love that would have been a terrible thing to happen. They wouldn't have known what hit them, to go from fully loved to nothing through no fault of their own would have been a great injustice. Especially when they would be grieving for the loss of their previous owner at the time, they wouldn't have known she was in a nursing home, they probably thought she was dead, either way she was lost to them and they would have been feeling her departure dearly. I was grateful the daughter did the right thing by Tommy and Lilly, and I am very happy that we were the ones who ended up with them. We kept that circle of love going for those two pugs, we got to have them share our life and we were thankful for that.

    I felt it right to talk to Tommy about his previous owner. I used to tell him how much she loved him, I told him this over and over again because I didn't want him thinking she didn't care about him anymore. That would have been an awful thing for him to be carrying around. It wasn't her fault that they weren't living together now nor was it his fault. It's just how life turns out sometimes and it's heartbreaking for those involved. I knew what I was telling Tommy to be the truth, I imagined that lady sitting in the nursing home, her mind going from foggy to clear then back to foggy again. I know in those times of remembering that she would have thought about

Tommy and Lilly. She would have been missing them, her heart would have ached so much for them in those moments, then all of a sudden, she would have forgotten about them once more until the fog cleared again. I didn't want Tommy thinking he'd done something wrong and that she didn't love him any longer. I wasn't exactly sure what thoughts may have been going through his mind about what he taken place, but I didn't want this to be one of them. I felt he needed to know how deeply she loved and adored both him and his little sister Lilly. I thought it would have been far easier on their previous owner than it was on her two pugs because eventually, as she worsened, she would no longer even remember having them, well not in her mind she wouldn't anyway, but I felt deep down in her heart that she would always remember them. But for Tommy and Lilly they would be remembering her every day and no doubt in very clear detail. I sat with Tommy in my arms and explained to him about what had gone on. As he lay on his back looking up at me I explained to him about his previous owner being very old, I wish I'd been given a name because calling her the old lady or his previous owner didn't seem as nice as it would have been if I had a name, but there wasn't anything I could do because it was never given to me. In the end I just referred to her as his first Mummy. I explained to Tommy that "First Mummy" was old and that she had dementia. I was going to try and explain to him what dementia was and I would have done it in the same way I would have done if I was talking to a small child. So, I paused for a few moments, gathering my thoughts, choosing my words, wondering how to best describe this cruel disease in a way he'd understand. Then I looked down at him again ready to begin talking and he just looked so happy, so I decided that maybe he didn't need to know what dementia was after all. All he really needed to know was that "First Mummy" never ever stopped loving him she just used to forget he was there sometimes, and as I told him this I imagined how hard and no doubt how confusing it would have been for him to see this happening. I wondered if he ever tried to remind her he was there, I imagined he would have done especially around meal times. She must have been in a bad way if the pugs dancing around her feet didn't remind her to feed them. I told him she didn't just forget to feed him and Lilly she forgot to feed herself too. Can you imagine how it would have been in that house, one day she'd be ok and life would be as it had always been since Tommy was a puppy and the next day she'd just be sitting there oblivious to what was going on around her. My heart broke for those two pugs, I wondered if they ever nudged her arm, or tapped her on the leg trying to tell her they needed to go outside for a wee. How heartbreaking and painful this disease is for loved ones to stand by and watch, with us the heartbreak is the same but at least we know what's going on whereas Tommy and Lilly wouldn't have had a clue.

I rubbed Tommy's chest and told him that "First Mummy" needed some help and special care, needed to go and live in a place where nurses could look after her the same way I was now looking after him. I told him she was being given some really nice dinners just like the nice dinners I was giving him and Lilly. I said "First Mummy" now had some lovely people who were reminding her to take her medication and that they would also help her walk around the grounds just like he was walking around our grounds, and I said that she would be just as happy as he was when she was out walking. I felt it was important that he knew all this and important that his sister knew it too, so I sat Lilly on my knee and told her exactly the same thing. Tommy sat beside me when I was talking to Lilly just as Lilly had done when I was talking to Tommy. I could have just spoken to the two of them together, but I wanted to look them in the eye, talk to each one personally and get my point across. I felt explaining these important facts to them would save them feeling hurt, feeling rejected, I wanted no confusion in either one of their minds about where their previous owners heart lay. Their first Mummy couldn't be here to tell them all of this herself, but their second Mummy was able to do it for her and after we'd had our special chats Tommy did seem happier in himself and little Lilly did too. I think it's so important to try and see things from their point of view, so when I take in a pug I like to try and get as much information as possible about their old life so I know how best to help them, how best to talk to them, of course sometimes it's impossible to do that, sometimes I have nothing and in those times I just give them a little talk about how much I love them and how much I so desperately wanted to be their new Mummy. I tell them that I chose them, specially chose them because I wanted them so much. I let them know very early on that this is going to be their forever home, that they have a big family here that loves them so deeply. I say "You are going to be living happily here on this little farm for the rest of your lives" And I can truthfully promise them this because I know they are more them likely going to die before me. And should I go before them, well, I married a younger man didn't I and he's got specific instructions to talk to them when I'm gone and explain to them that I loved them with all my heart and will be waiting arms outstretched when their times comes to join me.

If I don't have any information on the dog I've just taken in I don't worry about it too much because they always reveal to you what their previous lives have been like, I watch and observe and it's the little things you pick up on that can mean a real lot. But I also ask them to let me know if there is anything I can do for them. It's not just something I do once, it's something I do often with all the pugs regardless of how long they've been living here. This is something I began doing of a morning some years back and now I find that David has started doing it sometimes as well which is a really beautiful thing to witness, it was especially beautiful the first time I heard him doing it. I saw him drop back on the walk and crouch down next to Arthur who was sitting on the grass, I wasn't far enough ahead that I missed out on hearing him asking Arthur if he needed anything special from his dad today. I think it's good to talk to them this way because one, it makes them feel loved, special, important and that we care deeply about them and two, because should they ever feel unwell then I want to know about it as soon as possible so I can go ahead and help them. Of course, I'm not expecting a verbal answer, I mean I'm nuts but I'm not that nuts, although my husband would say that was debatable at times. But I tell you what being Dr Doolittle would certainly be a great asset sometimes especially in a house full of old pugs. I believe our animals show us how they are feeling by their actions, and I want them to know that they can do that at any time with me and I'll be there watching. So, what I do some mornings when we are about to start our day is ask each one of them the question of "What can I do for you. How can I help you today" It's just a quick kiss on the head and a quick ask as I'm lifting the pugs off the bed of a morning. Ok I do have days when I miss, when I'm running late or when one of the pugs needs to be taken outside for a toilet break very quickly before an accident happens. But I do it often enough that they know I am always here for them, always waiting and wanting to help in any area I can.

From Tommy's actions I could tell they were very close, him and the old lady, I think her husband must have died and Tommy used to sleep on the bed with her. He would have been such a comfort to his previous owner, a source of security for her being so huge and all, I think she would have felt safe going to sleep with Tommy by her side. He slept on her husband's pillow, he let us know that by his obsession with jumping on David's pillow every night. I thought it would have been really nice for her to roll over in the middle of the night and feel Tommy there. Tommy wanted to sleep that way when he first arrived here, but then where was David going to put his head. I give up a lot for my pugs but I felt asking David to sleep on the floor so Tommy could settle in faster wouldn't have been the right thing to do. So Tommy hops on David's pillow and goes to sleep while we are settling all the other pugs down then gets lifted off and put a little further down the bed, sometimes he won't even rouse when he's being moved. In the morning he just wakes up in a different place wondering how the heck he got there. You can do just about anything with Tommy, he's never been hurt by a human being, he's incredibly trusting, goes to sleep upside down in our arms and we gently rock him like a baby, and he'll just lay there snoring away happily. If only all the pugs we take in were as well loved as Thomas was, what a lovely world this would be.

There was many a time when I was looking at Tommy that his previous owner would cross my mind, in the early days of his arrival watching him made my thoughts instantly go to her. I was extremely sorry that they were no longer living together. I've always felt sad when those who love each other deeply are parted, it doesn't matter what the reason the result is the same, they don't get to spend the rest of their lives together, and there was sadness in me about that. It wasn't that I was unappreciative of Tommy entering my life because of course I was, I just didn't like the circumstances that brought the two of us together. I felt sorry for his previous owner sitting in the home wondering what became of her beloved Thomas. Well, he was our beloved Thomas to her he would still have been being referred to as her beloved Quick. If it were possible I would have liked to have written her a letter letting her know that I had her boy, I would have liked to have had the chance to say how much I loved him, how lucky I felt to have him as my son and how much he was enjoying life here on the farm. I figured when she was having a clear minded day she would have been able to read that letter and take it all in. But it was impossible to get in touch which was a shame because I would have liked her to have peace of mind, I think that would have meant a lot to her. One day that old lady sitting in the nursing home could well be me and I know I would feel a whole lot better if I knew where my babies went and what type of person was now looking after them. And if I do end up in a nursing home I pray to God that he allows me to keep my memories, I'd like to be able to sit there remembering all the pugs I've loved and shared my life with, the cruellest thing in the world for me would be to get dementia, to have those memories wiped, erased forever. It would be hard enough living without pugs in my life, but to have all those years' worth of happy times stolen, now that would be torturous. I've got all my pug photo's stored on my computer, perhaps I'd best print them out and make up album after album to help jog my memory should anything like that ever happen to me. And I'll write the name of the pug and a little bit about them underneath each photo, I mean you think you'll never forget a pug, but age does cruel things to a person and I'd like the pugs I've loved and cared for to stay part of me forever.

I mentioned earlier how much I knew our vet was going to love Tommy and he did, from the first time he met him he adored this big strong athletic boy of ours, but it wasn't just our vet who thought Tommy was fantastic he became a real favourite amongst our friends and family too. Tommy being the well-mannered old gentleman that he was made a friend out of everyone he met. When people dropped by the house all the other pugs would rush to greet the visitor but not Tommy, he was too laid back for that, he almost always made them come to him. And the funny thing was that's exactly what ended up happening. Once the others had all been greeted the next question was often "Where's Owde Tommy" and I'd point over to the wicker chair. Because if he wasn't out wandering the grounds he was generally asleep on his special chair at the end of the sofa, we put a cushion on the floor in that area once he let us know that's where he'd like to sleep. Then one day I thought to myself "I think we can do better than that" so I went out and bought Tommy a special chair of his own. The chair had a big comfy cushion on it which made it a little high, but he'd just leap up on it and either settle down to sleep or sit up watching me in the kitchen from his elevated view. He liked watching me cook and every so often I'd wander over and give him a little bit of what I was preparing for that nights tea. As Tommy aged he needed help getting up on his chair and I was always on the lookout for that, always made sure I was there should he need me. He'd come in from outside, have a drink, then go stand in front of his chair. Sometimes he'd place his two front paws on the chair, but that was as far as he'd be able to go and then as he aged some more he'd get a little bit confused and be on the other end of the couch with his paws up. But it was good that he was still able to let me know what he wanted so I'd go over and heave him up and he'd bound along and bounce over the end of the couch and onto his special chair and when he wanted to get down he'd rise up and look around for me, when he saw where I was, when he'd made eye contact with me he'd then give out one of his warrior cries and I'd stop what I was doing and go over and lift him down. When the visitors made their way over to his chair Tommy would roll over on his back so they could rub his tummy and he'd be there like that, mouth wide open, looking so happy. And why wouldn't he be happy, I mean he'd made people come over to him and was now getting half hour long belly rubs. Tommy sure did love being up on his special chair, well up on any furniture really. I remember the first night he got here, how quickly he made a beeline for our couch, jumped straight up on it with that big body of his, he looked like a lion springing up on a rock. Then it was a quick look over his shoulder to make sure he was allowed on the furniture, he was, they all are, and once he knew it was ok he got comfortable and flopped straight down and went to sleep with one of those huge paws of his tucked underneath his chin. I don't think he moved all night from that position because he was in that exact same spot in the morning and the blanket I'd draped over him was still arranged in the exact same way I'd arranged it the night before, slightly tucked underneath his back legs to keep them warm.

It wasn't just our friends who loved Owde Tommy my brother in law adored him too. And Tommy adored him right back, he would sit on the back of Chris's chair when he was visiting and the two of them would fall asleep together after dinner and you'd be hard pressed to know who was snoring the loudest, but I think it could have been a draw. We had a BBQ one summers evening, it was around Christmas time and all the boys sat outside looking at the stars and talking into the wee hours of the morning. Us girls all came inside and went to sleep. I remember falling asleep listening to my husband and his brother talking and laughing outside the bedroom window. I couldn't hear what they were saying just heard them murmuring but I sure did hear the laughter because that was pretty loud, of course there were innuendos, in jokes and things they had been laughing about since their childhood. I thought it was a lovely thing for them to be doing. They were best friends as well as brothers, so it was really nice whenever they got to spend some time together. The next morning David told me they had seen two shooting stars and I suppose Tommy would have seen them too if he hadn't been fast asleep underneath his uncles chair. Chris had never even seen one shooting star in his entire life and was ecstatic at seeing two in the one evening. He was lucky that he happened to be here on a night where the sky was crystal clear, not one single cloud in sight, you can normally see stars here but on magical nights like this the stars look like diamonds and there are thousands upon thousands of them twinkling down at you. He couldn't believe how clear and beautiful everything was. We had gotten used to it, but with him living in a heavily built up area he'd never seen anything quite like our amazing night skies. You feel like the stars are so close to you when you are out there, you lay back in your chair and look up and it's almost as if you could literally reach up and touch them. There's just you and this huge chandelier of stars and it's an awesome feeling, and in a way it makes you feel kind of small and unimportant, because really in the scheme of things that's exactly what all of us are.

I sometimes stand out there and think about the people who have been standing there doing the exact same thing I am doing for thousands and thousands of years. All those little eyes looking up in wonder and amazement the same way I am doing now, the millions of people who have gone before me who are now no more. It's like you have a bond with them somehow, like those stars are what links us all. And I start wondering about those people, who they were, what they looked like, what were their names, what made them laugh and what made them cry, who did they love, did they live good lives. What were their hopes, dreams and aspirations, did they do all they wanted to do while they were still here. And what ages were they when they became one of the stars I am looking at right now. I mention things like this to my husband and at times he'll answer me, and we have a great in depth discussion, other times he'll just look over at me and say "You are far too deep for me baby" and we'll laugh and have a much lighter conversation until next time. I remember when David and I were first going out together, the things I'd come out with would have him shaking his head at times, he thought I was too deep for him back then and told me so quite often. He said he'd never met anybody quite like me and the things I'd come out with either made him laugh or completely blew his mind and not always in a good way either. On the morning of our 24th wedding anniversary I was reminding him of this while we were having breakfast and over Wheat-Bix we were laughing about it. As he left for work I shouted out to him "How's me being too deep working out for you now? And in amongst the sound of pitter-pattering paws on wooden floorboards he answered "Just fine baby, just fine" then he smiled at me and turned and walked out the door. And as I stood in the middle of the lounge room holding a sick pug and watching his car going down the driveway I thought to myself "Damn straight it's just fine, it's just fine indeed"

Sadly, my brother in law Chris died of cancer when he was just fifty years old, we lost him far too young and that was a real hard blow for both David and me. Chris had more empathy in him than anybody else I know. I used to share the stories of my pugs previous lives with him and with an understanding heart he felt for each one of them, he loved them all but Tommy was definitely his favourite. I remember in his final weeks of life Chris asked if Tommy could be brought to the hospital so he could see him one last time. That was a thing he really wanted, and we thought it was nice that he'd asked to see our boy so David and Tommy took off for the long drive to the hospital. As I write this I have a picture in my mind of David's car going down the driveway with Tommy's smiley face peeping through the back window. Many years have passed but that image is as clear to me now as it was on the day it happened, and it was nice to remember. I haven't thought about that day for a very long time and enjoyed the mental image. I was going to go with them but decided to stay home and keep the pugs to their regular routine. Well, it wasn't just for that reason that I stayed behind, I did so because I felt it was important for the brothers to spend some time together without me being there. They could talk and laugh about whatever they liked when they were on their own and they deserved to be able to do that. Conversations can sometimes change when women are around and I wanted the two of them to be able to talk about whatever they liked, what interested them the most, not try and frilly it up for my sake, which I know they would have done if I was in the room. David told me the nursing staff all took a huge liking to Tommy because I guess they wouldn't get too many big smiley frog faced pugs in their ward. One nurse after another kept creeping into the room and sneakily feeding Tommy biscuits, well Tommy loved biscuits almost as much as he loved his uncle Chris, so he had the best time at the hospital. He sat on the side of Chris's bed and his uncle stroked his ears as he had one last long conversation with his little brother. Chris died a week after David and Tommy's visit.

I think Chris took to Tommy because he was a big beautiful polite quiet gentleman, and you could pretty much describe my brother in law the same way. Or maybe it wasn't that at all that drew him to Tommy, maybe Chris just took delight in Tommy's big old smiley face. And I can fully understand that because a whole lot of people did. I know he delighted me whenever he was standing there looking upwards. You couldn't help but smile when seeing Tommy's face. And although Tommy was my squishy faced wide smiley frog I do believe he had come from good stock and was an extremely well-bred pug, his side profile was amazing, thing is you just didn't get to see that part of him very often because he was 99% goofy froggy faced. And most people thought that was all there was to him, but those who lived with him day in day out knew differently, and you'd tell people about it, tell them how stunning and striking his profile was but they'd look at you like you were telling a huge fib and Tommy didn't help the situation either because he never sprang into action when anybody else was here. But being with him all the time we got to see a part of Tommy others never did. He'd be sprawled out in front of the heater in winter and suddenly his head would come up, he'd be instantly alert and gazing out the front windows and he was so regal looking then, he reminded me of a lion statue, he just had this magnificent silhouette. He wouldn't move, wouldn't actually get up and walk over to the windows, he'd just bring his huge head up and lay there watching what was going on outside. And that magnificent silhouette could disappear then reappear in less than a heartbeat too. He could go from all goofy like to royal and regal in the blink of an eye. But because he was relaxed and chilled most of the time that's the image most people saw of him and that was fine really because the most important thing you wanted for him was to be happy and Tommy sure was that.

A lot of the pugs we take in come to us around the ages of nine or ten and by the time they get to those ages their faces and bodies are very different to how they once were, and that's fair enough I find that I am the same way as I age, but sometimes they'll give you a glimpse of their younger selves and it can be a pretty special thing to see. Harper was not a well-bred pug, and she didn't have the best life before coming to us, not well looked after in the slightest, but even she could have moments of transformation but her moments of transformation only came when there was food around. Nothing sparked Harper's interest like food did and she was very fond of being given special treats. I remember being with Harper at the vet one day. It was a new female vet we were seeing and she'd just given Harper an injection and poor Harper really wasn't feeling at all well. She wasn't interested in walking so David had carried her in and put her on the table and she just sat there looking like a sack of spuds. All slumped over, tongue hanging way out, totally pathetic looking and very disinterested in life she was and yes she was ill so looking like that was understandable. Well, this new vet was trying to be extra nice to her first time customers and especially nice to their little depressed looking pug, no doubt in the hope of us asking to see her the next time we were in. So she walked over to get Harper a treat. She had her back turned and began violently shaking the treat out of a jar, the jar was full of these odd shaped bits of dark dried out liver and due to them being all clumped together they weren't coming out of the jar so easily. By the time one actually dropped on the countertop much shaking had been done and of course Harper could hear all this and smell it all too, by this point the entire room smelt like liver. David was standing with Harper making sure she didn't fall off the table. I was standing to one side with full vision of both the vet and Harper. On first shake of the jar Harper had sat up really straight getting herself ready, she flicked her tongue about then sucked it in waiting for the treat. Her eyes were huge and fixated on the vet, but the vet had her back to us so couldn't see what Harper was doing. When she finally turned around her whole face changed, she did a double take, she looked at Harper and then started looking on the floor at the two other pugs we had with us that day, she thought we'd swapped pugs on her while she had her back turned. She asked where the pug she'd just given the injection to was and David and I both pointed at Harper sitting on the table. The vet looked at us and said "No way". She couldn't believe it was the same pug. David and I laughed because we were well aware of what Harper could become at treat time, but this vet wasn't and thought we were playing a trick on her. Anyway, it was the exact same way with Tommy. He could look instantly different whenever he felt like it, it's just that he didn't feel like it too often.

Tommy had been living with us for about two years when he decided that he wanted to help me herd up the sheep. I have no idea what caused this sudden interest in being a sheep dog but one night as I was on my way out the door he let me know that he wanted to come with me. It was a snap decision on his part and that surprised me because Tommy didn't normally make snap decisions. I remember the first day it happened, Tommy was asleep on his special chair and all the others were sound asleep too, so I thought I'd take this opportunity to sneak out and put the sheep away. But Tommy clearly had other ideas. As soon as my hand was on the door handle he sprang into action, leapt from his chair and was instantly by my side and very eager about coming with me. Steffy must have been really tired that day because even his heavy thud didn't wake her up. Tom had watched me putting the sheep away from the time he first arrived and never seemed all that bothered, he didn't even bark as he watched my movements through the glass like some of the other pugs did. I'd often glance up at the house and there would be a line of little woofers at the windows and there towering above them all was Tommy not saying a single word. His head and his eyes followed me, but he wasn't interested enough to bother offering up an opinion and his sisters going nuts beside him couldn't even motivate him to do so and those little old ladies were a pretty enthusiastic bunch. That's why it surprised me when he suddenly wanted to tag along. I guess at some point during the day he must have thought to himself "I reckon I'll have a go at doing that myself tonight" and he must have been waiting until it was time to go out. He must have just been resting his eyes, not in the deep sleep I thought he'd been in when I headed for the door. They say dogs can't tell the time and this may be true, but I tell you what they are very much aware of it. They know our schedules better than we do.

    I looked down at Tommy standing next to me and thought "Oh why the hell not". I mean I couldn't really see the harm in it. I knew it'd be easy to keep an eye on just one pug if the ewes got nasty, if all the pugs were involved it'd be an absolute nightmare trying to keep them all safe and I wouldn't even consider attempting that, but the others showed no interest in coming out, so Tommy and I put the sheep away together that night. He kept very close to me, his saunter got faster or slower to match my stride, and when I stopped he stopped. I don't think he knew why I was stopping but he must have realised there was a reason for it and there was, it was to let the sheep wander along at their own pace, we don't rush anybody here. Tommy seemed to be really enjoying himself out there, a bit of a warrior cry was heard every now and then and his face looked so happy when he was doing it, still like a wide faced frog but deliriously happy to be in amongst all the action for once. He really did love being able to make those sheep move, make them go in the direction he wanted them to go, he was in his element and very proud of himself too you could tell by his expression. A few of the sheep weren't too happy about the situation though, with me they were calm and even natured but with Tommy by my side they weren't impressed at all, and much foot stomping was being done. The rams were fine but Agnes Griffiths, our lead ewe, looked at Tommy like he had no right being in the paddock at all let alone trying to tell her what to do. She walked over to Rose and they both stood together stomping their feet as if to say "What do you reckon about this bloke then, who the hell does that frog faced pug think he is" Rose looked over at Tommy standing here doing his warrior cry with that wide mouth of his and decided that she'd like to take him on. Tommy was ahead of me by this time, but I could see what was going on. I saw the other ewe's watching Agnes and Rose and knew what was about to happen and nobody was going to be ganging up on Owde Tommy while I was there sticking up for him. When you've been around sheep for a while it doesn't take much to know what they are thinking and if the top ewe and her best friend decide something "Is on" then "It is On" and a lot of head nodding and foot stomping signalled that. But Tommy being a newcomer to sheep droving wasn't picking up on their signals, he was still in his delirious bubble, but I knew he soon wouldn't be if the ewes got to him. The rams were still calm and collected but the other ewe's saw Rose and Agnes Griffiths sizing Tommy up and thought they'd get in on the act too and the lot of them started moving towards him at once. So I quickly ran and stood behind Tommy and started waving my arms around making them all think twice about having a go at him. And of course Tommy couldn't see what I was doing so thought it was all him and once he thought he'd made the sheep turn and run all by himself, well his confidence level went through the roof. He seemed to think he had some form of magical power and started doing his warrior cry louder than I'd ever heard him do it before. To be honest he looked and sounded a little bit silly, but the job was getting done and he was happy doing it. So night after night he leapt from the couch and stood by the door while I got my gumboots on, then we'd fly down into the front paddock together and heard the sheep into the back. Tommy was big bold and fearless and once the ewes sensed this they did as they were told, they didn't even consider taking him on. Less and less foot stomping was being done each night until they stopped doing it altogether. I reckon I could have actually gotten Tom to a point where he would have been quite the sheepdog, well a sheep-pug anyway, but after a month or so of coming out with me every evening he totally lost interest in the game. So, I just left him inside sleeping and went out and moved the sheep on my own. His obsession with the sheep was lost almost as quickly as it had begun, one day he was with me, the next he didn't bother coming out, just lay on his chair as if to say "You are on your own tonight Mummy I'll stay here where it's nice and warm and wait for you to come back in". So, I grabbed my coat and paused for a few seconds by the back door just in case Tommy changed his mind but he didn't even bother to raise his head. So I called out to him, "Are you coming Tom", nothing, "Tommy, Thomas, are you coming with me", again nothing, he wasn't for moving just acknowledging me with his eyes only, he didn't even bother lifting his head just sort of staring at me out of the corner of his eye so as not to act too interested. He'd done that one time before though then jumped off the couch fast when he saw me closing the door and I had to walk back and open it for him on seeing him staring through the glass. I didn't want to be halfway down the paddock that night and have him suddenly decide he wanted to come out with me after all because by that time it'd be too late. I'd have already gotten the sheep moving and I couldn't muck them around, couldn't leave them and run back to get Thomas. I would have just gotten on with finishing what I was doing, and poor Tommy would have been standing by the window crying. I didn't want him upset, so I was making doubly sure he knew that I was going to walk out the door, "Tom, Tommy, Thomas", "The sheep", "Last call", "Colonel are you coming with me to put the sheep away tonight or not" and he just smushed his face further into his blanket. I definitely had his answer then, no question about it, so with that I turned and walked out the door by myself.

To be honest I did rather miss having my big boy out there with me. I'd kind of gotten used to having a helper by my side, sure I had to be constantly on the lookout for his safety so the job took a little longer, but I would have had it take three times as long and it wouldn't have bothered me one little bit, just as long as Tommy was out there with me. But he didn't want to come, and I didn't ever make him. It was like he thought "Well I've conquered that game now, what's next on the agenda" But it did prove to me that Tommy wasn't as unintelligent as I'd previously thought. He must have just not been interested in doing things before and once his interested was sparked, well there was no holding him back. I suppose they are just like us really, they are interested in what they are interested in and you can't force a pug or a person to have an interest in something they don't want to. That's like forcing a child to learn a musical instrument just because you play one or like the sound of them. Mum did that with me for a while but me and that organ never became friends. It's the same with all these animals you see online or on TV doing these amazing things and you think to yourself, well I might try and get my dog to do that and when you can't you are disappointed and really you've no need to be. Because all that's happening there is that the dog is just doing what it likes doing, what is part of their individual personality and dogs just like us all have different quirks and traits. And you can work with that trait, set it up in a situation where the dog looks like it's actually doing something incredible. And you being a proud owner will film it and post it and yes it'll go viral because the people who are seeing it think it's the most intelligent, cutest or funniest dog in the world, so it gets shared and shared and shared. It's just how people market things. And then yes you will have these dogs that truly are super smart and can pick up on anything fast and a lot of the time they'll have been found in the pound by a dog trainer looking for their next prodigy and to be honest I do love hearing stories like this. Because any dog saved from death row and given plenty of attention and praise and rewards in the form of treats, well that certainly beats the alternative doesn't it.

Tommy blessed us by sharing our lives for five wonderful beautiful years. And he had very little illness during that time. The last few weeks of his life he had a cough and was on antibiotics for it, but it wasn't making much of a difference, he was old and both David and I felt he was nearing the end and it would soon be his time to go. After you've been doing this a while you get to know the signals, he wasn't really sick, he was just old and had started slowing down. We tried stronger antibiotics just in case it could ease his cough and give him a bit more time but again, not much change. I said goodbye to Tommy many times in the last few weeks of his life because I had this strong feeling that he'd pass away quietly in his sleep, so each day when he was still with me and breathing I told him how much I loved him and how grateful I was that he had been part of my life, he would be the fifth pug we had lost in the past eighteen months so there were a load of family members on the other side ready to greet him. And I let him know this so he wouldn't be afraid, well that's if he was afraid, but Owde Tommy didn't seem all that fazed by anything, not when he first came and not now nearing the end of his life, but I felt it best to let him know who would be there waiting for him anyway. Maybe I told him more to make myself feel better, I don't know, all I know is that every day I'd tell him stories about my babies who were already in heaven. I told him that Harper and Lilly and Ruby and Grace and Sarah and Horton and Uncle Chris would be there waiting for him and that he could hang out with them until Mummy and Daddy got there. I also told him to go find his first Mummy, the one who had dementia, the one who forgot to feed him, the one who forgot to feed herself so had to go into a nursing home to be looked after. I said to Tommy "It's ok sweetheart she will remember you now" I told him to go and leap onto her knee and give her a huge snuggle and smother her face with tender little kisses because she would have missed receiving those kisses in the last five years.

Tommy died in August 2012. He was 14 years old when he died. What I remember vividly about his death is our vet holding his paw, looking him in the eye and telling him that he was sorry. I thought it was a nice thing to do. We'd had many weeks of vet visits before finally putting old Tommy to sleep. He had been on medication, and he'd show a bit of improvement then go back to how he was. The thing with Tommy was that he had just lived all the years he had in him, he was old, and the coughing fits were really wearing him out. I remember when we were in the car going down our driveway with Tommy that last time, he was sitting on my knee and started coughing and chocking so we stopped the car at the front gate, and I hopped out and put Tom on the ground so he could get his breath. I had to hold him up because he had gone limp. David came around from his side of the car and we just gave each other a quick look. It was a look that said do we let him go here, now, on the farm, or do we get him going again and proceed to the vet. It was a split second look because it had to be, there was no time for deliberation. But I knew what David's look meant and he was the same with me. When you've been together as long as we have you don't always need words. So I got Tommy into the best position to catch his breath and he did just that, then straightened up again and shook himself a little bit and then we got back into the car, and I held him on my knee talking to him all the way to the vet. As much as both of us would have liked Tommy to have died here on the farm, we just couldn't let him leave the world choking and gasping for air. Both of us felt that was not a very nice way to die. I suppose it may sound strange to some of you that we got a dog going again only to have him put to sleep an hour or so later. But we both knew it was the right thing for us to do. If Thomas had gone peacefully in his sleep it would have been a different matter. But seeing him like that with that look of fear on his face, well we couldn't do that to our boy. So, we went to the vet and sent him off to the bridge with a simple prick of a needle. It was quiet, it was gentle, Tommy went out of this world in David's arms with me standing beside the two of them stroking his head. And then I once again sat Tommy on my knee and talked to him all the way home. Before the needle was administered I did ask our vet one last time if he thought there was any more we could do for Tommy, anything else he could think of that we could try. And I already knew the answer to that question because we had done all that over the past two months, but I think sometimes you are wanting to double check for your own peace of mind even though deep down in your heart you know that this is the end and there is no more to be done but let him go.

That night David decided he wanted to light a candle for Owde Tommy, and a candle has been lit here at Grace Farm every night since. Even though it all started with Thomas, and we still refer to it as "Tommy's candle", it's now lit for every pug we have loved and lost. Even when my husband was rushed to hospital he called over his shoulder "Will you do something for me while I'm gone" and I answered quickly "Yes of course, what", and he replied "Don't forget to light Tommy's candle for me will you". Until then it was David who had always lit the candle, for his boy you know, and I started lighting it while my husband was away from home and am still lighting it today. The candle used to be out hanging on the veranda inside a beautiful green and gold decorative lantern, we used to watch it flicking outside our bedroom window and it was a lovely sight to see. But it gets pretty windy here and some nights that glass lantern would be almost tilted on its side, and we thought it was a bit dangerous, we didn't want it falling on the deck while we were sleeping and burning the house down. So I left the lantern outside and brought the candle into our ensuite and that's where it still is today. And every night I watch the pattern it makes on the ceiling before I drift off to sleep. Even now all these years later I still miss everything about Tommy. I miss his size and his way of sauntering around the place. I miss his big lovely smiling froggy face and his beautiful gentle nature. I miss him sleeping against my back. And God bless Tommy because he changed my heart and paved the way for a lot of male pugs to come into our home. Now I don't even think twice about it, male or female it doesn't matter to me anymore, if they need us we are there for them. And that's all because of Tommy being the beautiful soul that he was.

Our house was a lot different after Tommy had gone, not quieter because he wasn't a loud pug, just different, like something very special was now missing and of course that's because there was. Our big beautiful boy was gone and he left a huge space. I felt it, David felt it and so did everybody else. Ruben and

Arthur were the ones that seemed the most upset that Tommy had gone, they hung their heads real low for a few days afterwards, perhaps it was because they were both so much like Tommy was in nature, perhaps they shared a bond that I wasn't fully aware of. Or perhaps it was just their way of honouring a fallen brother. We were feeding Tommy with a syringe the last two days of his life and his siblings had been there watching all of this, then on the third day Tom clenched his jaw shut and said no more. He let us know that he wanted to go. And although it was hard it did give us peace that we were doing the right thing. Yes you still cry and yes you are still sad, but it does help having that peace within. Walking past Tommy's special chair was hard for me, of course it wasn't empty Steffy had claimed it as her own, but not seeing him sitting there was difficult. She was so tiny in comparison to him, she would fold herself into the back of the chair, I'd walk by and not even realise she was there sometimes. With Tommy you'd clearly be able to see him sprawled out from a distance, but you had to actually stand in front of the chair to see Steffy laying there. Over the course of a few months Buddy decided to join Steffy and they slept side by side for a little while until she choose to go back to the couch and sleep next to Emily. After that it became solely Buddy's chair and I think Tommy would have been happy knowing his lovely docile soft natured brother was getting joy from it. These days Tommy's chair is stored in the shed with a sheet over it. After we lost Buddy a few new pugs entered the house who thought it would be more fun to destroy Tommy's chair than to actually sit on it and I wasn't going to let that happen. These two little blessings started chewing on the bottom of the wicker and nothing I could do or say would deter them from doing so. They became obsessed with it, there were plenty of chew toys in the house, but they took no notice of them and attacked Tommy's chair on a daily basis instead. It was like they were unravelling a jumper, like they'd found a thread and begun pulling on it. The wicker kept disintegrating and moving further and further up the chair. I'd shake toys in their faces or hold two toys up and squeak them rather loudly while standing on the other side of the room, but they barely acknowledge what I was doing. To me that chair was full of sentiment but to the two new pugs it was nothing more than a form of entertainment, I remembered the beautiful boy that chair was bought for, but they never even knew he existed. So while there was still something left of the chair I scooped it up and rescued it. I said to them "If you can't play nice then you're not going to play at all" and I had an echo of my mother's voice running through my head as I uttered those words. I then marched Tommy's chair out to the shed and came back inside and swept up the half chewed twigs that were scattered all over the floor. I did feel sad that the area was now empty. In a way it only magnified that we had lost those two lovely old boys who'd occupied that seat. Even today there is still an empty space where Tommy's chair used to be, a few of the pugs go and sit in that area during the colder months because the floorboards get heated up nicely by the morning sun. I know that's why Tommy chose that area to sit in in the first place and today it's still one of the most popular spots in the house. In fact, it's not unusual for me to have four or five pugs sitting in that warm sunny spot watching me preparing their breakfast. And once the bowls are full they all come trotting over and bark and dance in circles until a bowl of tasty goodness is put down in front of them.

CHAPTER THREE

Lilly

I have thought hard about how to start this chapter because it is a tough one. I think the best way to describe Lilly is as a shooting star, she came, she shone and then she was gone. From the last chapter you'll already know that Lilly and Tommy came together and were a bonded pair. And in every way Tommy was big Lilly was little, you couldn't get two pugs that were as different as these two were. They were a bit like the odd couple, complete opposites in every single way, but unlike the odd couple they got on really well together. Lilly was female, Tommy was male, Lilly was black, and Tommy was fawn and they had very different personalities too. But it didn't matter at all to them, they loved each other deeply, that was clear from the moment they walked in the door. They used to wrestle on the lounge room floor, not gentle wrestling either, but really getting stuck into each other. There was absolutely not an ounce of nastiness there, don't get me wrong they were not trying to draw blood or anything like that, they just played incredibly rough with one another, no holding back. Tommy would be there opening his mouth real wide and sort of snapping her up, but he didn't have a whole lot of teeth so there were no concerns with that action. I did get really worried that Lilly, being so tiny was going to get hurt, but she was actually the roughest one out of the two of them and more often than not it was her who initiated the rough play in the first place. I had an idea that this was the way they'd been playing together all their lives, well he was a year older than she was, but as soon as she arrived on the scene I think that's how they would have been amusing themselves. She did manage to get herself trapped underneath him a few times so I would go over and lift him off her. But by the time I'd walked back across the room she would be under him again biting and squealing and having the time of her life. I think

Tommy used to get half on top of her to give himself a bit of a rest. Like trap her there so he could get his breath back because she was a full on tough little bugger and him being so laid back I think she used to take it out of him a bit. He was only a year older than she was, so it wasn't an age thing. She was just way too much for him to handle sometimes. I was hoping that in time she'd go off and play with one of the other pugs in the house and give Owde Tommy a bit of a rest. I thought Emily would have been an excellent playmate for Lilly. But Lilly never once sought her out, she loved her Tommy, and he was the only one she wanted to play with. And I couldn't begrudge her that, he was her brother after all and this was the way they had chosen to live their lives. Sometimes I thought that maybe I should just let them get on with it and stop interfering. And for the most part I did, but every now and then I'd intervene because I felt I had to, I didn't like that amount of weight pressing down on that tiny frame of hers. I mean even though they were having a ball it didn't alter the fact that he was too heavy a dog to be on top of her. I even tried to get them to play differently, kept pulling Lilly out from underneath and putting her on top just to keep her from getting squashed. Sometimes that worked out nicely, other times she wasn't having any of it and would be once again trapped underneath Tommy biting away at his stomach with all her might and nothing I could do would make her stop so I'd take all the pugs for a nice little wander around the farm just to get their minds on other things.

And where Tommy sauntered Lilly would trot, she had quite a beautiful little trot on her actually and because she was so tiny she looked even cuter when doing it. But then again I think tiny pugs look extra cute no matter what they are doing. I have always loved watching pugs moving along quickly. The slow stroll is nice of course it is, but when they speed up it's a bit of a different sight. They become almost comical. Ears begin flapping up and down, legs move quite differently when there's a spring in the step, even their tails begin bouncing about, it's like everything about them that is already adorable gets really brought out when they trot. Sometimes even their jowls will start flapping up and down and it's at these times that I wish the human eye could make things go in slow motion. Like whenever we wanted to we could slow the sight in front of us down so that we could better capture the image and enjoy it all the more. Then go back to viewing it normally when the moment had passed. Like you blink your eyes once and everything immediately starts to slow down, and you blink twice and everything goes back to normal again. I'd be blinking all the time on my walks around the farm if such a thing were possible because it'd be fantastic for not only watching the pugs but all the other animals we have living here as well. Imagine how the horses would look galloping around the paddocks in slow motion, tails and manes lifted up on the breeze, it'd be quite the sight to see. Same with the sheep chewing, imagine that long drop of the jaw in slow motion, some of the older ewes chew quite slowly anyway but it'd be slowed down even more giving you time to think of comical things they could be saying. And the birds flapping their wings in slow motion would be a calming sight to me.

    I'd called Lilly by her name and she'd instantly turn and come trotting over to me, she took to her new name quite quickly and I was glad of that. Lilly was a beautiful name I had been saving for that one special pug, the right pug, the perfect pug for a much loved name and when I met Lilly I knew I had found the receiver of that name. Lilly was a sweet old fashioned name that I have loved for a good many years, I loved the sound of it, the ring of it, it rolled off my tongue beautifully like music. And Lillian was not only my own grandmother's name but David's grandmother as well, so it was extra special because of that. I even love "Lilly of the Valley" perfume. Not so much for the smell, I'm more of a "Devon Violet" girl myself, but I love it because it was the perfume my grandmother used to wear. There was always at least one bottle of it underneath the Christmas tree for Nana every year. So whenever I smell it, and that doesn't happen very often these days because it's classed as an old fashioned perfume now, but on the rare occasions I do come across it I am instantly taken back to being by my Nana's side. I like that about scents, they have this amazing power to transport you to another world, another time, another place. Our sense of smell is very powerful.

I remember looking at this little black pug that had just gotten off the plane and thinking to myself "Oh wow I think I finally have my Lilly pug" On the way home I ran it by David, and he said he thought it fitted too so Lilly became Lilly instantly. Dave already knew I had that name on my pug name list because when Steffy arrived I did for a little while think that name belonged to her. And for a day or two she was in fact called Lilly and I would use it when out in the paddocks, even though she was deaf I still used it, but she'd be there looking up at me and as much as I wanted to call her Lilly she didn't in any shape or form suit that name. She was a beautiful pug, and it was a beautiful name but for some reason that made very little difference, the pug and the name did not go together. I used it for another day, just in case it would fit better the more it got used, but it didn't, it was a lovely name sure enough, but it just wasn't the right one for Steffy. And I can't tell you exactly why that was, but it just did not fit and there was no point pushing it, so I stopped using it on her, left it on the list for a future pug and set about giving Steffy her own name. And for a while I actually thought that name would be Gillan, but David had other ideas about that. He loathed the name so much he refused to use it, he started calling her Steffy and in the end I started calling her Steffy too. So Gillan became Steffy, and I can't see her as ever being called anything else now because it's the most perfect name for her.

When Lilly and Tommy finally got off the plane it was late, and we had been away from the farm and the other pugs for a very long time and that was on my mind a bit. I had wanted our new family members to fly in around mid-day, two o'clock at the latest, that way we could get them back to the farm with enough daylight to show them all around the place. I always try and look at things from a dog's point of view. You put yourself in their shoes, you are old, you are fragile, you're scared, you're tired and sometimes you may even be sick. Your body, your ears, your eyes aren't what they used to be and so you feel vulnerable. And by no fault of your own you've been made to leave your home, the choice is made for you, you have to go regardless of the reason, and so you and any trace of you, your bed, your toys, your bowl, your comb, your lead and collar are packed up and driven away. You may need to stay in two or three different homes before a forever home is found for you, but you don't know that at the time, each home is new to you, each one takes some time to get used to, and you may have only just gotten settled when it's time for you to leave again. Our farm is their final home, but they have no way of knowing that when they get here, they may think they are just passing though yet another home and sometimes it makes them unsure of everything. I think older dogs are exactly like older people, they take a little bit longer to settle into a new place, a new routine, new people. Of course, we try and make the transition as easy as we can on them but it generally takes some time for them to finally settle in. We've had pugs who've taken quite a long time and as much as you want to help them feel secure as quickly as possible no pug can been rushed, they've all lived different lives, had different experiences, each pug is different and so is the amount of time they need to feel secure. All David and I can do is patiently wait and love each individual little soul while they are working everything out.

That's why I wasn't thrilled about getting home so late. Being on a plane would have been hard enough on these two pugs I didn't want to stress them out any more then I had to and I felt that wide open fields of pitch blackness would be unnerving to them. As I rule I don't like putting dogs on planes, probably because I myself don't particularly like flying, I don't fear it, just don't like it, but I think that has more to do with actually leaving home then it does the plane ride. David doesn't share this point of view, then again he's flown all over the world on business so he's used to it. When we were finally able to collect Lilly and Tom the night air was chilly. The plane had touched down, but they were in no rush to bring our pugs out to us and I worried whether they were in a drafty area getting cold. That tarmac was really windy as well, if they'd been left sitting out in the open, fully exposed to the elements for lord knows what reason then they would be suffering, and I didn't like the idea of that at all. Would the rescue people have thought to put coats on them, probably not, they'd left the rescuers home earlier in the day, all dogs have to be at the airport an hour before the plane takes off and it wouldn't have been cold when they left. Besides you have to be careful putting a jacket on a pug, they can overheat so easily, and it can be disastrous.

We paced the length of the reception area many times, stopping every so often trying to peer through the open door behind the counter. But it was only a small door so you couldn't really see much. We went outside and pressed our noses against the high wire fence trying to see if the buggy dragging a cart behind it was the one holding our precious cargo, thank goodness David is tall, he could see a lot more than I could and kept a running commentary on what was going on. I always find airports to be the most fascinating places, especially the area where livestock comes in, it's amazing what types of animal's people have flying in from other states. A lot of the time its people traveling with their pets or people who have bought from a breeder intestate. Over the years we've seen some really funny sights and some even funnier and slightly weird looking people waiting to take possession of whatever is in the crate. Then again I guess those people are looking over at David and me and thinking the exact same thing about us. Some will talk to you and you'll get to know their stories and I always like that because it's interesting to me. Other times they don't want to talk to you at all and the look they give you is like a warning, they tell you with their eyes that the last thing they want to be doing is making polite conversation with a stranger. So I leave those folks to themselves and just watch on from a distance. I mean you have to amuse yourself with something while you wait and I turn it into a bit of a game, sit there trying to guess by the look of the person the type of animal they are collecting. Some people actually do look an awful lot like their animals, which I believe is why they are drawn to them in the first place. I saw one lady lining up and said to David "She's here to collect a cat" and I guess he was bored on that occasion because he decided to humour me and play along, although he did at first say that a lady collecting a cat was a no brainer. Then he asked "What type? I said "Persian" he said "Colour? I said "White" and so we both sat with our eyes glued to the lady as the man behind the collection counter brought over a box. It was a cat carrier and I thought "Tick" and we heard a meow and I stood up to get a closer look as the cat was transferred from the airport cat box to the one the lady had brought with her. I saw all the fur and thought "Tick again" but the Persian was grey not white as David pointed out and I said "Well you can't win them all" and that I thought getting two out of three things right was pretty good going. To date it's the highest score I've ever gotten. The man behind the cat lady looked like he was there to collect a bear which David said disproved my theory. He was picking up a German Shepard instead and I thought that was a relief because by the look of him the bear he would have been collecting wouldn't have been a cute cuddly teddy bear, more a big wild human eating kind of bear and I didn't want such a thing on the same plane my new pugs were on. Sometimes when the wait is excruciatingly long David is more than happy to join in on the game with me, we'll both be sitting there with our eyes fixated on the door wanting to be the first one to have a guess. And then one of us will say something like "Dog, Pomeranian, Tan" then we'll wait and see if we got anything right. Most times you won't but it makes the time pass faster so we keep on playing. One time three men walked in looking like they were members of the Italian Mafia. And because they looked so shifty neither of us said anything about what we thought they were there to collect, we just watched them going about their business, well I did anyway, after a while David was bored so he got out his phone and started checking work emails. But not me, I wasn't bored at all I was totally captivated by them because I'd not seen anybody like them in here before. But boy did we laugh on the way home because they were there picking up some pigeons, of all the things we would have guessed pigeons would not have been one of them, a gorilla maybe, a couple of snakes perhaps, but not something like a little bird. And what was even funnier was that there were only about six pigeons to collect. I didn't get close enough to see inside the box but from the size of it there wouldn't have been any more than six and I couldn't understand why it took three big burly men to collect six little birds. I said to David that they must have had blue diamonds hidden underneath their wings. All the way home I talked about why I thought these men needed to travel together. My stories about them got bigger and bigger, David started off being amused but soon got over it, but I was sitting there holding my new pug listing all the illegal activities these men had done in their lives. They were hit men I said and could never travel alone in case somebody decided it was payback time. Or that the man signing for the pigeons was "The Boss" and the other two men were his bodyguards. And perhaps the pigeons weren't diamond smugglers at all, maybe they were just his pets, he was like this big tough Mafia boss who had a soft spot for pigeons. "They were a gift from his father" I blurted out at lightning speed, pigeon breeding was a passion they had shared while he was growing up, something they could do together as father and son, they had aviary's filling every inch of the back garden which irritated the mother and I was about to go into his childhood and the type of upbringing I thought he had when David requested that I stop. But me being me I had to get one last word in otherwise I'd burst so I shouted out quickly "Loving but very disciplined" before finally shutting my mouth. At which David was very grateful I could tell by his face.

When David said he saw a dog trolley being pushed our way we ran round to the other side of the fence and waited by the gate. Your heart goes a hundred miles an hour when you know you are moments away from coming face to face with your new pug or in this case new pugs. "The female is only little" the rescuer had told me over the phone. I was a bit worried that we were getting a male, I had a few old nanas at home and the last thing I wanted was to have a male dog bossing them around. The only reason I'd broken my no-male-rule and relented was because these two pugs had been together all their lives and I felt to split them up would be like splitting up a married couple and putting them in different nursing homes. As much as I worried about the pugs I had back home I just couldn't let this male and female be separated, it didn't sit right in my heart. I knew I would have never forgiven myself if I had done that, so I'd just have to watch the male around the nanas and teach him to treat them with the respect they deserved. Of course, I had absolutely no idea how big Tommy was at the time, if anything I was guessing he was small too on account of being told the female was. But no, he was huge, but as it happened Tommy was the most docile loving lovely boy and not one ounce of trouble. Tommy was a perfect fit for us. When our pugs were finally pushed out towards us I couldn't get over the size difference of the two, the rescuer was right the female was certainly tiny the male was a giant next to her. The airport worker unlocked the crate and David bent down and put the harnesses on while I signed the paperwork to release them to us. I looked at the male pug closely, was he really that big or did he simply look massive next to this tiny little girl. David had to make one harness smaller for the female and extend the other for the male, it was the largest harness we had, and it was opened up all the way yet it barely went around his chest. I knew exactly where these two pugs would fit in our pack size wise even before getting them home because we'd used Harpers harness on him and Grace's harness on her. I knew the male would tower over all our other pugs and that the female would now be the tiniest pug we had in the house. I smiled to myself wondering if Harper would be happy that she was no longer the biggest pug in the family and how Grace would feel about having a dog in the house smaller then she was, it would be a new experience for her that was for sure. Once the harnesses and leads were secure we took the giant and the little fairy for a walk around the grassy area so they could stretch their legs and relieve themselves before the long ride home. The two of them trotted along happily on their leads, if the plane flight had bothered them they weren't for letting on. David took the male and I the female, even though we'd been delayed for many hours and I was anxious to get home we still gave them a walk, because really you have to. They had been in that crate a long time, they needed to have a walk and a wee for their own comfort and I wasn't going to rush them through it, we let them take as long as they liked. I thought about the girls back home and how their little old bladders were holding up. I never like to have their routine interfered with but sometimes it can't be helped and beside our two new pugs needed to have a break and a sniff and a bit of a breather, so I concentrated on them and got to know them a little bit better. I can't remember exactly when it happened, but Lilly had become Lilly in my mind by the time we reached the car. On the way home from the airport David asked what I was thinking,

I'd been quiet for a while, just sitting there with one arm around Lilly and the other one bent backwards trying as best I could to give Thomas a reassuring pat. But he was incredibly chilled out as was fitting his wonderful personality so he really didn't need one, but I didn't know him well back then so was doing all I could to make him feel that everything was going to be ok. David wondered what was on my mind. I've always been a deep thinker and if I'm quiet for a good length of time he knows my mind is concentrating on something. I carried on thinking for a little while before answering, I often do this because when I'm that deep in thought I like to stay there for a few moments before coming out of it, when I was ready I turned to my husband and told him how incredibly happy I was feeling. We finally had our much longed for farm, we had our four old pugs that we arrived with, then we'd taken in two younger ones that desperately needed our help and now we were driving home with our two new family members, my heart was just about as close to bursting as it had ever been. I felt so much contentment in that moment and told Dave this and a few other things I was feeling. David smiled at me but didn't say anything much in response, but that's not so unusual for him. He's the silent type and I'm the talker. I watched his face as he concentrated on the road, he looked tired, it had been a very long day.

It was so dark when we arrived back at the farm, due to the lengthy delay the fire we'd lit and left choked off on night mode had long gone out and with the old pugs having been left in the house for hours there was a mess to clean up on the floor. We don't have a doggy door here, of course it'd be handy, but with foxes you just can't have the dogs going outside at night on their own. Imagine little Gracie with her old eyes going down the ramp for a wee and being carried off by a fox. She wouldn't have been able to see it coming, wouldn't have been able to outrun it and gotten back inside the house in time and even if she did the fox would have just followed her in and dragged her out by the neck and what a terrible death that would be for her. Actually, now I think of it the foxes probably wouldn't even wait for the pugs to come outside, they'd be in the house as soon as the lights went out stealing sleeping little old pugs from their beds like chickens in a hen house and you can't have that. I cleaned up the puddles and David set about relighting the fire, it was colder in the house than I would have liked it to be, but it wasn't freezing which told me the fire had not that long gone out. Still, I didn't like that the pugs had been left in a house with a dwindling fire. At their ages I always like to make sure they are kept nice and warm. There were some parts of the fire still slightly glowing red, so all Dave had to do was bash the blackened logs around a bit and put some kindling on top then leave the choke fully open and in no time at all the fire was away again. I noticed that Tommy had wandered over to see what David was doing, he seemed fascinated by the fire, I don't think he'd seen a Coonara before, he watched the sticks being shoved in with great interest. He stood alongside David with a look on his face as if to say "What you doing new daddy". I smiled seeing the two of them together like that, then went into the kitchen to get the chicken organised.

Lilly I can clearly remember following me into the kitchen to see what I was going to do with that delicious smelling chicken, she'd had a bit of roast chicken at the airport before we left but she was obviously very hungry and wanted some more. It was quite bright in the kitchen which gave me a chance to properly look at our new daughters little face. She sat on the kitchen floor with her head tilted upwards. I looked down to say "Hello" and as I did I saw these two little cross eyes looking up at me, it was only then that I realised Lilly was cross eyed. Being busy at the airport and dark on the car ride home I hadn't been able to clearly see her eyes, just that tiny cute little body that I thought was so adorable. And because her eyes were full of gunk and very dry it was hard to see them properly anyway. I snuck Lilly a few bits of chicken and shouted over to David that we had a little cross eyed girl in our midst and that when he got round to seeing her eyes that he mustn't laugh because I didn't want her being self-conscious. Dave closed the door on the fire and came over to see what I meant, Lilly trotted over to him as soon as he crouched down on the floor, and he smiled as he cupped her little face in his hands. He, like me, thought her cross eyes were beautiful, they only added to her overall cuteness as far as we were both concerned. He reached up and grabbed some chicken off the bench and fed it to her, Tommy nudged his face under David's arm, so he reached up again and got some more chicken off the bench. Then we both washed our hands and I held Lilly while David put some eye drops in both eyes, we didn't want to just wipe her eyes when they were that dry, so we flushed the gunk out with lubricating eye drops which served two purposes, it got rid of the gunk and gave those extremely dry eyes of hers a bit of relief. Eyes that dry would have been irritating for her, painful too, she seemed so much happier after we put the drops in. Daily eye drops would now become part of her life. And she was always good about letting us put them in, some pugs will have a fit about it, try and fight you off, but not little Lilly she seemed to know we were putting them in for her own good. I could even do it one handed while David was at work. I'd scoop Lilly up, hold her in one arm and put the drops in with my free hand and there were rarely any missed drops, two to three times a day I did this, I'd tilt her head slightly backwards and she'd just let me. I think she was more interested in the treat I had on the countertop ready to give her once we were done and she knew we weren't done until she had two drops in each eye. Then she'd get her treat and off she'd go.

Once Lilly's eyes were sorted out it was time for all of us to have something to eat. The pugs began doing circles when they saw me putting the chicken on the table, the house quickly filled with heat as we all sat round eating tea together. Seeing as their tea time was meant to be a few hours ago the pugs were all really hungry, if a pug skips a meal it's like the end of the world is nigh, so David and I sat there dishing out chicken to all of them with the two new ones sitting in amongst everybody else like they'd been living with us for years. I think it's nice to share a meal when new pugs enter the house, it's like a bonding time for everyone, we are just one big happy family sitting down and enjoying food together. And yes even though they are pugs and its chicken, which is an all-time favourite with everybody in our house, they are still happy to share, we don't have any arguments, not with the first meal we don't anyway, even if the new pug is food aggressive I find the first few meals are always eaten in peace because everything is new to them. There are too many new siblings and too many new things to concentrate on. Their true personalities take a bit of time to come through and if they reveal themselves as food aggressors, well we deal with it, and some will come in as food aggressors and then stop after living with us for a while and others are always going to have problems in that area, so we'll be on guard when offering the pugs a treat. It's just a matter of knowing your pugs, you are aware that some of them have a problem so you work with it not against it, like I wouldn't throw a pile of treats on the floor for everybody to pounce on because you are certainly going to have problems if you do. But you can still offer a round of treats to everybody quite peacefully and happily, you just have to keep an eye on the one who is going to be shoving the others out of the way. And again, it has everything to do with the personality of the pug and they are all different. The shoving we deal with pretty quickly here because we won't tolerate that, some of our delicate oldies are unsteady on their feet and we won't let anybody go pushing them to the ground. You learn to position the pack accordingly before bending down to give them their treat, I like them to all have their treats together as a family, not singled out, so I'll move the pack in a certain way to keep everybody happy. And after a while they tend to naturally line up that way themselves at treat time because they are so used to doing it. I keep the food aggressor on the end so that way he or she will not be making trouble for the rest of the pugs. You learn to dish out the treats real fast here too because that works best. It's like "Treat, treat, treat, treat, treat" and then we are on our way for a walk or a sniff around the place and a wee. You are always going to have a pug who just has to be given their treat first otherwise all hell will break loose, so you go with that because it's a matter of whatever it takes to keep the harmony. You are not rewarding the pug for being who he or she is you are just doing what needs to be done to keep a peaceful flow in the pack and remember we have a lot of pugs here and some of them are blind and some of them are deaf and some have other issues and so the rules in our house are slightly different to how they'd be somewhere else. Although even if I only had two or three pugs I would still work with the personalities of the pugs, work out who is better off getting their treat first, last or somewhere in the middle. And it's not like favouritism with who gets their treat first, it's just basic common sense. Some pugs will not mind being the last one to be given a treat, with the personality they have dwelling within they won't give a hoot, as long as they get one they won't mind at all, so you'll have a little laid back sweetheart patiently waiting their turn and not be at all bothered by it but if you tried that with a different pug you'll find they'll become really upset to the point of being annoying to the others and I don't like to have old blind or deaf pugs being upset at any time in their lives let alone at treat time because treat time is a happy time, that's the entire point of giving them a treat. So, you work out a system and stick with that and you'll have no issues at all. And it's not always the food aggressor who wants the treat first either, you think it would be but it isn't always the case, some will really want that treat but will learn sit for it and so you know you can leave them until the middle or even the last pug to be given a treat and they will just sit there goggle eyeing the treats in your hand until it's their turn to have one. We've had visitors to the farm who want to give the pugs their treats so we have to explain to them not to stand around idly chatting giving one treat out at random intervals because with a pack you can't be doing that. If a treat is going to be given then it's got to be given fast and that's all you have to be concentrating on at the time. You focus because you need to. And it's not just being pushed around that the treat routine is set up for. If you don't have some form of order then one pug will end up getting two treats while another misses out. We do have a few extra treats in our hands though just in case somebody drops theirs by accident and one of the more able bodied pugs picks it up before the little blind soul can locate it. I mean come on it'd be pretty unfair for an elderly dog to drop their treat due to something like lack of teeth or a hanging out tongue and then miss out on getting one altogether. So spares are taken out with us and everybody is happy, especially me because I think I become sadder than the pug that's dropped their treat is if they miss out.

I have lived with many different packs of pugs over the years and treat time differs depending on who is in the pack at the time. At one time I was feeding all the delicate pugs their treats first then I would feed the blind ones then I'd very quickly take a few steps backwards drawing the others away so that the ones who'd already gotten their treat could eat it in peace. Then I'd give the black pugs their treat and then concentrate on the fawns and dish out the remaining treats at high speed because all the pugs I'd drawn away could see and hear. Then you lose a few pugs, and some new pugs will join the family so everything about the treat routine changes to compensate. During the week I'll work out a new routine that's best suited for the newly formed pack and try and get them all used to it, then I'll tell David how things are so that when he's giving them their treats on the weekends he knows what the deal is. And I'll just stand back watching on, telling him who has dropped a treat and needs another one or if he's accidently given one pug two treats because the sneaky little thing has eaten their treat fast then quickly shot around and come at him from the other side. David likes to be the feeder when he's home because it's a pretty fun thing to be doing, seeing all those little old faces tilted upwards is a very special experience so it's nice for him to be the weekend treat giver or as he went through a stage of calling himself "The Sweetie Man". The term came from a movie called District 9 we were watching many years ago where a man was trying to lure in a little alien to capture in order to clear an area. It's a funny movie, well we thought it was anyway, just the way he was saying it and the fact that he actually thought he could capture an alien with a bag of sweets. The actor was using a South African accent and I have always loved South African accents. The first time David used the term I almost dropped to my knees laughing because I'd forgotten all about the movie and my legs were fast buckling under me I was laughing so hard. It's like we were just doing our normal happy treat giving thing and I was concentrating on that, then out of nowhere this saying came floating through the air and I wasn't expecting it. He was mimicking the actor in the movie as well which made it all the funnier and David is a very good impersonator, he always has been. I was laughing at the voice he was putting on and the actions he was doing. But I was also laughing at the poor little pugs standing there in a line all looking up at him, some of them were tilting their heads a bit and if I wasn't laughing so much I probably would have been telling him off for not giving the pugs their treat quickly enough. But of course, I was in no state to do that so I just stood there hunched over, at one point gripping onto a tree to steady myself because I am uncoordinated at the best of times, my legs turn to jelly and I'm even worse. So there he was with all the pugs gathering around saying things like "It's the Sweetie man here" "Now who wants a sweetie, who wants a sweetie" and I'm getting weaker from laughter by the minute and the poor little old pugs were just waiting for a treat like they always do. And David was laughing and I was laughing and the pugs were looking up at him like "I know you are saying something stupid and your movements and gestures are not your own, but we don't care Daddy just hand over our treats will you" I guess our behaviour is nothing new to them, they are used to us behaving like idiots and laughing our heads off about it. I bet some of them think we are two lunatics who are easily amused, and they'd be right in thinking that because we are, we truly are. At times like this it helps to be living on a farm, if we were still living in suburbia we'd have been locked up by now I'm sure of it. One of the neighbours would have heard all the continuous loud laughing and called the police and they would take one look at us both there laughing our heads off over nothing and perhaps think we were on some illegal drugs or completely off our heads for some other reason and take us away and neither me nor Dave would help the situation much because we'd only have to look at one another to start laughing again. Sometimes I think we could live on a desert island just us and the pugs and be completely happy doing it, we wouldn't need to be connected to the outside world, we could very easily keep ourselves amused. About year or so back David even bought us matching t-shirts from the District 9 movie, he came across them by accident while looking on a website for something else. They don't have "Sweetie Man" written on them but another funny quote from the movie and I swear the pugs cringe whenever they see us wandering around the farm dressed exactly the same. I bet their little minds are thinking that they didn't think their parents could embarrass them any more than they already do and then we go and start dressing identically like a couple of goofballs.

After dinner all the pugs went out for another quick toilet break then we locked up for the night, there'd be plenty of time to show Lilly and Tommy round the farm in daylight. We could have gone for a short walk with a torch but nothing was so important that it couldn't wait until the morning, so we threw some big logs on the fire, made sure it'd last the night, then did the pugs nightly eye routine and gave Lilly another drop in each eye too. After that we all settled down to sleep, in our nice warm house with our nice full tummies. Tommy chose to sleep on the couch, but Lilly came into the bedroom with us and climbed into one of the dog beds that were scattered around. I fell asleep quickly which is unusual for me, but I did wake a few times during the night, which isn't so unusual for me and when I did I got my torch and went and checked on the two new pugs just to make sure they were ok. They were fine, both sleeping soundly and neither one of them seemed aware I was there. They'd had a big day and were no doubt completely worn out by everything that had gone on. As soon as daylight broke I left David sleeping and took all the pugs for a walk around the farm, I thought it'd be nice for the two new pugs to spend some time exploring their new home now they could fully see it. Tommy went off and had a good look at everything on his own, but Lilly stayed close to the pack. She liked being outside sure enough, trotted alongside the others quite happily and enjoyed sniffing at things but even from day one Lilly was never much of a walker. Her body was fine visually but it was like she didn't have the energy to do it, I noticed that she got tired very easily. All she could manage to do was walk down to the front gate and then she'd be worn out and have to sit under a tree and catch her breath. And there's nothing unusual about that, a lot of the pugs we take in will take a while to get used to walking around the farm. It can take a few weeks for them to build up to it, especially if they haven't done much walking in their previous home. So my new little black pug sitting under a tree resting wasn't so uncommon a sight for me to be seeing. I kept an eye on her, so I always knew where she was and if she didn't want to walk back up the hill by herself then I'd go and carry her up once the others finished their walk and were back inside the house. Over the years I've had to carry quite a few of the newcomers when they got tired. You just have to be constantly monitoring them, so they don't overdo things until they are able to cope. They are pugs and they are old, they have to build up their stamina slowly, there are no races here, everybody goes at their own pace and walks as much as they are comfortable walking. That's the beauty of being on a farm everyone can walk at their leisure and can be left sitting having a little rest whenever they like, and I know that because all our fences are secure no harm is going to come to them. On around day four or five of their stay I noticed something wasn't right with Lilly. She had a runny nose, and her breathing was a bit heavy. I picked her up and pressed my ear against her little chest so I could hear things better, I often do it this way because it can be pretty hard to hear anything when you have a pile of pugs tap dancing by your feet. I listened hard and I didn't like what I heard so rang the vet, it was just on closing time, so an appointment was made for first thing in the morning. I mean pugs are normally pretty nasally, some more so than others, but this wasn't the regular pug sound. If Lilly had arrived in a home where they'd never had a pug before they may have just assumed it was normal but having had pugs for a good many years I knew something wasn't right and felt she should be looked at by a professional. For one thing I didn't know this pug, didn't know her history, didn't know anything about her or her health, she'd only been in my care for a short amount of time, and I didn't want to take any chances. If it was one of our other pugs we may have waited a bit longer to see if things cleared up. When you've had a dog for a while you get to know them and their health issues. You know whether you can help them yourself with the knowledge you've acquired over the years or whether it's time to see the vet. Some can have funny tummies from time to time as they age so we always have something on hand for that, there's a shelf in our fridge for pug medicine and the various eye ointments are kept on that shelf too. We keep everything together so should one of the pugs not be feeling well we can go to the fridge and get them started on something right away and a lot of the time things will clear up in a day or so and if they don't then off we trot to the vet. But I don't like the pugs to be sick when they are trying to settle into a new home, everything is strange to them, you don't want the added stress of them being ill. The next morning, I noticed that Lilly was now coughing a little bit too, clearly she had an infection, and I was really glad that I'd made the appointment the night before. Our vet is wonderful with our pugs, and he spent a lot of time checking Lilly out, he said she had a throat infection and that her lungs were heavily congested. He gave her an injection and we were given something to help break up the goo and get it off her chest as that was so important. We were also given a two week course of strong antibiotics and home we came with our tiny new daughter wrapped up in a blanket.

I thought Lilly had gotten sick because of the lateness of the flight and the chill in the air. I wondered if these two pugs had been left sitting out on the open tarmac for far longer than they should have been or if maybe the crate they'd been transported in had last had a sick dog in it. I figured all the crates would have been cleaned or if not at least wiped down with some form of disinfectant before being allowed to be used again. I just assumed this crate had not been cleaned properly before Tommy and Lilly innocently got put into it. I mean it could have happened to any dog put into that crate, it was just my two that were unlucky enough to be placed in that particular crate that day. Either way I blamed human error for Lilly getting sick or should that be a human being with a couldn't care less attitude and I was irate about it because I felt if they had done their job properly then she would be settling into her new home now without being sick. Half way through the second week Lilly's illness had spread to the other pugs. They all sat in their beds looking completely miserable and there was a chorus of coughing constantly ringing through the air. Tommy was the only one it didn't affect which was strange because he was the one who flew down with Lilly. But if he wasn't sick then it can't have been an infected crate or anything that happened on the flight down. So your mind then, as it always does with a houseful of pugs, starts going over the week's events to try and narrow down the cause of the illness. Was it maybe one of my original pugs that had first become ill, had Lilly caught it off them and was it always going to spread to other pugs in the house? Also, we have foxes in the area, did one of them sneak onto our property in the middle of the night and brush up against a tree and then did one of my pugs do the same thing on one of our walks around the farm because disease can very easily be spread this way. And I'm sure is often spread this way on farmland. This may seem like a lot to be thinking about but it's not really, you stand in the middle of the lounge room surrounded by a pile of sick pugs in beds with these thoughts and more rushing through your mind and it'll only take a few seconds to sort through them. You'll either negate a theory or you'll look deeper into it and run it by your husband when he gets home from work to see what he thinks. If at all possible I like to know why my pugs have become ill in the first place because it can help you prevent further illness happening down the track. And sometimes it's great, you'll be able to work it out, other times you simply won't have a clue. Like if I knew for sure that foxes where the cause then I would then lead the pugs to another part of the property to have their walk. And then set out to deter any foxes from entering our property again. We have secure fences, but foxes are cunning they will slither in wherever they see even the tiniest of gaps, they are a bit like mice in that way. A better way of deterring a fox is to mark your territory yourself. And as gross as this sounds it really does work. Because foxes are territorial animals they will respond to such a thing, it's like you are speaking their language. But you have to have the male in the house doing it. You can never use urine from a female as this will attract foxes rather than deter them, a fact which I am incredibly grateful for because the idea of me having to squat by the fence does not appeal to me in the slightest. So, it'd have to be Dave weeing on the fence line and he couldn't just do it the one time either, it'd be a case of repeating it every few days in order to convince those foxes that your farm is not for them. After a few weeks they will simply move on to another property and leave yours alone. We've not yet had to resort to weeing on our fence lines but some of our neighbours have done with great success. I often laugh about it actually, I can just imagine me forcing my poor husband to drink a litre of water then shoving him out the door when it comes time to urinate. And it'd have to be done at night time too because you don't want him being fined for indecent exposure. I mean you could risk it because there isn't a lot of traffic on these roads, well not compared to suburbia there isn't anyway. But knowing our luck some little old lady will be having a nice leisurely drive in the country and then come across Dave out there protecting our farm from foxes. She'd either run into the nearest tree from staring or have a heart attack from the shock of it all and run off the road into a ditch. Imagine being in court and having to explain to her grief stricken family exactly what had gone on, be sitting there looking at a row of innocent searching eyes and have to explain to them why grandma died. We certainly don't need that so should we ever find ourselves in the situation of needing to deter foxes it will most certainly be done after dark.

So, there I was for days on end dishing out multiple courses of antibiotics to all the little old ladies in the house and also running from bed to bed with syringes full of cough medicine and because I didn't want to be reinfecting somebody who was nearing the end of their illness by using the same syringe I'd just used on somebody who was on day two or three of getting sick. I had a syringe for each individual pug and so I didn't get confused I wrote their names on them and once a dose had been given I'd thoroughly wash the syringes so they were well sterilised then pop them on a tea towel to dry. And as I was dashing about taking care of everybody I'd look over at Tommy and he was sitting there in the middle of the couch smiling his big froggy faced head off looking as healthy as a horse and almost as big as one too. I kept wondering that maybe his immune system was in great condition and that's what had spared him getting sick and I just figured that Lilly's immune system wasn't in great shape because she seemed to be the sickest out of all the pugs. So, while everybody else in the house shuffled off to bed and slept their illness off Tommy had a ball playing with all the toys and running out to the hay shed, then down the path and out into the front paddock discovering his new home. The fact that nobody else showed any interest in going with him didn't seem to bother him at all. He'd pause at the door for a second or two, not really waiting to see if somebody was going to join him, more gathering his thoughts I think, more planning which direction he was going to take off in and once he figured that out he'd fly down the back ramp and off he'd go on his own for an hour. I'd be tending to his sick siblings but always kept a close eye on him from the windows, so I knew what was going on, I'd see that large frame of his sauntering this way than that. Sometimes he'd stop and sniff, other times he'd stop and stare at something on the other side of the fence and then off he'd go again. If it started to rain I would put the pug I had in my arms down and go bring Tommy back inside because I knew he wouldn't think to come in of his own accord and because I was dealing with all these sick pugs the last thing I wanted was Tommy getting sick as well. I was very happy that he'd been spared this illness and I really wanted to keep it that way. So I'd go find him and he'd look up at me like "It's only a few drops of rain new Mummy, what are you spoiling my fun for" maybe in his mind he thought I was being over protective, but I always took treats with me when I went to bring him in and once he saw them he'd happily follow me back home and I'm glad he did because otherwise I would have had to carry him all the way and my arms would have been aching like crazy from doing so.

During this time of illness there were many trips to the vet, as each new pug showed signs of getting sick we knew what we were dealing with now so appointments were quickly booked and off we'd go with one or two sick pugs in tow and there would be Tommy always at the window watching us go. I bet he thought this was how it was in this new home of his. Because he didn't know any different I guess he thought that we constantly drove down the driveway leaving him behind and then returned a few hours later with treats for everybody. While we were gone his sick sisters slept and I'm sure Tom did that as well but he also spent a lot of time weeing in the house and I felt this may be due to him being upset and unsettled because we were always leaving him, but he'd wee inside just as much when I was home so I figured perhaps not and so didn't feel quite so guilty when seeing him sadly staring out the window watching us drive away. It was late spring and so there were a lot of rainy days, but there was also bit of sun around, the mornings could still be pretty cold but the afternoons were really beautiful so I would take all the pugs outside and sit in the sun. I have always thought a bit of sunshine was good for healing and also good for lifting everybody's spirits. It was nice watching the pugs sleeping on the deck, nice to see Lilly as small as she was laying there surrounded by her new family. She spent a lot of time sleeping on her back and so did Tommy and I thought that was a funny thing for these two to be doing, I wondered if it was just naturally them or if their old owner had taught them to do it at some point in their lives. I personally couldn't see a point to doing such a thing but maybe she could, either way I thought they were both pretty cute laying there upside down while the rest of the pack slept on their tummies or their sides. The sun would be shinning, the different types of birds would be chirping, and the wind would be making the leaves on the trees dance ever so slightly and there in the middle of all that beauty would be the sound of snuffly snoring ringing through the air. It was a lovely way to spend an afternoon. I'd have a cup of tea and the phone by my side. I took a magazine out there with me as well but spent most of the time catching up on phone calls and watching my contented little family sleeping as I chatted away.

Most of the pugs came good with a two week course of antibiotics but a few didn't so had to be taken back to see the vet for another course and Lilly was almost always in amongst the pugs that were going to see the vet again. This infection had hit poor little Lilly the hardest of them all and it was sad seeing her constantly being reinfected. I was double checking myself all the time just in case I'd accidently given her some medicine out of somebody else's syringe, but I was fairly sure I hadn't, I was really paying attention because you have to when you have a houseful of elderly beings. They are old and as with all things that are old they need special looking after and a whole lot of tender loving care and you really have to pay attention to what you are doing at all times because the health of your babies depends on it. And I was being especially careful when doing anything with Lilly because she was new to me and so I was looking after her but also making note of what her weaknesses where as far as health went because I knew this would be beneficial in my long term care of her. I used to ask our vet why Lilly was the one who was the sickest out of everybody. I asked him if he thought there was anything more serious going on with her. And each time he saw her he checked her out thoroughly and said that no he didn't think so, just with her being so tiny, runt of the litter kind of thing, he said she may just be the kind of dog that is always going to take a little longer than the others to get well again. And I had to agree with that analysis because runts of litters in any animal do tend to be a bit that way, I've bore witness to it before. Her being a runt made me love Lilly all the more and feel so very sorry for her too, I didn't like seeing this darling little thing constantly unwell. My concern caused me to ring the rescue group who'd sent Lilly and Tommy down to me to find out more about her history, but they said she was absolutely fine while they had her there. So that put my mind at ease a bit, that made me think it was merely a virus that had come from who knows where and that she would eventually get better, especially as the weather got warmer and if we had to keep her on strong courses of antibiotics until then well that's just what we would have to do.

So, David and I took turns of nursing Lilly and fed her extra special food just to get her well again. If she didn't want what the others were having something else was gotten for her and we didn't mind that at all because really this was not about spoiling this was about a pug not feeling well and us doing everything to try and get her though it. The last thing you want is for them to stop eating altogether so you just give them whatever they fancy on the day and go with that and repeat it the next day, but what she wanted to eat differed from day to day, so we were always swapping and changing. Normally I don't like to keep altering their food, but this wasn't a regular settling in period, so we went with whatever Lilly wanted. Nourishment is important especially when they are unwell and on medication, we never fed her rubbish as we wanted her to be as healthy as she could be so yes the food was special, but it was also good for her as well. When Dave was home Lilly used to sit on his knee and have her meals hand fed to her and she looked so cute being so tiny sitting there on this big blokes knee. I thought once she got well and once she settled in then she could be put on the diet the other pugs were on and she could also eat with the others as well, but that would come in time. For now, none of that was important.

Both David and I quickly fell in love with Lilly and because she was so much smaller than the others we tended to baby her a bit as well. I think the ones that need that extra bit of attention tend to soak into your heart real fast. We'd be there tending to her and making a big fuss of her as well and then we'd both breathe a sigh of relief when she was doing well health wise. And when she was feeling good she was just like any other pug. There was no holding her back, she'd play, and she'd potter about the place, she was fascinated and interested in all that went on both inside and outside. Still not much of a walker but I was putting that down to her needing to work up to it and that fact that she was constantly becoming infected by this damned virus, I mean how could she possibly be interested in walking when she wasn't feeling well. There was the odd day that I'd leave her inside the house while the rest of us walked but she didn't like being left behind, she still wanted to be with everyone so most days out she'd come. But always sitting at the top of the hill watching us go and on the odd occasion she did come with us she would always be sitting at the back of the pack, lingering a little, having a bit of a sniff and she looked gorgeous doing it, just her mannerisms, her way of doing things made me smile. Her way of sniffing was especially cute. She'd lean in and have a sniff then pull back think about things for a moment or two and then lean in again for another sniff, it was like she almost always had to double sniff things. I don't know why she did this or what was going through her mind at the time. She did it both when she was sniffing on her own and when she was sniffing with the pack. Like she'd see the others gathered round a tree and once she caught up to them she'd shove herself in between to see what it was they were so interested in, and they'd move on and she'd still be there leaning in sniffing and re-sniffing the base of the tree. It was like it was important to her to double check everything and I wondered if maybe she was a little bit neurotic. Was it like me leaving the house then wondering if I'd left the iron switched on or not turned the oven off and having to turn the car around and go home and check. I used to do this a lot at one time, when I first got married it was, before I had a lot of elderly pugs relying on me I used to do it, now my mind is so full of everything else that's going on that I don't have time to be wondering about such things and also because I have so many little beings depending on me I do tend to unplug irons right away and turn ovens off once, check I've done so then completely let it go. The thing is when I was returning home full of worry it was all for nothing because I never left anything switched on, not even once, I guess it was my first home and I didn't want to be responsible for burning it to the ground.

On the days Lilly felt good she'd be back to playing rough with Tommy, she'd wrestle him to the ground then jump all over the top of him and he would just lay there letting her attack him. She'd go from being on top of his head to being underneath him biting at his tummy and kicking away at him like crazy, little black legs kicking and kicking and kicking. It was like she wanted to attack him from every single angle. She was super speedy too, like a little ninja. Flying all around him biting and kicking and having the time of her life, she'd yelp and squeal and at times I thought she'd really hurt herself, but she hadn't she was just in a super excitable mood and being very vocal about it. He was so placid and laid back he'd just roll from one side to the other while this tiny little thing dived on him. He'd lay there watching her come running at him and lay there watching her go again. But when he'd had enough he would stand up and when she came flying at him this time he'd pin her down just long enough for him to have a breather. It was nice to watch Lilly playing again, nice to see her with some energy, after how she'd been it warmed my heart seeing her so well. She had many days where she was feeling really great, you could tell how she was feeling by how she chose to spend her time. And her favourite thing to do in the whole wide world was to play with Tommy so that's how she spent her good days. That was her form of entertainment. I thought back to the old lady who used to own Lilly and Tommy, about the amount of joy she would have gotten from watching her two pugs playing. I pictured her sitting in a chair knitting while her very big and very little pug amused themselves. I imagined her glancing up from her knitting every now and then to watch them play. Thing is I had no idea whether their old owner used to knit or not, but in my mind she did anyway and I envisioned her in a warm lounge room in the middle of winter, TV on, favourite show playing, Murder She Wrote or Midsomer Murders perhaps, or was I just putting impressions of my own Grandmother onto this lady and in reality she was nothing like her at all. She could well have been one of these old broads who played cards and drank gin and tonic every afternoon, she could have even been a chain smoker sitting in a room thick with smoke. Either way I bet she did take joy in seeing her pugs at play, I mean show me a person who doesn't enjoy seeing their children happy.

 Lilly and Tommy really did love being in each other's company and my other pugs all sat back and watched them play. Normally at least one of them would have joined in, mainly Emily, but no she never did, it was as if they were all respecting the special connection that these two pugs had and simply left them to it. Lilly and Tommy would be on the rug in the middle of the lounge room going at it and the other pugs would be in the row of beds along the windows watching on or sleeping depending on how long the game went on for. I stood back and watched them too and what amazed me most about Lilly was how very rough she was, I suppose because she was so tiny I expected her to be dainty, like a little butterfly, but she wasn't like that at all, she flew at him with no fear of whether she was going to hurt herself or come off worse for wear. She reminded me of a little fruit bat, the way she'd fly at him like that, little, black and fierce faced she was and as she neared him she'd leap up into the air. All four paws left the ground, she really did look like she was flying, and she'd body slam him as she came down. Sometimes she'd have a colourful coat on which by the way made her look even cuter. The weather was getting a little bit warmer now but because she'd not been well I wanted to protect her, so she kept her coat on longer than some of the other pugs had theirs on for. I still do that kind of thing today, the little delicate oldies will have their coats put on well before the others get their coats put on and they will keep them on long after the others think it's too warm to wear them. Mainly at night and first thing in the morning the coats are left on and then the sun will show its face and I'll go running around pulling coats over little old heads because they've started panting.

With Lilly if we went outside she'd always have a coat on, even if the sun was out she'd still have a coat on, the wind can be cold and if she went and sat by a tree well she'd be sitting in full shade then so her keeping a coat on was a very good idea. I was concerned that Lilly kept getting sick but felt that once she'd gotten over this and been living here a while and I'd had the chance to improve her overall health that the next time an infection hit our home she would be able to cope with it a lot better than what she was doing now. I felt confident that she would improve a hundred percent with the right care, I kept wondering if she had been left outdoors, not by the old lady but by her daughter as that wouldn't have been good for one so small and fragile. Well not good for Tommy either but this little girl was a lot needier than he was. Your mind thinks about all these sorts of things as you are looking after them, you spend a lot of time with them on your knee and it gives you plenty of time to let your mind wander. And yes you worry too as I tend to do that a lot with my pugs, especially when they are not well. But then Lilly would come good, and I relaxed a bit, I thought "Right here we go, she's finally gotten over this, she's turned the corner and is now on the road to recovery" I thought ok, this is where the real improvements will begin to take effect. I figured this was where I could really help her out. I believed with excellent care and a great diet that this little pug was never going to be affected like this again. She was in my hands now and this level of nurturing is what I'm very good at and I was really looking forward to watching Lilly go from strength to strength and your faith is restored too when you see her playing with Tommy at those times she looked like the healthiest pug in the entire household. The others were all sleeping, and Tommy was laying down and here was this energetic little girl whizzing all around the lounge room. And I'd see this and David would too and I'd say to him "I wonder why she's not that energetic on our walks" and he'd tell me that this was just her way of doing things and I agreed with him because some pugs are like that, lacklustre with certain things unless it's the thing they are most interested in and then they go at it like crazy which was exactly what little Lilly was doing. So she'd come good, and you'd think she'd finally kicked this thing and then the next week or the one after that it'd all start up again. So again to the vet and again he just didn't find any evidence that there was anything else wrong with her. Ruby got this thing back again three times and so I just assumed it was a very nasty virus and there was a lot of it going around we'd been told. I figured that my most delicate oldie and my new little runt of the litter were having the most trouble kicking it due to them being who they were. I was also glad that Grace hadn't gotten it more than once because she was the oldest pug in the house and sometimes when things like this hit it's when you'll lose an older pug. I used to sit with Lilly on my knee and wish that she'd been blessed with some of Tommy's stamina. I bet he would have given her some of his robust health if he could have done so. Again, I told myself she would be ok once I'd had time to build her health up and also once the nicer weather hit. She was probably having trouble adjusting to the cooler temperatures down here that's what the lady who sent Lilly down to me had said, she had come from a warmer state and the rescue group said there was nothing wrong with her when she was with them, so it had to be the temperature that was adding to her getting sick. The weather can be all over the place here in Melbourne, we are well known for it, it can be hot one day and cold the next and fluctuations like this really do muck little old dogs around a fair bit. Lilly was just having trouble with the change in climate and would be ok once she got used to it. But she was never to get used to it, she was not here when the warmer weather came. It was a cool summer anyway and took a while to get started but that didn't make any difference to Lilly because she was already gone.

We lost Lilly in December 2007, she had been with us for only four short months, and she was the first pug we buried on our new farm. Never in my wildest dreams did I think we were going to lose her. I had only just gotten to know her I wasn't ready for her to go, it was too early for good byes and anyway she was far too young to go to leave, she was only eight years old after all. I was beside myself about the unfairness of it all, just so unfair for Lilly not to be granted a longer life. I felt I hadn't been given long enough with her. And then of course the blaming game begins. I felt like I had let her down by not seeing that she had something more wrong with her than a virus and that played havoc with me. Also, to go from that much happiness to the depth of despair overnight is a big thing to cope with. I was mourning the loss of my little girl, the one I had given that special name to and I was also mourning the loss of the perfect little family until I had. And being so close to Christmas well that broke my heart a little bit more because Lilly didn't even get to spend one Christmas with her new family. I normally love Christmas, but that Christmas went by in a daze. There are only two things I remember about it actually. One was David's mother coming over and not understanding why I was acting the way I was. I wanted to cancel the visit and asked David if he would take his Mum out to a nice restaurant instead and leave me alone with my pugs. But he thought the visit would be good for me, it wasn't, he thought it'd make me feel better, it didn't, it made me feel worse. I would have been far better off being on my own and it was a really wet Christmas too, the paddocks were sopping so he couldn't even take his Mum out for a walk around the farm so I could have a rest from having to make pointless conversation about nothing. That can be hard at the best of times but harder still when it's the last thing you feel like doing.

The other thing that clearly sticks out in my mind is my poor husband putting up the Christmas tree because he thought if I had a tree I would be happy because I usually am when I have a Christmas tree in the house. But I couldn't be bothered with the tree, nor the cooking, the carols, the cards or the decorations either. I just didn't want anything to do with Christmas that year. It was our second Christmas on the farm, and I had been planning it for months. And when Lilly and Tommy got off that plane I began looking forward to the family Christmas we were going to share together. But I just couldn't face it now, I didn't care, and I didn't want to care. I just wanted it to be over and done with. David kept waiting for me to put up the tree, he didn't care about it for himself, Christmas has never been a particularly happy time for him due to his childhood, but he knew the joy it gave me and wanted to see me happy again. He would come home from work and glance at the area where a tree should have been and saw the empty space. I had even planned where I was going to put my Christmas tree when the real estate agent was showing us round the farm and there was a glorious looking six foot heavily decorated fine specimen of a tree standing there this time last year. But now I felt nothing, the only time I did feel something was when I came inside one day after walking the pugs and there was my wonderful husband struggling with our new Christmas tree. I'd bought a white tree that year because I'd never had one before and I wanted this Christmas to be something extra special. The sight of my husband doing the best he could to see me smile really melted my heart. He was doing a heck of a lot of cursing, and I think that was the funniest part of it all. So I sat on the couch laughing at him. He was really trying to do a good job and battling with this tree that seemed to be not wanting to cooperate with him at all. I watched on as he circled the tree a good many times making sure the branches looked nice but then he quickly lost interest and so began chucking the decorations on. And I do mean chuck because he stood a few feet away slinging baubles at the tree and if they got caught in amongst the branches and stayed there so be it, and if they fell to the ground well one of the pugs started chasing them across the floor, luckily our baubles are all shatterproof. I don't think there has ever been a Christmas tree put up so fast or so roughly before, the tinsel was also thrown on from a distance and he's tall, so he got it all the way to the top. But he looked like he was doing some kind of ceremonial dance to be honest, like dancing with ribbons and then he'd run and pick up the baubles the pugs had lost interest in playing with and began once again chucking them back at the tree. The normal me would have been saying to him that the tinsel goes on first and the baubles and trinkets after that and that there should be a balance of decorations evenly sprinkled across the tree, but I didn't say anything because the grieving me couldn't have cared less, I was just enjoying watching the show. And I'd like to say that all of this changed my mood around and that we had a lovely Christmas from that day on, but we didn't, sure it lightened the atmosphere a little but it didn't completely lift it because I was still distressed about losing Lilly, so sad about what had been taken from both her and me that I thought shouldn't have been. She had been robbed of life and I had been robbed of sharing a part of my life with her and that thought kept going round and round in my head. Still Christmas day came and went, and we got through it, we laughed a bit and got joy from the pugs and each other, but it wasn't one of the happiest Christmases we've ever had and I blame myself for that. I felt if only I could flick a switch and put all I was feeling to one side then everybody would benefit, but I've never been the type to be able to do that. If I'm feeling something no matter what the feeling is then I'm all in, heavily invested, I am really feeling it and in this case sadly so was everybody around me.

I'm often asked if I only had Lilly for four months why did I grieve for her for as long as I did and why did I take the loss as badly as I did. And I think it was because I was mourning the loss of so many things at the one time, the loss of Lilly, the loss of having what I thought was the perfect family unit, the loss of feeling such contentment, so many things had been snatched out of my hands. I was angry that Lilly had only been given eight years of life, to me it seemed too short an amount of time to be given on this earth. I wanted Lilly to have a chance to grow old, to have grey take over her face, to live on our farm for a long time, but she didn't get to do that, to me four lousy months was a very unfair amount of time for us to be together. I cried over my own loss, and I cried a lot for Tommy's loss too. And I was upset because this was the first two elderly pugs we had taken in since moving to the country and I couldn't even get one of them to live longer than sixteen weeks, to me that really wasn't a very good start for our little farm. They weren't good odds at all as far as I was concerned. I figured if I couldn't get a long life out of them then what right did I have doing this. Because I lost Lilly in the blink of an eye I also lost a lot of confidence in myself. I kept saying to David perhaps I was wrong, maybe this is not my calling after all. Maybe I was just not up to the challenge that I thought I was born to do. I was doubting myself left, right and centre and piling all these thoughts onto David each time one shot into my head. And he reminded me that Ruby and Grace were elderly too and I'd gotten them to these ages no problems at all and what about Harper, he said "Just look at the improvements you've made in her". I was blessed to have David. He was the voice of wisdom as he always is when my world is spinning out of control. Without him adding reason and sense to my upside down catastrophe then I don't know where I would be. The thing was if I'd have lost either Ruby or Grace four months in I think I could have accepted that better because they did look so very old to me when I first met them, and I do remember thinking that even if I can give them six months or a year of love and happiness then I'd be happy with that. So the thought of loss was already in my mind at that time and because it was I think it would have been easier to cope should one of them have left me so soon. But I believe because they went from strength to strength I thought this was going to be the case with every pug I took in and I quickly found out it wasn't. And of course, if you think about it logically, which I never do right away, it cannot possibly be. That's like thinking every human being on the planet is going to live the same length of time and that's not how it is in reality and it's the same with our dogs. Yes eight years old is far too young for a gorgeous little pug to die but it's the same if a human being dies young, it's heartbreaking for their families and it's not fair but life is not in the business of being fair is it. And some say you just have to accept it and I don't do that so easily. My uncle often tells me that his mother, this lady wasn't my grandmother because my uncle George is an uncle who I adopted and sometimes adopted uncles are the best kind to have, anyway his mother believed that each living being is given a certain amount of time on this earth and they are not going to live a day less or a day longer than that which has been allotted. But I have a lot of trouble accepting such theories, I rebel against them actually especially in cases like Lilly and Horton. I accept them very easily when death comes from old age but I'm not so good with those I love being robbed of life and maybe that's not realistic of me and maybe I need to grow up and look at things the way they truly are. But the biggest part of me is always fighting, always hoping, always praying for a better result and in some cases a miracle. I am always wanting to beat the odds, I just can't be accepting and take things laying down, that's not in my nature and I don't think it ever will be and so I think that's why I take things like this so hard. And should I work on that, no I don't believe so because to me accepting is giving up and I don't want to give up or give in, I'll always fight on until there is no fight left in me and that hasn't happened as yet and sure it could happen tomorrow or in a weeks' time or in twenty years' time but until it does I'll keep on plodding along as I am.

Lilly's sudden death was a huge blow because in my mind I thought getting this farm was going to make every pug I took in have a healthier longer life. I had rescued dogs while living in suburbia and done quite well with them and I thought if I got bigger and better then it would up my odds of success. But I think that was all me because I wanted it to be that way. After the first Grace Farm book came out I had somebody write and ask me why I forgave the man who attacked Ruby so easily and I said because I had to. I explained that it was because I didn't want to come to this farm with anything but a pure heart and the reason for that was because animals feel things about us, they are very sensitive that way and I wanted to have them feeling nothing but goodness and happiness coming from me. If I wanted them to heal and thrive, well I felt they wouldn't be able to do that fully if the person taking care of them had resentment in her heart. I didn't want to bring any negative feelings here with me, dragging them around like an anchor, they would have stifled what I wanted to do on this farm, the world I wanted to create. And also, I wasn't about to let some creep ruin this farm for me or any of the animals I was about to take in. Looking after elderly animals was very important to me so I let his actions go, in my mind I did everything right before coming here and yet I still lost Lilly and that gutted me. I'm still glad I forgave the man though because it really was the right thing to do, I couldn't be carrying that resentment around with me for the remainder of my days, which wouldn't have been good for me or my health, it would have taken a toll.

When Lilly wasn't coping with the infection she was full of life and happiness. But I was looking at her from the outside only having no idea what was going on inside, and because there were no other signs of illness other than the infection, me, David and our vet, none of us thought to go looking for anything else. If she had shown any other signs then tests would have been done and yes something would have shown up then and we would have acted on it. Even with not having as much experience as I do now I still would have had the sense to look deeper if, like I said, there was anything else out of the ordinary happening there but there wasn't. I mean nobody is going to put their dog through a pile of tests when there is nothing to support that anything else is going on other than that which she is being treated for. You just wouldn't do it, you wouldn't put a dog that is battling a virus through a pile of tests where they would need sedation, especially a pug, because you put a pug through anesthesia when they are already ill, and the chances are they will not come out of it. And of course, if our vet had picked up on something that Dave and myself missed then he too would have suggested looking deeper, drawing blood or doing scans and x-rays, doing all the things one does when they are looking for something that the human eye cannot detect. I just think that sometimes dogs are good at hiding things from us, some dogs are very good at it, and Lilly I believe was one of them. I've talked to a lot of people in rescue and animal health, and they say the same thing, they've had similar cases, a lot of people in the industry have. Does it make losing Lilly any easier, no not really, I still lost her and that still hurt but it did give me a bit more understanding of what may have happened. And did it help with my confidence in my ability to care for old dogs, well yes and no, as I was still pretty hard on myself for a long time afterwards. In fact, I didn't take in another dog for quite a while after I lost Lilly because I really didn't think that I could, and I suppose it was always going to take a very special situation and a very special little pug to alter that. And that's exactly what did happen because the next pug I took in was Horton.

Looking back on all this now I can see things a bit clearer than I once did. I think if I'd taken in a whole lot of pugs and they'd each been given a lot of years with me and then sadly I lost one four months in then I think I may have been more ok with that, I wouldn't have doubted myself as much because I would have been able to see what I could do. And of course, that's exactly what I did go on to do, I went on to do it over and over and over again and with some extremely difficult cases too. I have taken in many pugs at the ages of eight, nine and ten, some that were on their last legs and still been able to get them through to the ages of 14, 15, 16 and even 17. All this was coming for me, I had a big future ahead with a lot of successes, but I just didn't know it at the time I lost Lilly, so I allowed the rot of self-doubt to set in and once it took hold it was very hard to get rid of. I wish I could have waved a magic wand and made everything alright for Lilly, but the reality is I can't do that, such things are beyond my human capabilities. I was talking to a friend one day about Lilly, sharing everything I was feeling at the time, and she told me to be strong for Tommy and to be kind to myself. She said I had done all I could do, which was way more than anyone else was willing to do for these two old pugs. She said perhaps not all the animals that come to my farm are going to live to ripe old ages, but they are meant to come here regardless. This friend also said that she had no doubt Lilly was sorry she couldn't stay longer but she was probably happy with the outcome. It was quick but Lilly did not suffer and nor did I. She said that Lilly did not want to languish for weeks or months and see me in pain trying to help her. And that thought didn't make me as happy as my friend thought it would because that had already been kind of happening hadn't it because Lilly had come down with that infection not long after arriving here and I had been doing all I could to clear her of it. I did a lot of crying over the loss of little Lilly but in the end I decided I was not going to cry anymore in front of the other pugs. They pick up on all of our emotions far more than most people give them credit for and I didn't want to upset them, if I felt like I was going to cry I did so in the shower or walked alone amongst the gumtrees in the back paddock and let everything out so that when I came back inside again I could pat my little blessings and act as though everything was alright. They needed to feel that and besides the tree walks did me a world of good, I wasn't gone too long because I didn't like leaving the pugs, but those short walks were healing for me, nature is a wonderful healer. I always felt so much better when I walked back into the house. And also, how could I be sad when there were all those little flat faces pressed against the window watching intently for that first sign of my head coming over the hill, they'd go nuts barking and I knew that I'd been spotted, I could hear Steffy like a foghorn and a whole lot of mini growly woofs coming from the others whenever Steffy drew breath. With Lilly there was guilt suffered, putting one of your beloved dogs in the ground is bad enough but walking away with a nagging voice in the back of your mind that perhaps there was a way you could have saved her, well that kind of thing takes a toll. And it makes things all the harder. The "If only's" claw at your soul and the "What if's" can tear your heart to pieces. But they, as I have found out many times over the years, are all part of the grieving process and these days I am able to deal with them so much better than I was earlier on. When these thoughts come flying at me know I am able to talk myself through it because I know the truth, I know why this is happening and that you can do everything perfectly and still be plagued by these thoughts. David has always been able to sit back in the knowledge that there are times when the life of one of our pugs is going to be taken out of our hands, he always had a better understanding of it, but I really struggle. I think if there's even a tiny splinter of doubt in your mind as to whether there was anything else you could have done then it's enough to feistier and of course me being me I allowed it to turn gangrene there for a while.

On the flip side I've been very lucky in my life in that I have had some wonderful people to help me when I needed them the most. I was talking to one of my dog rescue friends a few months after Lilly died. She'd taken in a little mix breed that lasted only two months in her home, a measly eight weeks. She was telling me how those two months were the happiest of that little dog's life, how she had pampered him silly, and I noticed there wasn't any hurt on her face and no anger in her voice as she was talking to me. She spoke about him with such joy, telling me all about this little dog, how lovely he was, his likes and dislikes and the cute things he used to get up to. And she was pleased, genuinely pleased with what she got to do for him in the final two months of his life. She got to love him, care for him, showed him that he was special. She had peace about it, she had done all she could do, and she let go of everything else and concentrated on that. And I had two thoughts running through my head about her reaction to this, in a way I thought she was being heartless and in a way I envied how well she was dealing with it. I sat across the table from her and when she paused I said to her "Why are you not angry about this, why are you not kicking and screaming about the unfairness of it all" I fell short of saying "Why are you not behaving like me" but she knew what I meant and started talking to me some more. She was an older lady and as is the case with such people had gained an awful lot of knowledge and understanding along the way and she was more than happy to share some of what she'd learnt with me. I guess to her it wasn't all that long ago that she'd been in my shoes and perhaps somebody had been kind enough to talk to her when she was struggling. She had been involved in rescue a lot longer than I had and she had seen a lot more than I had seen, in a nutshell she had far more experience than I had so was coming at this from a different angle to how I was, she was looking at it very differently to me. And the biggest part of me wanted to be a bit more like her, to feel the bliss she was feeling, I tried to learn a lesson from her, look at it the way she chose to look at it, certainly it was a much happier place to be in and I wanted some of that. I wanted to look back on the time I had with Lilly and have that be enough. But I just could not do it at the time, I don't know if it was because I was angry or because I was being suborn or even if it was because I was just too dumb to be able to see things the way she saw them. I after all had an extra two months with Lilly then she had with this dog, and I probably should have been grateful for that. And I suppose deep down I was grateful, but I let everything else I was feeling come boiling to the surface instead. This lady had learnt to look for the good in these situations because you have to really, but it was all new to me. I would learn that lesson much later on. But for now, I was broken hearted. And not just that, I mean I was glad Lilly had come to me and didn't have to live out the final months of her life with the old ladies daughter who clearly didn't want her. But I was still as mad as hell that Lilly didn't get to live longer. And of course, anger is no good, no good to me, no good to anybody really because it doesn't alter the situation that has taken place. It more or less just wastes your time, uses up all your energy and keeps you stagnated, it prevents the healing process and keeps you from getting back to what you should be doing with your life.

Lilly died at 1.30 in the morning on the 12th of December. She was restless so I moved her from our bed to the floor so she could hopefully make herself more comfortable in one of the dog beds down there, but she didn't, she was still sitting up when I checked on her again a little while later, so this time I carried her outside thinking she may have needed to go out for a wee. She didn't she just sat there on the grass, I could see her from the porch light not even attempting to get up and sniff about. I figured I'd gotten it wrong, she didn't need to wee at all so I picked her up again and brought her up onto the veranda. The house was in total darkness, I hadn't turned on any lights when I carried Lilly out because I didn't want to wake everybody else up. But due to how she was acting I wanted to have a better look at her, so I put her down on the deck to try and see what was going on, the porch light was brighter now because we were right underneath it. As soon as I put Lilly down again she took one last breath and passed away. I quickly picked her up and raced back into the bedroom, David was awake by this time, Lilly and I must have woken him up as we walked out of the room, he was in our ensuite and looked up and smiled when he saw me carrying her in. I guess he just thought I was bringing our new little daughter back inside after a toilet break. His face instantly changed when I told him she had just died, he gave her CPR, tried to get her going again but it was no good, she was gone. David rang our vet the next day and he was as shocked as we were at her passing, we asked what he thought could have gone on with Lilly, he said it could have been cancer, probably in her lungs. But he didn't know for sure, it was just a guess really and as no tests were done we will never have an answer to what caused Lilly's death. I didn't think of doing an autopsy at the time, looking back now I wish we had of done one because at least I would have an explanation then. But our thoughts weren't on that at the time, so we picked an area of the farm for burial and David dug a little hole. To be honest up until that day none of us had given a burial site much thought, we hadn't been here long enough to think about such things. I suppose we should have at least had a bit of a conversation about it, we were living with a few elderly pugs after all, but we were still in that dream stage of happiness and newness at living here and life, lovely wonderful beautiful life, that's where our thoughts were at the time. We were living in a state of pure bliss. Death wasn't on our minds back then as much as it is today. I don't even know if we chose the best spot for our cemetery, it was chosen in hast because we had a little girl that needed a resting place. David chose the spot in the end because I couldn't think straight. My mind was more on why we had lost her, if it was cancer then I think she must have had it all along, before she even entered our home. But as is the case with some cancers you don't know they have it until the end. If Lilly had it when she was with the old lady then she definitely wouldn't have known what was going on due to the dementia. And her daughter barely looked at these two pugs at all, and the rescue group thought she was healthy too, I don't think they deliberately sent a sick dog down to me, I just think that nobody knew that Lilly was as ill as she was. And that is a thing that makes me very sad. Looking back, I think that perhaps the reason she never fully got rid of the infection was because her immune system was under attack from the cancer. I so wished there was something we could have done for her, even if it was just being able to give her a few more months of life. Losing Lilly made me fearful too, I kept getting my bedside torch out and checking and rechecking the pugs all throughout the night. You think if you can lose one so quickly and unexpectedly then you can lose others just as fast. I'd not be sleeping because I was constantly worrying about the pugs and the lack of sleep only added to everything else I was feeling. I'd go to bed the next night and tell myself not to do that, to sleep because everything was going to be ok, but I'd find myself tossing and turning and have to get up and make sure that everybody was alright. I was like this ghost creeping throughout the house making sure all was well. I stopped short of going out into the paddocks and checking on the horses and that's only because I watch far too many murder mysteries that I think I'm going to be somebodies next victim and if I'm standing alone in the middle of a paddock in the middle of the night I figure I've just upped the chances of that happening. The night time checking and rechecking thing lasted about a month or so, after that I reasoned it out in my mind that everybody was going to be ok. And by that time, I was too exhausted to keep it up anyway. It was like I was constantly doing double shifts, loving and taking care of everybody during the day then neurotically creeping about with a torch four or five times a night and also I had to think of the pugs, it wasn't very nice for them to keep having a torch shone in their faces. I would put my hand over the top of the torch so that it dimmed things a little, gave me a bit of light, enough to see if they were still breathing but not too bright for those little pugs eyes but I was still startling a few of them awake and I didn't like doing that, I think in the end that's the main reason I stopped. And I believe the pugs breathed a sigh of relief when I did.

When I first saw Lilly I remember thinking "Wow I've hit the jackpot here" I've got this unique small black pug and she is wonderful, she had my heart from first sight. And because Lilly was younger than Tommy I just automatically assumed I'd have her longer than I had him, but the universe had other plans and I've since learnt that the universe usually does have other plans. Still, I'm very happy at how things worked out for Tommy. I am so glad he came to me, if he'd just been a single male pug looking for a home then he would never have become our son and that would have been really sad, sad for both him and for us. It wasn't the way I would have liked to have adopted my very first male pug though, I think seeing an old pug face, falling in love with it and not caring what sex it was would have been my preferred option. A lot less heartache if it had happened that way that's for sure. But when I'm hugging him and telling him how much I love him, how happy I am to have him with me it really doesn't matter much how we came into each other's life, the main thing, the only thing to be thinking about is that I am his Mum, we are together, and I felt we were meant to be together. Well not only me but all of us living together as a family. Imagine if somebody else had taken Lilly and Tommy in, the poor old boy would have been all alone once Lilly died, and I think he'd really feel that loneliness, but he didn't have to worry about being lonely, ever, because he had a big family. And also, I was with him 24/7 and he would have been used to somebody always being there with him when he lived in his previous home.

There was a time when I wondered if Lilly or should I say losing Lilly had been a form of punishment from the universe for me or if not the universe punishing me then a way of it teaching me a lesson, a lesson I should have learnt a lot earlier. There was a pug about a year or so before I got Lilly that I decided not to take in, I didn't open up my home to her and always felt that I should have done. The pug would have been coming here to die. I was asked along with a handful of other specially chosen people to take in this little pug, the rescue group said it wouldn't be quantity of time with her but quality and at that point in my life I just didn't think I could do it. I didn't think I had it in me. Her name was ItsyBitsy. I cried when I read the e-mail. In a short paragraph I found out that ItsyBitsy was ten years old, raised on a raw diet, had very little grey in her face and due to having her rear patella's misdiagnosed as a youngster now dragged her back legs, it said that she was in no pain and that it didn't stop her from getting around and today I know this to be the truth because of the time I spent with Horton and all the other pugs I've shared my life with who have similar conditions. I also read that this pug suffered from a little bit of dementia, again I've had few with dementia over the years and I too know that such a thing isn't the end of the world. That they just need some special looking after, lots of extra care and you always need to know where they are at all times in case they are having a bad day and need your help. When I read all this about little ItsyBitsy it didn't put me off, none of her special needs put me off, if anything it made me feel sorrier for her, that a pug like this was looking for a home at that stage of her life. I wondered who had let her down. I didn't know what happened in her previous home, why her owners no longer wanted her as none of that was in the email. If I'd taken her in I'm sure I would have been told more. It also said that eventually she would lose the use of her back legs and then whoever took her in could get her a cart or put her to sleep. And I thought that I'd go with the cart first just to give her every chance possible of living a better life for a little bit longer, well if her dementia wasn't getting any worse that is, because you have to weigh up quality of life too in these cases and every case is different and every week with them is different too.

I spent the next few days thinking about ItsyBitsy wondering if I would be strong enough to take on this important role. And again, it had nothing at all to do with her legs or the dementia, extra care is where I excel, it was just my heart I was concerned about. I know the pain felt by loss, all my life even as a small child I have always sunken to great depths when losing one of my animals. I've always taken it hard and so that was the only thing holding me back and it was a big thing to me. For days I gave myself little pep talks, tried to talk myself round for her sake because this farm of mine is lovely to spend any amount of time on. And it wouldn't have hurt to have this little old pug spend her final days here surrounded by love and all this beauty. ItsyBitsy could have dragged her little legs round the place, spent her time sleeping on the lush green grass or on the veranda in the sun and a beautiful cart would have been sought when the time came to get one and then eventually when everything that could have possibly been done for this dear old soul had been done we would have buried her beside one of the trees and put a plaque there. But that didn't get to happen because I said no. Protecting my heart won this debate because I didn't think I would be able to cope with losing a pug so quickly. I thought this isn't me, this isn't what I am good at. I didn't want to fall in love with her then be heartbroken when she died. I knew I would be having to look at this pug every day wondering if this would be the day we'd lose her, and well I just didn't think I was strong enough emotionally to take on such a role. I talked to David about it, and he thought I shouldn't do it either, he didn't even have to think about it, he just said "No, no" And I looked at his face and when his face looks like that it means what he's said is the end of that discussion, no more talking about it.

Nobody in Melbourne who was asked to put up their hand for ItsyBitsy did, so she was put on a plane, sent interstate and died a few months later. When I heard this news I cried my eyes out. I wondered if I'd let ItsyBitsy come here would she have perhaps lived a little while longer, was that plane ride too much for her to cope with, did the atmosphere in the plane make her condition worse, could it have accelerated things, did it make her life even shorter than it was going to be. I thought about this with ItsyBitsy, and I thought about it with Lilly too, but I'll never have an answer to either one of those questions. But it did lay heavily on my mind especially with ItsyBitsy. I didn't know it with Lilly I thought I was just flying down two healthy pugs. But I had full knowledge of the situation with ItsyBitsy, and I couldn't get past the fact that it was me who'd made her get on the plane. I was disappointed in myself for making her do that, well disappointed in myself about the entire situation really. But of course, it wasn't just me who had said no. None of the others wanted to do it either, not sure what their reasons were, probably the same as mine. But I bet they weren't beating themselves up about it the way I was, but that's just my nature, it's the way I am when it comes to animals I feel I have let down.

Looking back now if I had a chance at giving ItsyBitsy a home no matter how long she may have been here I would definitely have done it. I would have brought that little pug home to the farm and loved her with all my heart every second, every hour and every day that she was with me. But of course, coming to that realisation too late didn't help ItsyBitsy did it and to this day I still have huge regrets about that. I mean I have done a lot of good for a whole lot of animals in all the years I've been alive but it's the one you say no to that is going to tear at your heartstrings every time you think about them, and you do think about them an awful lot over the years. I am always going to remember ItsyBitsy's name, it's imprinted on my heart now because she is the one I let down. I felt the loss of her would affect me emotionally for a very long time but the rejecting of her to protect myself has affected me even more so. I felt that I should have been stronger and stayed stronger for the amount of time she needed me to be strong. Piled all my resources to do what needed to be done for this little pug and then fall apart when she left, once I'd given her what she needed me to give her. She would have only been around for a short amount of time, she deserved to be looked after no matter what it took, me, well I had the rest of my life to live. I would have only been her Mum for a short time, and I should have done it, I should have been there for her and I wasn't and I have to live with that now. David's thoughts on the matter were that he didn't want me to have to go through all the sadness, see me get myself to that high level of upset, he has always been protective of me, my human guard dog. At times he has saved me from myself and so I do trust his judgement. He genuinely thought I would not be able to cope and perhaps so, perhaps I needed to go through some other things in life first in order to be who I am today because I am a very different person now to whom I was when the ItsyBitsy email came through. I have changed a lot over my time here on the farm, I've had a lot of experiences that have been very hard to go through, but they have made me a stronger person. A lot stronger than I ever thought I could be that's for sure, but of course at the time you don't feel strong at all you feel like the saddest, weakest most vulnerable soul on the planet. And the strength doesn't come in that you can go through anything now and no longer feel it, because I still feel everything very deeply. The strength I am talking about comes in the fact that you can go through it all, be brought to your knees, then stand back up again and keep on going. That is where the true strength lies and in that I am very strong. Protecting my heart isn't my first thought anymore, the dogs that need me are, I don't think I have a right to protect my heart when there are so many dogs out there needing my help. They come first now because they have to, they are too important not to. Also, my experiences have made me a better person too, not better in the fact that I'm not badly broken because I am due to what I've gone through, I mean better at coping with what life decides to throw at you. You don't know how much you can take until you are made to take it. And so, in that I am better than whom I was before. I feel with all important lessons in life that if you don't learn them at one point you are going to be made to learn them at another. The lesson keeps coming round and round until you are ready to learn, ready to grow, and life can be a harsh and merciless teacher at times. But the truth of the matter is that when you are rescuing older dogs you never know how long you are going to get with them. Lilly was with me four months, to date she is the pug who has shared my life for the shortest amount of time, nobody can predict the time you are going to have together that's why you have to make every moment count. Lilly came here and lasted around the same amount of time ItsyBitsy lasted in her interstate home. I survived Lilly's loss and I would have survived ItsyBitsy's loss too.

After Lilly passed away I feared that Tommy wasn't going to cope so well without his lifelong friend, I thought he may mourn her loss to the point of leaving us too, so David and I made sure to be aware of Tommy's feelings at all times. We both made a special effort to make him feel treasured. And he responded in kind, he was happy, he did his big goofy froggy smile and lapped up all the extra attention. I wanted him to feel loved and wanted, that we thought he was the best thing ever, so that he wouldn't even think of going anywhere. He did miss Lilly I could tell that he did, but he also took a great deal of joy in being around the sisters he had left. I knew he no longer had his little playmate, but I saw that he was happy being in amongst everybody else, I think what would have been much worse for Tommy was if he had to live as an only dog. Such a thing wouldn't have suited him at all, some pugs can be completely ok with that, and some pugs don't like it and I believe Tommy wouldn't have liked it. I think he would have died pretty soon after Lilly did, from grief and from loneliness. But there was no lack of company for Tommy around here. He would wander off on his own and he would saunter along with the pack. He would sleep on his own on his special chair but if somebody decided to hop up and join him he was alright with that too, he just moved his big body into a more comfortable position to accommodate his sibling. He had suffered loss but he was ok, and I think David, me and all his sisters played a huge role in making him feel that he was going to be ok. He had loved ones surrounding him and he liked that I know he did because he would often lift his big old head and look around to see where they were and once he'd spotted a few of them he then lay his head back down and drifted off to sleep again. Steffy seemed to miss Lilly a real lot, with her being deaf she could smell that Lilly was no longer in the bedroom at night and kept running into the lounge to look for her in there. And she'd scream, stand in the middle of the lounge room screaming out for Lilly and of course Lilly didn't answer her call, so she'd run back into the bedroom again and start screaming for her in there. This went on for a few days, maybe a week but then she seemed to realise that Lilly wasn't coming back, and she did look awfully sad about that. Steffy is the kind of pug who takes somebody into her heart fast and looks out for them and when they leave she feels the emptiness, she notices that unfilled bed or space on the floor and I think that's because Steffy is constantly watching, watching, watching. She's taken it upon herself to watch everybody and knows so much about them due to this. And somebody new will enter the house and nobody will tell her to, but she then starts watching out for them as well. It's a really beautiful thing for her to do but it also means that she'll feel an absence deeply and my heart goes out to her during these times because I know exactly what she's feeling.

Tommy handled Lilly's loss a lot better than I did which started me thinking that maybe he was in fact a lot wiser than I was and knew that she had gone on to a much better place and was not sick anymore. But I watched him more closely and yes the signs where there, but they were more subtle. Yes he missed her, but he was also alright with it, like he had an inner peace about it all. And I got to thinking that perhaps this was the way it was meant to be. I do believe that pugs find us, we think we are finding them, but I think they find us too and perhaps this was how it was meant to happen all along, that Lilly's time on earth was coming to an end and maybe Tommy was meant to come to us so that he wouldn't be alone. I believe there is something that's bigger than all of us, a thing that is guiding pugs to our farm. I do a lot of praying about this little farm of mine and when my Mum was alive she did too, perhaps that is why we get the pugs we do. Like there's a reason for it and behind it. And maybe I am to just sit back and let it all unfold the way it's meant to unfold.

Also, seeing the way Tommy was handling this made me think that maybe Lilly had lasted the four months she did because she wanted to make sure that "Her Tommy" would be ok and once she had that sorted she knew it would be alright for her to go. Perhaps she was holding on as long as she could for his sake. I've often thought that she could have died at the daughter's house before going into rescue, or at the rescue group itself, or even on the plane. But she didn't, she came here and stayed until she saw that Tommy was settled into a loving caring home and then decided it would be ok now if she moved on to what comes after our time here on earth. Maybe Lilly and Tommy even had a conversation about it so that he knew what was going on. Certainly, that would explain how well Tommy was handling things now. Sure, I would have given anything for Lilly and Tommy to have both been able to stay here for as long as Tommy did. But perhaps all this had been worked out long before they came into my care, and I was nothing more than a loving bystander with no control over what was about to take place. Maybe all my role was ever going to be was to show Lilly love for those four months and Tommy for the next five years. Perhaps that is all our roles really are and all we are meant to do in these circumstances is watch and learn. Really gives you something to think about doesn't it. These days I am able to look back on my time with Lilly with a better understanding, it's been over a decade since her passing. I now don't concentrate so much on the bad, I focus on the good. And the good in this situation was that Lilly had love and kindness, she had somebody who was attentive to all her needs all day long. She had somebody helping her and looking after her and she had a quiet farm routine for those four months. She had pats and snuggles and knee time and lots and lots of talking to. She knew she was special, she would have felt that she was important to David and to me. And when the time came Lilly died with somebody who loved her right there by her side, she wasn't alone and her brother, the one she loved so very deeply wasn't alone when she had gone, he never spent one single day alone in the five years he was with us and when his time came to leave, he wasn't alone then either. Tommy had two people that loved him right there with him, one was cradling him in his arms and the other one was gently stroking his head and he merely did what little Lilly had done five years earlier, he closed his eyes in this world and opened them up in heaven. And for both Lilly and Tommy their first Mummy would have been there waiting to greet them with outstretched arms. If I could paint a picture of this scene it would be of an old lady and a little black pug standing happily together in this beautiful place high above the clouds and below would be two parents, a vet nurse and a veterinarian standing together in a small blue room. In the tall man's arms would be the body of a rather large fawn pug and floating upwards in a faded fashion would be that same large fawn boy with angel wings and a big froggy grin and he would be looking up towards the clouds and the closer he got to them the more he would be smiling, his focus now would be solely on where he was going and he would be happy, really happy, that reunion for all three of them would be a wonderful one. And while much rejoicing was going on in heaven here on earth two people and the body of a dearly loved docile fantastic gentleman of a pug will be making their way back to a small farm. To dig another hole, to mourn their loss and to love the pugs who are eagerly awaiting their return and then one day the phone will ring again or an email will be sent and the answer to the question will be "Yes" and their life on the farm with you will begin and you yourselves will go on and on with the lives you were born to lead, loving and taking care of these elderly blessings until the scene you've just read about is ready to be repeated again.

CHAPTER FOUR

Gerald

One of the first things I did once I landed on Grace Farm was set about finding myself a horse but not just any old horse, I wanted a Clydesdale. I had shared my life with horses before but never a Clydesdale and that's where my heart was being drawn. I had been dreaming about having a big solid horse with huge fluffy feet my entire life, ever since I was a little girl. I had plenty of toy Clydesdales growing up and even lovely shinny china ornaments that I'd bought as an adult, I'd lined shelves with them and got joy out of dusting, I always stopped and studied each one as I did so and then stare dreamily off into the distance with visions of fields full of beautiful horses dancing through my head. But no more daydreaming for me, the time had finally come for the living breathing thing to entre my life and I was beside myself. I now had a farm, finally my very own property that I could put anything on it I liked, my heart was giddy with excitement, no more battling with irritable land owners for agistment, the only two people that had to be in agreement about this was me and David and one of us was already fully on board. It was freedom at last for me, and freedom in any area of one's life where there was once containment is a very beautiful thing.

I can even remember the very first Clydesdale ornament I ever owned. I believe it was this ornament that first got me interested in the Clydesdale breed because before that I don't remember having any knowledge of them. I won it on a spinning wheel, a one ticket win. It was at a fete at my younger sisters kindergarten so that's how young I was. We hadn't been in Australia all that long, me and my older sister were in primary school and my younger sister had just started kinder and this fete was to raise some much needed funds. All the children in attendance and their families were encouraged to go and show their support. I personally didn't have much interest in going to be honest. I would have rather been outside playing in the streets, but my family was going so I had no choice but to tag along. Well my Dad wasn't going because he always worked on the weekends, worked during the week as well but had a different job on the weekends just to try and make a go of life here in Australia, he worked really hard did my Dad and always came home exhausted, but I had a feeling that even if he wasn't working that day he still wouldn't have come along because fetes weren't really his kind of thing. Anyway, the rest of the family trudged along. Mum gave us three girls our pocket money just before we entered, there was a lady selling tickets at the gate, not to gain entrance because that was free. The tickets were for rides and stalls and things like that, in fact those tickets could get you anything from anywhere once you were inside. I bought six tickets with my pocket money and my older sister did the same. My younger sister stayed with Mum and went on some of the little kid rides, but me and my older sister took off to see if there was anything more to our liking. The spinning wheel was in the entrance of the kindergarten and at first I didn't give the prizes on the table any of my attention, mainly because I couldn't see them properly due to crowds of people standing in the way, they weren't looking at the table more trying to make their way inside and I got pushed along with the movement and found myself outside near the candy floss stall before I knew what hit me. I also found that I had been separated from my older sister and so set about trying to find her, or if not her then Mum and my younger sister, basically I went off in search of anybody with a familiar face. I made my way back inside the main building and was once again swept up with the crowd in the room and found myself yet again right near the spinning wheel. I didn't know what fate was back then but now I wonder if I was always meant to be pushed towards that table, see that horse ornament, and have my heart leap with joy. When I found Mum I told her what I'd seen. I thought the ornament I'd come face to face with was for sale, so Mum came with me to find out how much it was. When the concept of the spinning wheel was explained to me I didn't think I had a hope in hell of ever securing that horse, as young as I was I could still see that my chances were not good. And what about all the people in the line in front of me, what if one of them chose my horse for a prize, he would have been lost to me forever. But being the kind of kid that wasn't so easily put off I lined up with the others and prayed like mad while standing in the queue. My older sister was in front of me, a girl with long frizzy red hair was directly in front of her and there were a few other kids in front of the redhead but I couldn't see them properly because they were concealed. And I was madly trying to look as well because I wanted to find out how many tickets would be handed over before I got to hand over mine. I knew each ticket lessened my chances so strained my neck out as far out as it would go but it was no use, I was blinded by the boof headed girl in front of my sister, from where I was standing she looked a bit like Cousin It, well a bright red Cousin It anyway, a Cousin It that only used shampoo on her locks never conditioner. If she'd tied her hair in a ponytail I may have had a chance to actually see who my opponents were. But all I knew about them was that they were shorter than Cousin It. All the younger kids handed over their tickets, gave the wheel a spin and were offered a prize. All tickets were winners was what the man kept yelling out, but most tickets only allowed you to put your hand inside a rather badly put together lucky dip. I looked at the shabby box with the ugly paper wrapped around it and wondered if the prizes inside would be as equally offensive to my eyes. If my ticket got the lucky dip would I simply turn and walk away rather than have to put my hand in there. I figured that would make me losing the Clydesdale ornament all the worse. As I stood in line I was weighing up which way I was going to go should that be the outcome, still praying for a miracle win but also planning what I would do if I didn't get my prayers answered. And by the time Cousin It scurried off with her prize I'd decided that for me it was going to be the little Clydesdales or nothing because I knew deep down in my heart that no consolation prize was ever going to come close to being good enough for me, especially if it came from such an ugly looking box. I've always been artistic, I've always liked things to look a certain way, a beautiful way, and I've always felt that if you are going to do something then you may as well do a good job of it but whoever threw that box together clearly didn't share my views, perhaps it had been put together by an overworked overtired kindergarten Mum. A Mum who was the type to say "Yes" to everything before realising how long each task was going to take. I watched on as my sister walked over and spun that wheel with all her might, then sigh and shove her hand into the lucky dip. She searched around for the longest time, she seemed to be picking lots of things up but changing her mind and blindly searching around again. The man who ran the spinning wheel had the patience of a saint because he didn't bother how long the kids were digging around for as long as they came out with only one prize he was happy. And in a way I was hoping she'd hurry up and in another way I was ok that she was taking so long because it gave me more time to pray.

Finally I was first in line, I handed the very last ticket I had over to the man and in a loud voice he told me I could now step up to the wheel. I took my time with this, again giving myself more time to mutter to God. I passed my shinny Clydesdale as I stepped up, I gave him one last look then closed my eyes and gave the wheel a spin. My spin wasn't as hard as my sisters was, in fact it wasn't as hard as any of the other kids had spun it either and as I stood there eyes closed and praying I was thinking that perhaps I should have spun it harder. I couldn't breathe, couldn't open my eyes, all I could do was wait for the wheel to stop and for the man to tell me what I'd won. Time and time again I heard him say "Lucky dip little fella" or "Lucky dip young lady, your ticket has won a lucky dip" and I was hoping like crazy that he wasn't about to say those same words to me. Suddenly there was clapping and then somebody said "The boy has won a table prize" and I'm thinking to myself what boy, I'm the only one spinning here. I thought I'd been standing there so long with my eyes closed that they'd brought somebody else up to have a go because my go was over, and I still wasn't moving on. I quickly opened my eyes and looked around fast expecting to see a boy standing on the platform beside me, but I was the only one there. I looked at the man and realised he was talking to me, "Son, son you've won a table prize, go over and pick whatever you want" and he didn't have to tell me twice, I shot off that platform, dived over to the table and scooped the little shinny Clydesdale ornament up. I didn't even care that he had mistaken me for a boy or even if everybody in the crowd thought I was a boy, God had answered my prayers, no ugly lucky dip prize for me, the Clydesdale was mine and I was ecstatic about it. And besides it wasn't the first time I'd been mistake for a lad. My hair was short, a no fuss style that I could quickly run a comb through and then be on my way, and I went around wearing jeans and t-shirts all day long, well except for Sundays Sunday was church day and for church I was made to wear a dress. But I took it off as soon as we got home, and it was back to jeans and a t-shirt again and I would wander round the neighbourhood with my hands shoved in my pockets thinking about life and patting other people's dogs because at that point I still didn't have one of my own. But I did have a crocodile, not a real one although I pretended that he was, but a rubber crocodile that I always carried around with me wherever I went. If I was at the dinner table he'd be sitting on my shoulder, walking round the streets or outside playing and he'd be hanging from my back pocket by his tail, or I'd hook his tail through the loop of my jeans where a belt should have gone. Came in handy that his tail was curled because I could secure him with that, and I'd feel him banging against my side as I walked along. I lost him a couple of times, but he was always quickly found again by retracing my steps and I wish I could tell you that he had a really cool name but sadly he did not. I just called him Crocky. And Crocky was a pretty good friend to have, he would sleep beside my pillow and at bath time he'd be swimming amongst the bubbles.

I loved my little spinning wheel prize with all my heart but sadly life with him was very short lived, only one day to be exact, within a measly twenty four hours he was broken in pieces. That night I put him on the floor beside my bed, I'd made my Clydesdale a stable out of an old shoe box because I wanted him to have somewhere nice to sleep. I made a door for the stable too, well a half door actually like Mister Ed had on the tv show I used to watch, I wanted my china Clydesdale to be able to peep his head out like Mister Ed did when he was in the mood for talking to Wilbur. I loved how talented that horse was, I especially loved how he used to pull the door shut whenever he didn't want to talk anymore. I adored the concept of a talking horse, and that horse was so beautiful, the show was in black and white but that horse was a Palomino. Part Arabian and so very stunning, incredibly intelligent too, his real name was Bamboo Harvester and he lived to be twenty one years old. Oh, how I loved that horse. I couldn't wait for the show to come on every afternoon. I loved the antics he got up to and how he blamed everything on Wilbur, it was nice for a human being to be the one getting into trouble for once, nice to have the tables turned. I think that was half the reason I watched. Well, my Clydesdale ornament slept all night in his Mister Ed style stable but in the morning when I was sleepily getting out of bed I accidentally stepped on the stable squashing it and my poor little horse in the process. And I guess I did a fair job of it too because there was no talk of him being glued back together. So, while our relationship was short lived the love he instilled in me for Clydesdales wasn't, it would go on to last me the rest of my life.

My favourite horse list reads like this, Clydesdales, Shires, Friesian, Percheron, Gypsy Cob you know all the heavy horse breeds and then the colours come into it, the Palominos, the Pinto's and the Paints. And I also adore big black horses and any little white horse with a pink bit on its nose, sure you need to watch that they don't get sunburnt and pay extra attention to that but it's worth it. My favourite pony is the Welsh Mountain Pony. I have trouble seeing the personality of the horse first because for me it's all about vision, the way they look is so important. I had a friend who would tell me off for being like this, in her eyes I was being a little unfair. She thought I was overlooking a lot of wonderful natured horses just because they were not visually attractive to me and she was right, I was, I do and I still am. And I don't feel guilty about this either because we all have a right to love what we love and there are plenty of people out there who don't like the bigger heavier horses as much as I do nor Palomino's either and that's ok, there are a lot of people in this world and so no horse breed goes completely unloved. It's the same with pugs not everyone is a fan but as long as all the breeds have somebody who adores them that's all that really matters. Also, I wouldn't ever turn my back on a horse at a sales yard just because it wasn't my favourite colour, if it was calm and I had the room I'd take it in rather than have it killed for dog meat, if nobody else was willing to put up their hand for that horse besides the doggers, then I, regardless of what it looked like, would do so. This friend of mine had two bays and a chestnut and when they passed away she went on to get another couple of chestnuts so I suppose she had a type too and I guess I could have said something to her about this but I didn't, I just let it go, but while I patted her horses whenever I was at her farm I still thought my horses were far prettier. It was the same when we first came to Australia and I was about to get my first dog. Dad thought because we were living in Australia that it would be fun to get an Australian terrier, but I had other ideas. I was really excited to be finally getting a dog but when we arrived at the breeders and got out of the car my face dropped. I started looking at all the dog runs and wondering where all the cute dogs were. But run after run had the same boring looking tan coloured dog in it. Don't get me wrong there is absolutely nothing at all wrong with the Australian terrier, but I just knew they were not the right dog for me. Maybe if some of them had black in them I may have been more visually drawn but these ones were all plain tan. The breeder came out all happy and chatty and Dad was leading me over to some adult dogs asking which one I wanted, I think the breeder was looking for a good home for her older breeding dogs and yes ours would have been an excellent home, but I just didn't like the look of the them. To me it was merely a huge sea of dogs that all looked exactly the same and I wanted this dog I had built up in my mind for so many years to be more than just one of many. More than a production line dog which is exactly what all these dogs looked like to me, they may as well have been filing by on a manufacturing belt. And really because she was such a big breeder that's exactly what her poor dogs were, production line dogs, looking back I so wish I had freed one of them, but I was a child and so wasn't thinking about such things, today my mind thinks about nothing else because that's the world I live in now but back then I was just a little kid getting her first dog. I wanted it to be an individual, something special and these dogs weren't. And also, how could I possibly choose one of them, I mean which one would I pick, they all blended into one another, it'd take at least a day to sort through them and come to a decision and even then how would I know if I had chosen the right one. Being as young as I was I think I probably found the entire thing a bit overwhelming. When I said I didn't want one Dad's head spun around the fastest I've ever seen it spin. He said "What did you just say? I don't know if he couldn't hear me over the breeders loud talking, the dogs loud yapping or that he couldn't believe what I'd just said. So I repeated myself and this time the breeder got involved. She and Dad were both staring at me now, looking down at me like I was the most ungrateful little turd on the planet. She said to Dad "Is she saying she doesn't want one" and just before I was about to pipe up again he turned to her and said "Yes". Well now she started glaring at me with eyes of fire, she was not at all happy and dad had driven me all that way, so he wasn't happy either. Also, he may have felt like a fool in front of the breeder because he said to me that it was either one of these dogs or nothing at all and I looked up at him and said "Ok I'll have nothing" and with that he pointed towards the car and told me to go and sit in it. And I did and I glanced back at the terriers, and I felt sad for those dogs being in pens but that's all the emotions I felt, I just couldn't make myself like them, I wish I could have done but they were not appealing to me. I thought I'd rather not have a dog at all then have one of those. I had been dreaming about a dog for a very long time but the images I had in my head didn't match the Australian terrier. I was set in my ways, I knew I wanted a dog, desperately wanted a dog but that dog wasn't it. I watched Dad talking to the breeder for a little while longer, I guess he had built this whole scene up, told her on the phone how the only way he'd gotten me interested in coming to Australia was by saying that I could have a dog when I got here. I bet the two of them had expected me to race from the car in raptures, throw myself in amongst those dogs and come out carrying the one I'd decided on. None of them had expected me to react the way I had done, and now poor Dad was standing there backpedaling and trying to pacify the breeder. He got in the car and after driving in silence for a while said that if I changed my mind in a few days the breeder said he could bring me back again, I told him I wouldn't ever change my mind and I didn't. When we got home Mum came into the yard and asked where the dog was, and Dad told her that I didn't want it and she couldn't believe it either. I think they thought I'd be offered a dog and that'd be the end of the story, I'd take the first thing that came along and be happy. But I've always known what I wanted, even at that young age. A few days later Mum asked me what kind of dog I would like and I said "What kinds are there" and she said she didn't know. A few weeks later Dad came home from work and told Mum he knew of a couple that were moving overseas and couldn't take their dog with them. I'm not sure how he found these people or how they found him, but it was arranged for them to bring the dog to our house on the weekend. I knew nothing about this dog, Mum told Dad it had to be small because I think she was afraid of having a big dog around her three little girls, I wouldn't have minded how big it was but she did so I knew the dog would be little otherwise there'd be no point in it coming.

So, Saturday morning I found myself sitting on the front steps waiting for a car to pull up and I had a dress on and a ribbon in my hair because that's what proper English folks did back then when company was coming. I can clearly remember that dress, it was the colour of a clear summer sky and had a white bib and collar, short white puffy sleeves too. The dress I could cope with the ribbon gave me a headache. I wanted so badly to pull that thing out of my hair and sling it across the yard but I knew I'd be in big trouble if I did, so I left it in. And besides I thought it may make me look cuter to the people bringing the dog and I really wanted another shot at having a dog, so I needed these people to like me. My little sister was so beautiful, blonde hair, blue eyes and tiny, cute as a button, if these people were bringing the dog for her they would have handed it over in a second. Me I wasn't half as cute as she was, so I had to try harder. She, just like my older sister, are like my Dad's side of the family, all little folk, me I'm more like Mum's people, bigger, not like Mum she was little, I'm more like her mother, my Grandmother and my great Grandmother, that's who I take after. Sure, I could win people over with the personality I had but I was sadly lacking the cute factor and that's the only reason I let that ribbon stay on my head. I figured I needed all the help I could get. I didn't want these people turning up, looking at me and doing exactly what I had done to the Australian terriers. It was important for them to like me, so I sat and I sulked until a car pulled up then sprang to my feet and started smiling like an imbecile. But that fake smile was soon taken over by the genuine thing because this little black dog was adorable, I mean super adorable. I loved her instantly and Kimmy instantly loved me. She started jumping all over me while her owners watched on. They were nice people, they loved their dog that was clear to see, they wanted a home where she would be loved just as much as they loved her, and I guess they saw that in me because they allowed her to stay. Kimmy was a terrier, scruffy, cute, a cross breed, really gorgeous and funnily enough not too dissimilar looking to the Australian terrier in the face. A different colored coat and her body sat lower to the ground than theirs did, her tail was much longer too but it wagged like mad and where the Australian terriers ran back and forth barking, Kimmy slithered along the floor then rolled over on her back when she reached you so you could scratch her tummy. Kimmy had personality plus. There was none of that in the Australian terriers that I saw, but it did get me thinking that if perhaps they'd been given a chance there would have been, if I'd met them one on one the outcome could have been much different. Not that I gave the Australian terriers much thought after that, I had Kimmy now and she in my eyes was perfect. I don't recall how old she was when she came to live with us but she had three house moves with us so I'm guessing she was only young, although she could have been older and just lived to a ripe old age because if any dog is going to make it to eighteen or older you can bet your life that a terrier cross will do it, they just seem to have fantastic longevity for some reason. And Kimmy really did have a huge amount of energy, I often wondered if her owners weren't really moving overseas after all but had just made up a story because this little dog of theirs was too much of a handful for them.

But she wasn't too much of a handful for me, she was wonderful, and I'd race home from school just to be with her. My life changed for the better once Kimmy arrived on the scene. She was everything I'd imagined my very own dog to be and then some. We did everything together, my young life was complete. I had a dog now and to me that was everything. And when my first horse came into my life Kimmy would come out into the paddocks with me. She'd sniff around while I groomed or fed my horse and then she'd follow me back through the gate. Then one day she didn't come when I called, and we searched everywhere for her to no avail. I walked that paddock many times calling out her name, but I never found her, Dad thought she'd gone off into one of the other adjoining bits of land and gotten bitten by a snake. It was summer and the grass was long, that seemed like a good enough explanation. I went looking for her in that bit of land and all around the streets, after a few days I was now looking for a body and I wish I'd have found one because then at least I could have given my best friend a final resting place.

We put ads up in all the local milk bars with a photo of Kimmy and a decent reward. We kept getting calls that somebody had found her and then they'd come to the house, or we'd go to their house only to find another dog sitting looking up at us. But each phone call gave me hope and each time my hope was shattered, shattered by the very same dog time after time. It seemed whoever owned this terrier was allowing her to go wandering around the streets and people having seen our ads and the decent reward kept catching her and then giving our number a call. The dog smelt like eggs, so we started calling it Egg. So one of us, usually me unless the call came when I was in school, would go off and there would be Egg running around somebodies garden. Somebody who was pretty sure they were about to get a nice big reward. After a while the phone calls stopped so I guess the owner of Egg finally secured their yard. And my life went on without Kimmy in it and I was really sad about that, sad that she'd gone and sad that I would never know what really happened to her. Maybe she was just very old and took herself off somewhere to die and maybe somebody found her body long after our ads in the milk bars came down. If that did happen I hope they did the right thing by her and put her in the ground and not just into a rubbish bin as that wouldn't have been a nice end for her at all, not after all the years of joy she'd given to me. For years afterwards I'd find my mind drifting towards Kimmy and there was always that unanswered question, the first thought was a nice happy memory and there were so many of them coming flickering through my mind and once I'd enjoyed those there was always the second thought of what actually happened there. I don't think anybody stole her because she wasn't much to look at, just a scruffy little black terrier really, well a scruffy little black terrier with an enormous personality and a heart of pure gold and I was grateful to have shared a large part of my childhood with her. I think that's why I still adore terriers today, because of Kimmy I know what big comical personalities they have.

After Kimmy I got Scamp another terrier. I bid on Scamp at a livestock sale I went to with my Dad. It was mainly for cattle, but they had a small area to one side where they'd auction off chooks, geese and a few other kinds of domestic birds like budgerigars, canaries and finches. They also sold the occasional rabbits, puppies and kittens. I saw Scamp cowering in the back of a darkened cage, I'd been peeping in at her while Dad was looking at the cows, when it came auction time the auctioneer dragged her out and held her up in the air and there was so much noise, this little pup was absolutely petrified and so was I about speaking up in amongst all the adults gathered there, but I really wanted this dog and I was a shy kid but Dad said "If you want it you have to bid on it" I think it was his way of making me come out of my shell. At first I said nothing because I was too terrified to, but I kept looking at this poor trembling pup so I yelled out in the biggest voice I could muster, and I thought I'd got the dog but the woman behind me did. Dad said she was from a pet shop and if I went over and offered her more than what she paid that she'd probably let me have the puppy, she'd bought a few dogs that day, this puppy meant nothing to her but everything to me. So, I approached her and with all the noise she couldn't hear what I said, she thought I was just saying what a nice dog this puppy was. Dad was standing behind me and he intervened, he said "She's saying she wants to buy the dog off you" the woman looked down at me and said "How much for" so I offered her five dollars more than what she'd paid, and she couldn't hand that puppy over to me fast enough. Dad paid her the money and then we all went home. Scamp lived to around the age of ten and then I had to put her down because she was full of cancer. She was the first dog I ever had to put to sleep, and it was the hardest thing I'd ever done up until that point. I carried her into the vet and in those days you weren't allowed in with them when they were being put down and I always felt sad about that. I just handed Scamp over to them and they took her into a back room while I paid the receptionist. I cried all the way home. After Scamp came a line of Chihuahua's, some of which I bred myself, then a few pugs, a few pound rescued cross breeds, another few pugs, an elderly English Mastiff, then David, the Great Danes and back to pugs again. And in writing this I've just realised that I've made my husband sound like he was one of my dogs but that's not what I

GRACE FARM | 255

mean at all. I'm merely recalling my life and the course it took from Kimmy until now. I'd lost a really great pug not long before David and I started getting close and I remember telling him about her and he reacted in a very sensitive and caring way and I loved that about him because some of the friends I'd told said she was just a dog, but not David Comer, he fully understood my grieving heart. I looked deeply into his eyes, and I saw something very special there, he was a dog person, he loved them and he spoke so kindly to me about her, he was full of empathy and that really stuck out in my mind about him. I guess that's when I first started to recognise David as being more than just my friend Chris's younger brother.

I love all horses, but I will always be vision driven first and I think that has a lot to do with the fact I myself am not much of a rider, I can ride, I have ridden but it's not something that really interests me. And it works out pretty well being that way here at Grace Farm because most of the horses I take in due to age, injury, and sometimes both, are unrideable. Most people don't want a horse that cannot be ridden or any animal that can do nothing for them for that matter, but I do, such things don't bother me at all, my horses are purely beautiful lawn mowers. I mean I'm not saying that I would take a nasty biting kicking horse in just because it was stunning looking because I would never do that. I couldn't because I'm not a talented horse trainer, I don't think I'd have the knowledge to turn that horse around. I have more experience with dogs than I do horses and so I like the quieter ones best and that's regardless of colour because for me safety comes first, it has to, for both me, Dave and the pugs. In the past I have trained a few horses with the basics and did ok with that, I really enjoyed working with them, it's all about patience, gaining trust and not pushing them to soon so it's a pretty easy thing to do but I am not a professional, I did think of doing some form of training in that area many years ago but that's all it ever was, a thought, my interests got pulled elsewhere and stayed there so I never followed through with that. But I do ok with the horses I have, I communicate well with them, and they are well behaved and that's all I need them to be really. You can get hurt by horses, cows too for that matter, because they are so big and we in comparison are small, you can break a bone so easily and they'll just go running off down the paddock not fully understanding what they've done. You need to be careful around any large animal and give them the respect they deserve, always have your wits about you and concentrate whenever you are doing anything with them. And I think if you have this rule firmly in your head then it'll save a lot of accidents. Whenever I walk into the paddocks where my horses are I always do so with a respect for them, and yes over time I will let my guard down because you get to know their personalities, you can put your trust in them more. But being cautious is wise when in the company of those who are so much more powerful than we are, I learnt this with my first horse, not by getting hurt but by seeing the strength they have and what they can do. I was only young, but I was very much aware that those I loved were 1,000 kg flight animals. I saw they were a lot bigger, stronger and more powerful than I could ever be. And yes these are the things I love about them too. But I am forever mindful of where I am standing whenever I am around them, like you don't want to go getting yourself pinned against a fence or your foot stood on, you learn to work with them, run your hand over their bodies to let them know where you are especially if you are about to walk behind them, and this is doubly important if your horse happens to be blind in one eye like one of mine is. And then the rules are slightly different when you go from one horse to two or three because the dynamics in the paddock will have changed too. You need to know who gets along with who and who is going to be bossy with somebody, you don't want to be standing between a horse who is going to want to boss the horse behind you around because then you'll be trapped and get wrapped up in all of that. It's the same when standing in amongst a large herd of horses, it can be pretty intimidating when they surround you like that especially when it's with horses you don't know. It's just like a dog pack really, exactly the same thing, you'll have strong personalities and docile personalities, you'll have a boss and some followers but it's the size difference that can make the situation more dangerous, so you have to be careful. I mean have fun too because being in amongst a lot of horses is a really beautiful experience, you don't want to be standing there frozen in fear or gripping onto a fence post like a trembling mess, you just need to be aware of where all the horses are at all times. Also, they will pick up on fear so being scared is the worst thing to be around any animal, they are smart, they'll have you well and truly summed up before you've even stepped foot inside their paddock. The best way to learn about horses is by being around horses, you soon learn to pick up their language and this will tell you what they are thinking. I had a long period in my life where I didn't have horses and then when I started sharing my life with them again that respect and knowledge automatically kicked right back in. Communication is vital, through body language they always tell you what they are thinking, and you can pre-empt a move just by watching them. I've been really lucky so far in my life, I've only ever had one serious accident with a horse in all my years with them and that's because I allowed myself to be distracted by something else, stupidly let my guard down for a moment with a horse I'd just taken in and paid a price for it. But it didn't put me off horses, it couldn't, I love them far too much for that.

My very first horse was a Palomino. I called her Lisa. She was 14 hands, and she was aged, just a shabby looking pony left in a paddock because her owners no longer cared about her. But gee she sure was a beauty, a golden goddess, especially once I'd gotten a few months of really good food into her, her coat really shone then. I would watch her coat lighten and darken with the changing seasons. I was so in love with her. I thought when we came to Australia I was going to be able to get a dog, but nobody said anything about me getting a horse. It was like I was living the dream. For somebody who was hesitant about moving to Australia in the first place it seemed that life was working out pretty well for me. I loved being out in that open paddock, there was Lisa and a few other horses agisted there, so I got to spend my afternoons surrounded by them all and that was perfect for me. The other horse owners didn't seem to be there all that often, so it was basically just me and the horses and I liked that. The paddock was at the back of our house and Dad put a gate in so I didn't have to walk round the streets to get there, and it also meant that Lisa could be brought into our back garden. I rode a lot more back then, I even started attempting jumping, Lisa was such a calm horse. But she sometimes forgot to pick up her feet, she'd clip the jump more than she went over it so I'd jump off, run over, fix it up then take her over it again, it wasn't a high jump just a few feet off the ground and I was going to make the jump higher and higher but Lisa lost interest in it and when she did so did I. Dad built her a stable and all the other horses came inside with Lisa when it was raining, it was the only stable on that land and I wondered why somebody hadn't thought of putting some form of shelter up for those horses long before now. It seemed cruel to me to have no trees or stables for the horses to use for shade, shelter and to get out of the wind, didn't seem right that they were out there being exposed to the elements all day long like nobody cared about them. Australian summers are hot and yet these horses couldn't cool themselves down, they just had to stand there like that until the sun went down. But life got better for them once our stable was built, when it was raining, like heavy downpours, I used to get up on top of the kitchen table to see where the horses were, and I'd see tails swishing from the side of Lisa's stable and climb down again knowing all was well. I couldn't see who was in the stable because the entrance was facing away from our dining room window, it was built like that because you don't want the opening to be in the direction where all the weather comes from, you want it to be a wind block not a wind tunnel, but I knew by the tails hanging out that every one of those horses would have been sheltering in there together. This herd got on pretty well, nobody was made to stand out in the open, they all huddled up inside and that was a nice way for it to be. I wouldn't have liked it if one of the horses was being picked on and kicked outside, especially if that horse happened to be Lisa, what an insult that would have been, to have a stable built especially for her then have the other horses not allow her to use it. But these horses had been living together for a very long time and were all on friendly terms, maybe it was the lack of interest from their owners that fused them together or maybe they were just all even natured good tempered horses, either way no horse got pushed out and that was a good thing.

After Lisa came a little pinto called Comanche and a huge dapple grey called Bobby. Comanche was only around the 12 hand mark but Bobby was a giant he was over 16 hands and as docile as a puppy. Bobby was a vastly intelligent horse, in the right hands I think he could have been one of those trick horses and if owned by an animal trainer would have been on film sets or in commercials. I had both of them sharing my life at the same time and loved every second of it, they were not my horses I was only leasing them, but I got to be around horses and that was all I cared about, the fact that somebody else owned them didn't bother me at all. I had free reign to do as I pleased, I only ever saw the owners when there was a problem and there was hardly ever a problem, so I basically met them when I set up the lease and when the lease was up. I came upon these horses because I used to be hanging around their paddocks a lot, just wanting to be near horses again. I got to talking to people and found two whose kids had lost interest in their horses. The parents were the ones turning up now because the children had moved on, I don't know why the horses were not sold but they weren't, so I offered to free lease them and by free I mean I didn't pay for the horses I just covered the agistment fees, food, dentist and the farrier. It was good for me and good for those parents too, I got to be around these wonderful creatures once more and they no longer had to keep coming down to check on the horses each week. It was two different families' I was leasing from, but they were ok people, no trouble at all to deal with and neither were their horses. I shared my early twenties with those two horses but then the land got sold for factories so my relationship with them came to an end and I was back to once again being horseless and life for me just wasn't the same without a horse in it. I missed them, deeply missed everything about them, not being able to be in the presence of them was hard. And there were no horses near where I was now living or working so it was like they'd disappeared off the planet for me. I'd see advertisements on tv with these wonderful looking horses in them and instantly have a lump in my throat. And if that horse happened to be a Clydesdale well my heart ached, it lunged and yearned. They were so magnificent. I'd have that same feeling in movie theatres too whenever a horse came on screen, it wouldn't be a sad part in the movie, the horse wasn't dying and neither was anybody else, but I'd feel pain in my heart nevertheless, the pain of longing to be with those that I loved. My eyes would fill with tears too at times so the screen became a big blur until I blinked. But we all love what we love and if we love something so much that we cry because we miss them, so be it. Certainly, it's nothing to be ashamed of; well I'm not ashamed of it anyway. I've always been one to let my feelings out, expressing how I feel has always come naturally to me and I don't hide from it, I couldn't even if I tried. Our emotions are what make us real. I think trying to smother your feelings or bury them down deep is like you are betraying who you truly are. Also, I don't know if you've ever noticed this but the funny thing with horses in movies is that they more often than not have the sound of them whinnying accompanying the scene and sometimes it actually doesn't go with the scene at all. It's like they just throw it in because a horse has appeared, they do it with dogs in a lot of movies too, especially in older movies, they are getting a bit better in that area now, but a dog will appear on the screen and suddenly you'll hear barking and the dog on screen will have its mouth shut, just be standing or sitting there and not be interested in barking at all, the body language shows everything. I don't know why they do this but it's a thing I've been noticing for years. I first started noticing it with dogs because any barking dog on the tv will instantly start my pugs off, sometimes even wake them up from a deep sleep and have them running for the door. If they are all settled and I'm watching a movie with a dog in it I'll have my trigger finger hovering over the mute button in the hope of hitting it before the onscreen dog disturbs mine and sometimes I'll hit the button in time and other times the dog will get a bark or two in before I get to make the sound disappear, it can be hard to pre-empt, but you do your best. I only do it because I don't want the younger better hearing dogs to go trampling over the old deaf darlings when they are happily sleeping, I don't want them to be startled just for the sake of a tv show throwing a bark in for no reason. Anyway, after a while I started noticing the same thing with onscreen horses. I noticed it a lot more when I wasn't sharing my life with them and once I heard that whinnying it would be echoing through my head for days. It was like they were calling out to me and that made me yearn for them even more. I wondered how long it'd be before happy tears would be running down my face, how long it would be before a Clydesdale stepped its big fluffy hoofs on our land. One day as we were walking the pugs around the farm I was going to tell David that such a thing was more than likely going to be happening soon, but saved my breath on that and started up another conversation entirely, one that was more fitting of that day. There would be plenty of time to talk about my new horse once I actually had one secured. And the securing part was harder than I thought it would be. I was hoping to find an old farmer in the area who was looking for a good home for a Clydesdale that he'd owned for years, one that on his passing his family would be selling to the nearest abattoir at lightning speed. I would have loved to be able to do that for somebody I truly would, how nice would it be for an old person to know that his horse was going to be loved and well cared for for the remainder of their days. Yes it'd be sad giving it up, but I would have let him come and visit whenever he liked and it would be a lot better than the alternative. I know a lot of really lovely horses end up at the sales yards because their owners have passed away and not made any arrangements for them. But as hard as I looked I couldn't find anybody who fitted the bill. I wasn't involved with any horse rescue groups at the time, they would come into my life later on, back then I was going it alone, placing ads which were drawing all the wrong people and the wrong horses for me as well. Once somebody knows you are looking to find an older horse people start coming out of the woodwork with horses they no longer want or care about, but they don't listen so much to what you have to say, all they are concentrating on is getting rid of their horse, you are speaking but they are not listening. I had plenty of people looking to offload their horses onto me, well pushing them onto me would be a more accurate way of putting it. I was asked all the time, and sometimes in a very rude manner, why it couldn't be their horse, why it had to be a Clydesdale or at the very least a Clydesdale cross and I would go into a very detailed story about the toy Clydesdales in my childhood until they rolled their eyes and walked away. And that was ok, they could be as rude as they liked, they were not going to change my mind about something I had been waiting my entire life for. I'm sure they would have eventually found somebody to take their horses but for me it had to be a Clydesdale. They had not seen the hours I'd spent dreaming of these magnificent horses but I had and so I stuck to my guns.

I always had farm sets when I was a kid but the horses in them were never Clydesdales, Mum had to buy them separately for me, because whether in real life or just playing, my farm was always going to have a Clydesdale on it. And the older I got, a better quality of farm yard animals was available, the good ones were expensive though so I would have to save my pocket money up for those, but I tell you what they were worth every single penny. The details on them were so amazing that I half expected them to come to life at any moment and start galloping around my lounge room. The feet on those plastic Clydesdales were incredible, the strokes on the feathers were beautiful, somebody had clearly been studying Clydesdales as much as I had. I would sprawl out on the carpet and play with my farm sets for hours on end. Even today I can't stop buying well-made plastic Clydesdales. I use them as ornaments now though. I have a Clydesdale sitting on my kitchen windowsill that I painted to look exactly like Gerald. It was ok when it came, nothing wrong with it at all, but I wanted it to be exactly like him, a mini Gerald, this one's tone was nothing like the tone Gerald has so I got some hobby paint and mixed two colours together until I had just the right shade. I adore that little horse, but I move him off the windowsill in the heat of summer because I don't want him melting, don't want to be happily doing the dishes and come face to face with a melted plastic Clydesdale coloured blob.

The first horse I ever remember meeting was in England and I guess I was around four years old at the time. There was a big field across the road from my Nana's house. When I visited I would stand in her front garden and watch the horses, there were a lot of beautifully coloured horses in that herd, they were never doing anything much, just grazing and swishing their tails or shaking their manes then moving to higher ground, but that was enough for me, they held my interest. I never saw anybody riding them, they were always just on their own doing their horsey thing. Anyway, one day Nana decided to take me over for a closer look, I suppose she had more time on her hands that day and had seen how mesmerized I was by these horses. We had my younger sister with us, and she was still in a pram. So Nana had both of us to contend with and the horses too. Well, I just wanted to get as close to those horses as I possibly could and I wasn't wasting any time doing it either. While Nana had her back turned putting the brake on my sister's pram I used the opportunity to slide underneath the fence and was fast heading towards the horses when Nana spied me. I was called back and as much as I didn't want to I turned around and trudged back closer to the fence line. I thought that was it, that my first horse experience had ended as quickly as it had begun. I stomped my feet as I walked back because I thought I would be told to come back under the fence and be taken home. But my Nana loved me an awful lot, she could see how desperately I wanted to be near those horses, so she came into the paddock with me, and we walked over to the herd together. I remember stroking a big white horses head and Nana being the brilliant lady that she was had thought to bring some carrots with us. She lifted me up so that I could get closer to the horse and feed him a carrot. I thought it was the best experience of my life so far, I suppose that's why I remember it so vividly to this day. My next experience with a horse was a few years later when we were living in Australia. Dad put me and my little sister on a beautiful Palomino and we went for a short ride. Dad's friend was leading the horse and

Dad was walking beside us making sure we didn't fall off. That horse was quite big but really docile and I didn't know it was a Palomino, at the time I was too young to know about colours or breeds, I was finally on a horse and to me that was the main thing, it was only when looking at the photo some years later when a bit of knowledge had been gained that I realised what the horse was. And I do think it's funny that my very first horse turned out being a Palomino. It seemed that I was constantly being shown glimpses of this wonderfully coloured breed.

I wasn't looking to buy a horse, or should I say Dad wasn't looking to buy me a horse, but we had moved into a house that my Dad had just recently finished building and there was a paddock at the back of our new house with a few horses in it. I'd come home from school and couldn't wait to get out there and be with those horses, I wasn't meant to be in that paddock as it was private property, but I just couldn't help myself. So, I'd climb our back fence and disappear down the long paddock to look for the horses. It was a man that owned the land but an old lady who had a house at the opposite end of the paddock to where our house was, well for some reason she was in charge of it. She had no connection to the man that owned the land, not his mother or anything just an old busy body who took it upon herself to be the boss. Because she had lived in that home for sixty years she seemed to think she was in charge of the adjoining land, the horses and anybody who came near them. I'd go into the paddock and pat the horses, spend a bit of time with them then climb back over the fence and go do the chores that were assigned to me. It was usually collecting the chook eggs, sweeping my Dad's aviary floor and feeding and watering his budgerigars. So, I'd be in and out of that paddock in no time and back in again whenever I felt like it and I felt like it a real lot so I was always coming and going, I thought of it as an extension of my own back yard really. And when you are a kid who owns the property doesn't even enter your mind, you are not hurting anybody so you kind of do whatever you please and what pleased me the most was being in there with those horses. But unbeknown to me that little old lady in the house in the distance had been watching my every move. For weeks this old lady had been trying to catch me in the paddock and give me a good telling off. But she was very slow moving so by the time she'd come out of her house, get into the paddock and walk the length of it, I was gone again. She must have waited each afternoon for me to appear, sit by her window until I showed up then fly out her door as fast as she could, I was never aware of being watched. I was so busy hugging the horses that I never once saw her ambling along. One day though I must have been able to stay a while longer, perhaps I was extra fast doing my chores that day or maybe I just lost track of time, anyway one moment I was in my blissful little horse loving world and the next thing I was being grabbed by the scruff of the neck, shaken about and yelled at. She was only a little woman, but she really did scare the living hell out of me. She was angry too so that made her super strong, I suppose it was because I hadn't sensed she was approaching that she'd managed to scare me so much. Imagine being so utterly peaceful and blissful and then somebody grabbing you hard when you had no idea there was anybody there. I'm amazed the horses didn't tell me she was coming, but their mannerisms didn't alter at all, I guess that's because they were used to seeing her around, she was one of them just like I was one of them. Because she had been after me for so long when she finally got me she wasn't for letting go. Her adrenaline must have been kicking in as she walked along and when she finally got hold of me it started going nuts. Sure, she was ancient and her hands were wrinkly and worn but her grip was vice like and I couldn't wrangle myself away from her. She meant business too, she had me give her my address and wasn't going to let me go until she had it. She even dragged me all the way back to her house so she could write the address down. I suppose due to her age her memory wasn't so good, she was probably scared she'd forget it by the time she walked back home so she made me go with her.

So, there's me with this old lady dragging me along and behind us all the horses are following on. I guess the horses were just curious as to what we were doing so they thought they'd tag along. I suppose I could have given her somebody else's address and gotten myself off the hook but the thought of lying didn't even occur to me. She did scare me an awful lot though because I remember running home and crying and not wanting to tell anybody why. I think a lot of the crying had to do with the fact that she'd told me I was never again to set foot in that paddock. I wonder how many times she had come close to catching me only to have me slip away, I don't think she ever got too close though because if she did she would have been able to see which fence I was climbing back over, been able to count the houses and then done the same thing when walking down our street, that would have gotten her pretty close to my house, maybe the house next door or the one before that, either way all our neighbours knew me so I wouldn't have been too hard to find. I bet she was irate every time I disappeared from view. I bet she was coming down that paddock as fast as she could make her old legs go, she would have been sticking to the fence line too, kind of sneaking along sneaking up on me, never out in the open because I'm sure I would have looked up from time to time and I never saw anybody walking down the centre of that paddock. As far as I was concerned it was just me and the horses.

A day or two later this old lady came storming up our driveway when we were all having tea. I saw her from the window and almost threw up. My Dad went to the door, and I sat at the table a nervous wreck because I thought I was going to be in so much trouble. I'd already been banned from being around the horses, now I was no doubt going to get a loss of privileges too. After a long conversation Dad came back into the room, the rest of the family were all relaxed, but my eyes were right on him waiting for what he had to say. I felt for sure I would be in big trouble, but I think he knew how desperately I loved horses and having some close by that there was no way I could help myself, I just had to be near them. And also, even if the old lady was going on and on about how wrong what I was doing was I think my Dad would have been able to see the lighter side of it, she was acting like I'd committed armed robbery but he would have simply seen it as a kid climbing a fence to be with some horses. I bet she would have been even more angered by his lack of concern, she probably thought I was a chip off the old block and that would have made her even more enraged, and she was loud because we could hear her voice, not what she was saying just this loud croaky voice and then it would fall silent which would have been when my Dad was speaking and then the croaky old voice would be shouting out again. Don't get me wrong my Dad was a fairly good yeller, he could have yelled, he could have roared like a lion and sent her tumbling down the driveway, it's just that he chose not to. From my seat at the dinner table, I could see her there through the netted curtains, little white haired thing that she was, red jumper on, arms flying around all over the place. I'm amazed she didn't drop dead from all the yelling she was doing, and I also wondered why she hadn't come to our house sooner, was she just busy or was she sitting at home planning what she was going to say when she got to our front door. Or maybe she was just gloating for a day or two because she thought she'd won. I saw her turn and walk away, and she didn't seem happy at all, her arms were still waving about. Maybe she thought my Dad was going to be as furious as she was, perhaps she was hoping that he would drag me outside so the two of them could yell at me together, I bet the old biddy was really looking forward to seeing me being totally humiliated. But Dad took control of the situation pretty quickly and he didn't side with her.

Anyway, Dad and me talked about it all, then that night after dinner we went around to this man's house, the owner of the Palomino and Dad bought her off him. It seemed he was very behind on his agistment payments and so he and Dad worked out a deal that Dad would pay what the man owed, and he would give us the horse. He didn't really want her anyway, it was his daughter's horse, but she had lost interest in it, in all the time I'd been sneaking into the paddocks I'd never seen anybody with this lovely old mare. That's why I was feeding her carrots and apples, I would groom her with my fingers too, just to get the winter coat off her, she always looked so uncared for. I think that's what drew me to her in the first place. She wasn't a sad horse, well not when I had apples and carrots in my pockets she wasn't anyway but she always had the appearance of being sad, so I fed her twice as much as I fed the other horses. The entire thing worked out pretty well really, especially for me, the owner of the paddock got the money he was owed, the owner of the horse got rid of a burden he didn't really want, and I went from thinking I would be in trouble to ending up with my very own horse. To say that I was ecstatic was an underestimation. Not only did I have a horse I wasn't expecting to get, she was a golden horse, a golden goddess. I felt like the luckiest person in the entire universe. Would I have been drawn to Palominos if not for Lisa, well I don't really know, maybe, maybe not. I'm not sure. Are they special to me because she was my very first horse, yes they most certainly are because they will always hold fond memories for me. But I have loved Palominos for so long now I can't remember how it feels not to love them. When we first moved to Grace Farm there was a Palomino living next door, I didn't notice her when we were looking around the property with the estate agent. I met her a week or so in. She was so beautiful standing there in the long green grass, it made me feel even more at home here. Like that image of her was yet another sign that we were doing the right thing by coming here.

After Lisa became mine the old lady who thought she was the boss of the paddock started being a whole lot nicer to me. I guess she had to be really didn't she because I now had more reason for being in that paddock than she did, more authority too, but I didn't think of it that way. I was just a kid with a pony, that's all I was really concentrating on. And besides I didn't see her all that much at the start, she kept inside her house whenever I was around but eventually I guess she got over herself and decided she'd come out and treat me like a person instead of a pest, decided to see things for what they were. She started off just waving to me whenever she was in her garden, her house was a fair distance away and if I didn't notice her she'd call out to me using that big bellowing voice of hers to get my attention and it carried too even when the wind was blowing the wrong way. So she'd call out but never attempted to come near me. I guess she was still pretty mad at the way everything turned out. Then one day she came into the paddock and walked up to my end. She did it a few times a week and I would speak very nicely to her at all times because that's how I'd been brought up, she even invited me into her house for afternoon tea, it was only her and her daughter, no dad on the scene. The daughter must have been around fifty five years old at the time, just the two of them living there in that little house watching the world go by. No wonder she was so interested in catching me, she didn't have a real lot of other things to do with her time. Over the years I spent a lot of time in that house talking to the old lady. She wasn't half as scary as I first thought. And if I didn't have time to go up to her house she would come and talk to me while I fed and groomed Lisa. I took her an Easter egg one Easter and she acted like it was the best thing she'd ever been given. I don't think people gave her many gifts, it was just one chocolate egg sitting in a tiny basket with a little chicken on top of it. I carried that gift down to her house with such joy, I liked giving people things, liked seeing them happy. But I stumbled trying to get through the fence and the egg was solid chocolate and the basket pretty strong so they were fine but the little chicken got its face bashed in. I picked him up off the ground and blew the specks of dirt off him but I couldn't do much about his face, the fall had ruined it forever. Regardless she sat that basket with the bashed in faced chicken on her kitchen table for a very long time, like she was proud of it or something. She ate the egg but didn't throw the rest away like I thought she would have done, instead she displayed it like an ornament.

When Dad was building the stable the old lady took it upon herself to make sure to have a front row seat, again she had no right to be in the paddock but that didn't stop her. I would have liked to have seen the stable going up, but I had to go to school. Dad was a builder so he and some of the men who worked for him knocked that stable up in a day and my heart rested after that because I now knew the horses would be ok. The old lady brought a chair down and sat to one side watching everything they were doing, a crooked wrinkly old finger pointing at this and that, she even brought a flask of tea and sandwiches and sat there shoving them in while the men worked. Dad said she didn't exactly sit there quietly either. I heard him telling Mum that it wasn't so much as she asked questions more that she spat out her queries and demanded answers. And if she wasn't answered quickly enough she'd get up from her chair and be looking over their shoulders at what they were doing. Dad even put kick boards up in that stable to protect the horse's legs from going through the tin walls if they were in the mind to have a little kick. The old lady had a keen interest in this, at first she wondered what they were doing but once it was explained to her she went back and took her seat. I suppose she was scared of missing out on seeing something so that's why she brought lunch with her, it saved her having to go all the way back up to her house. Thinking back, I guess she wasn't as interfering as she was lonely and bored. Her daughter worked all day, so I guess that horse paddock was her only form of entertainment. She put an old bath tub in that paddock and she'd fill it up from her own tap so the horses were never without clean fresh water. After we bought Lisa we put a bathtub up our end of the paddock as well and that seemed to upset her because I guess she was happy when the horses came over for a drink, happy to be able to have something to watch and we had taken them away from her. Sure, they would have still drunk out of her bathtub but not nearly as often because they now had choices. After a few weeks she started walking up and checking if our bathtub was full and if it wasn't she'd walk up the street, knock on our door and tell Mum to go fill the tub up. And Mum being Mum invited the old lady in and the two of them would have a cup of tea and an hour or so chatting together. I often wondered if she'd actually been bucketing out the water in our tub because it really did seem to be empty a lot. I always filled it before I left for school and checked it again when I came home every afternoon, and I was sure that water should have lasted. Maybe on her most lonely days she traipsed all the way to our tub with a bucket, dumped half the water, went home and dropped off her bucket and then walked down the street to our front door. It did seem like an awful lot of effort to be putting in but I've never been lonely so I guess I don't know what lengths a person would go to for a little conversation. Maybe if I was in her shoes I would be doing the same thing. Mum said she'd often come home and find this old lady sitting on the doorstep waiting, I suppose she'd gone to all that trouble so wasn't leaving until she got what she came for and Mum would invite her in, and she'd chat away happily while watching Mum putting away the groceries. It's funny how life turns out sometimes, here was this lady coming to our house to complain about me being an ignorant little pest and I bet she was saying how much she had to do for those horses without having to deal with a trespasser on top of it. And I guess she would have been listing all her jobs, saying that their owners didn't care for them, especially the owner of the Palomino. And instead of giving her sympathy Dad would have seized the opportunity of getting his daughter not only a horse but a horse that was close by, so I didn't have to be out of Mums sight for very long. It was perfect really. In that conversation he found out where the Palomino's owner lived and found out who owned the land too. And that lady went on to make some new friends. It's like our paths were meant to cross for a reason and everybody involved benefited.

I spent all of my spare time in that paddock with Lisa. I wouldn't just groom her I'd groom all the horses if they were looking worse for wear and some of them were pretty big, much bigger than Lisa, Dad told me to stay clear of the larger horses, but I took no notice, I was in my element being right in the middle of them all. Dad would have had a fit if he'd known. But they were my friends I never came to any harm in amongst that herd. It felt like the safest, happiest, most natural place in the world for me to be. None of those horses ever did anything to me, after I'd hugged and groomed them I'd sit on the ground and watch them grazing. It was like I was one of them and I loved being one of them. Even today I still think about Lisa whenever I see a Palomino. I would love to get another one at some point and I have looked at a few but with the sheep and horses I have now I don't really have room, but it's on top of my wish list so you just never know. And there is a lovely old unrideable Palomino with a crooked ear that I keep going back to, a head injury is her problem so she permanently tilts her head to one side, she's with a rescue group and I keep trying to see how I can fit her in but for the time being I am unable to.

The first Clydesdale I ever saw in the flesh was at a livestock market. It was a Tuesday, so it was small sundry sales, Dad and I had gone because he was after some more chooks. The horse auction was on Fridays, and they got auctioned off in another part of the sale yard, all the way over the other side of the large car park. While Dad was bidding on the new chooks I went for a walk around the place and couldn't believe my eyes when I saw him there all on his own. I don't know why this boy had been brought in so early, but I had a feeling it was to try and quiet him down a bit because he was crazy. Huge, strikingly beautiful but going nuts in the small pen they'd put him in. Most horses are brought in on Thursday night but not this boy, I had no idea how long he'd been in there for, but somebody would have had to be checking on him daily to feed him and make sure he hadn't knocked over his water. He was the most magnificent specimen. A big black beautiful Clydesdale and I'd never seen a black one before, all the Clydesdales I had in my farm set were brown. I thought this big boy was the best thing I'd ever seen, I peeped through the cracks at him but couldn't see him properly, he was in a special fenced in pen that was a lot higher than all the other pens. And it was right down the back of the sales yard. I wanted to have a better look at him so without thinking I climbed the fence to see him in full view. Well doing that to an already enraged horse was certainly a mistake because once he saw me up there above his head he completely lost it. Banged into the side of the fence I was standing on sending me to the ground. I fell down hard on the concrete floor and although I was hurt I had to get up on my feet very quickly because with the noise this boy was making on the other side of that fence, well I thought he may have come crashing through and trampled me, the fence was really shaking and the wood holding it together was pretty old. I don't know why he wasn't put in a pen with a steel rail because there were plenty of them sitting there empty, but I guess they either wanted him hidden from view or the view hidden from him, either way it was a stupid thing for me to have done but my thoughts were only on seeing him better and in doing so I had upset him terribly. He was a stallion, no doubt one that had been left running wild on a large farmland servicing all the mares and they had rounded him up now that he was no longer of use to them. They were probably bringing in a different bloodline. His world had been turned upside down, no wonder the poor thing was behaving that way he did, he went from freedom to being caged, he must have been petrified of what was to become of him and I don't blame him one little bit because it's horses like this that don't do well on sale day. They generally go to a dogger unless there is somebody in the crowd with a whole lot of experience, and even if there is they have to want to put the time in and sometimes people think horses like this are not worth the bother, especially when there are so many other calm horses around. Big solid horses like this need a good amount of feeding and that's another reason they are overlooked, people just don't want to put that kind of money into keeping them from becoming skin and bones. There are all sorts of reasons horses get overlooked on sale day and of course there in the crowd are the doggers just waiting to pounce. They get these horses for very little money and if they are calm they can go on to have a second chance because they will be tested once back at the doggers yard and if good they'll be advertised for a lot more money than the dogger just paid. But if they are unapproachable and wild well sadly their lives quickly come to an end.

I decided the best thing to do was leave him alone and he seemed to settle down the further I stepped away from him. I limped back to the main sales area and never told Dad what I'd been up to. I think he would have gone ballistic if he'd found out how stupidly I had behaved, would have made that big black Clydesdale look like a placid little lamb if he'd known how close I'd gotten to being badly injured. I could have very easily hit my head on that concrete floor if

I'd landed a different way. Luckily I had enough sense not to have gotten into the pen with him because I reckon he would have killed me. I learnt a lesson from being knocked off my perch, I now knew never to climb up near a horse that is behaving that way again, it all added to my experience. But boy was that Clydesdale beautiful. And I do think that unless he was sedated on sales day he would have gone straight to the doggers, my heart hopes that this wasn't how he ended up, but I think it may have been. Horse auctions can be the saddest place on earth at times, especially when in the middle of a drought or when it's coming up to winter and people realise what it's going to cost to keep weight on their horse during the colder months. Pen after pen are filled with nervous horses that are standing there wondering what on earth has just happened to what was once their world. You see young horses there that have never been handled and mares in foal with foals at foot none of which should ever be subjected to a sales yard, you see mattered manes and tails, scared legs, and cracked and overgrown hoofs. Some of the horses smell like death. You see big heavy horses that are far too thin and pretty broodmares that are a bit too old to breed with, sure they have raised many a good foal and been excellent mothers to them but now they are aged so are no longer of any use to a stud. You see little pony's in big pens looking absolutely dumbfounded. You see eventers and pony clubbers that people have lost interest in. And you'll see many big striking ex race horses that tried their heart out on race day but were just too slow. The horse racing industry isn't a nice industry at all, sure everything looks glamorous on race day, owners in suits and ties, ladies with matching hats, dresses and heels, but not too many people see the dark side of it. A huge percentage of race horses bred don't make the cut, and not all are going to be sold through a private sale where a good home can be sought, there are just far too many race horses unwanted and a huge percent of these end up in sales yards where the only people interested in them are doggers and dealers. When your eyes are only viewing them for meat these big horses stand out, stand out to the wrong people. It's as vicious and as sad of a cycle as the pound system is for dogs. Somebody told me once that ninety percent of race horses bred end up as meat, I don't know if that's a correct percentage or not because I am not in the industry but this lady had no reason to lie to me so I took her at her word, the whole thing makes me sad. This is why I like rescuing horses, sure I can't have as many horses as I do pugs because I just don't have the room, but I do what I can and every little bit counts doesn't it, well it certainly counts to the horses who get rescued.

When I first started looking for a Clydesdale I was leaning towards a black one and I think it was due to seeing that horse at the sales yard all those years ago. And I did see a few black Clydesdales for sale, but they were not exactly what I was looking for, most were young and one lot could only be sold as a pair, a harness pair and they were not right for my situation, beautiful both of them but just not right for me. By this point I just wanted a Clydesdale, pure or cross it didn't matter to me anymore. I searched online and found out there was actually a Clydesdale Rescue. They had a huge white draft horse advertised on their site that I fell in love with instantly. I imagined myself riding him down the quiet country lanes around town, not fast, not ever a gallop, I didn't want to end up falling on my ass. I knew it would have to be a very quiet and a very slow ride for me, just the two of us leisurely ambling along pausing to look at scenery or animals grazing in paddocks and then just as slowly making our way back home again. But the rescue wasn't in my state and although there were so many wonderful beauties waiting for their forever homes I felt it would be cruel to make one of them embark on such a long journey. I pictured this huge fluffy hoofed darling standing up hour after hour in an enclosed space. I just couldn't do that to one of them, it didn't sit right with me, I loved them too much for that. But I did give it a lot of thought, I thought about it in an obsessed way actually, but after revisiting the site and gazing at the photos five, six and seven times I came back to my original way of thinking so set about finding a Clydesdale that needed rescuing in my own state. That's when I first started placing ads and I'd be offered all these nasty tempered ponies that bit and kicked. Little ponies with big attitudes, bigger attitudes then I was used to dealing with. And every one of them came with a sob story, and I was always their last resort before going to the knackery. I was new to this horse rescue business, and I'd read the email or have phone conversations with people and be left heart broken, and also made to feel like I was the most pitiful creature in the world because I didn't want to take these ponies on. The thing was I didn't want to take on something that was beyond my capabilities. This was mine and David's first horse experience together. I wanted it to be a good one. I didn't want David seeing the harm they could do then saying he didn't want horses on the farm anymore. David hadn't had much to do with horses, and I didn't want him to have to deal with the nasties. I felt a calm gentle soul would make the learning experience all the sweeter for him so that's what I set about looking for. On a regular basis I began placing ads.

Over time I became friends with a lovely lady who was heavily into the business of rescuing horses. She wasn't responsible for me getting the first horse I took in at Grace Farm, but she did help get me my second one. She contacted me due to one of my ads and after talking to her for a little while she offered me her Shetland pony Cinnamon. But Cinnamon wasn't exactly sugar and spice and all things nice, he too was a biter, so I said no and went on to explain exactly what I wanted and why. And she wasn't nasty or abusive she actually got it and helped me out with a few contacts. None of which lead to Gerald but at least I now had somebody who was willing to help, and she was a vessel of knowledge when it came to horses, they had been her life for a long time so there wasn't anything she didn't know about them. She was a great asset to me. She lived near an abattoir and the owner of that property wasn't as bad of a person as some of them are, he could spot the potential in a horse and wasn't always out to make a buck. Yes he was what he was, but he also had a soft spot for this horse rescuing friend of mine, they'd grown up together as kids. So, although they were both heavily involved with horses and were at opposite ends of things, they still made their relationship work and a whole lot of horses benefited from it. When he found out what I was looking for he let her know when a Clydesdale came in, which a few did but they were too much of a handful for me. By the time they got to him they were pretty wild but this lady helped them out with a more experienced horse home so they didn't get slaughtered, she was good like that, put her entire life into helping the horses that nobody else cared about. She was a wonderful kindhearted soul who would do anything for anybody and expect nothing in return. You don't find a lot of people in this world who are like that. Anyway, she helped me get the ball rolling and although her contacts didn't have what I was looking for it did give me an "In" into the world of horse rescue and I was grateful for that. Of course, I came across a lot of people who promised much and delivered nothing but that's human nature for you, it's a sad part of human nature but it's just the way some people are. Yet in amongst the "Bad Eggs" you come to meet the "Cream of the Crop" as far as human beings go. And it's like that with a lot of things in life really, you have to sort through the bad to get to the good and I'd go through it all again if I had to because the end result was fantastic. Sadly, this lady got out of the horse rescuing game a few years after I met her. She was constantly being attacked on social media for no reason and that cost her her husband, her home and her horses. The daily abuse from people who themselves were doing nothing at all to help any of these needy animals caused her to have a breakdown and she was such an enormous loss to the horse world that's for sure. Over the years I have tried many times to track her down with no luck which is a real shame because I so would have liked to remain friends with her. But I have a feeling that she wanted to stay lost, I think those keyboard cowards hurt her so deeply that she could no longer have anything to do with anybody who reminded her of that period in her life. In order to heal properly she needed to sever all ties and I understand that fully. I like to think she went away and started a new life for herself and in time took in a few needy horses and that they were able to help restore some of the damage that had been done. In my head I see her in a paddock with her arms around a big horse's neck with a couple of other horses milling around in the background. I hope she did go and get that for herself because somebody who loved horses as intensely as she did should never not have them sharing her life. I also picture her sitting on a veranda happy and content, laughing heartily with a mug of tea in one hand and a slice of lightly buttered toast in the other, as this is how I remember her the most.

Big John was the next Clydesdale to come across my path. And boy was he a beauty, all 18 hands of him was truly marvellous. Perfect markings, perfect form, perfect everything really. He was the only horse in a big paddock full of sheep and he towered over the sheep like a giant, then again that paddock could have been full of horses, and he'd be head and shoulders above them all. I thought he was brilliant and looked out for him every time I drove past his paddock. I saw him all the time when I was driving back to our farm. He was two towns away from where we lived so I got to see him every time I went to visit my Mum. And on the days I couldn't see him I was always so disappointed. Sometimes I would stop the car and walk over and give him a pat. After months of doing this and still not getting any closer to finding a Clydesdale of my own I decided that I would find out who owned Big John and see if they wanted to sell him. I never ever saw anybody with him, if I had of done I would have been right onto it. There was a small country Tea Room across the road from his paddock and I figured if anybody was going to know who owned this horse it was them. So one day I walked over and inquired. I had never been inside before and it was quite a nice little place, wooden tables with red gingham cloths draped over them, a bell tinkled as I pushed the door open and the handmade sign only added to the overall charm for me. I felt right at home there as soon as I stepped inside. The smell of sugary syrupy cakes cooking reminded me of my grandmother's kitchen, if I wasn't in such a hurry to go see my Mum I would have pulled up a chair and stayed awhile, perhaps even struck up a conversation with one of the other patrons who was sitting on their own. But instead, I quickly headed for the counter to do what I'd come there for. The staff told me he was owned by a man who didn't come to see him often. They said the man came by every two weeks or so to collect his mail and so I asked if I could leave my details for him and told them why. They didn't know much about Big John, his background or his age, all they were able to tell me was his name. And I couldn't think of a better name for him, because he sure was big and John kind of suited him. One of the ladies there said the owner probably would sell him to me because he didn't seem to have much interest in him at all and this got me so excited. I thanked her for her time, bought a crisscross almond cake for Mum and me and jumped back in my car.

 I had been busy on the farm and hadn't been past the paddock for about two and a half weeks, nor had I gotten a phone call from Big John's owner. And I was going to visit Mum again, so I thought I'd pull over and go back into the Tea Room to see if the owner had come by. When I got to the paddock I couldn't see Big John anywhere and I thought that was a bit odd because he had been in that paddock for about five years the Tea Room staff had told me. Anyway, I never saw Big John again and the people who ran the Tea Room said they didn't know what had become of him. But what I think may have happened is that once the owner realised somebody had an interest in his horse he must have thought he could get a bit of money for him. And I'd say that would have been about right because he was a really lovely looking horse. I reckon Big John would have then been advertised on one of the many online horse sites. And of course, with me not knowing about all of them I missed him. I mean the owner may have decided to keep him and bring him closer to where he lived, taken a new interest in him and started looking after him better but I don't think so. It was a real pity that he didn't even bother to ring me first to see what I would have paid for him, at least have a chat about things. And I didn't think about it at the time but later on I couldn't help feeling that the owner may have actually been working at the Tea Room, may have even been the person I had spoken too. I mean I could have been wrong, but it did seem kind of odd that a stranger who nobody knew much about was picking up his mail from a Tea Room opposite a paddock where he kept his horse, it would have made more sense if he was getting his mail sent to his home or his business and that's why I think the Tea Room was his place of business.

After the disappointment with Big John, I decided to go back to placing my own ads again and I thought I'd probably just get another round of false leads. I still had the idea of an old farmer looking for a good home for his aging Clydesdale running round in my head and I was constantly hoping the next ad would lead me straight to him but sadly it did not. At this point the odd Clydesdale and Clydesdale cross was still coming into the abattoirs yard and my friend was temperament and health testing them all for me but none of them were working out. So once again Cinnamon was mentioned but he still had a nasty bite and I couldn't allow that sort of behaviour here, I didn't want to be worried every time I entered the paddock and also David was away on business a lot of the time back then, so I was here on my own. I needed to be able to put some form of trust in the animals I was taking in and I couldn't do that with little spiteful Cinnamon. And once again my friend fully understood where I was coming from. I was in contact with this lady every few days and she was constantly telling me about incidents that had happened with unruly horses that came into the yard, broken human jaws when a horse had reared up, that sort of thing and if I hadn't had horses as a teenager and into my twenties and knew they could be calm beautiful creatures then these stories could well have put me off. David really wasn't one hundred percent sold on having a horse anyway so I kept all these little stories to myself, didn't breathe a word of them to him because I knew that would be the end of my horse dream if I did.

Then finally the phone call I had been desperately waiting for came in. The lady said she'd heard I was after a Clydesdale. I'd just come in from walking around an empty paddock when the phone rang. The pugs were with me on the walk as always but there was just something missing on our farm, and I was never more aware of it then I was that day. I listened to this lady talking about her horse and I couldn't believe my ears. She said she had an old gelding she'd rescued from a riding school a little while ago that she was looking to rehome. He sounded perfect to me. I wanted him. I didn't need to know any more, he was a Clydesdale and he had been rescued from a riding school, two things that were equally pleasing to my ears, but the part I heard most was that he was a Clydesdale, not a biting kicking problem pony but the horse of my dreams. We talked for a while, well she did mainly, asked a whole lot of questions. I think she was trying to get a feel for me, what kind of person I was, that kind of thing. She wanted to know who would be taking in this horse of hers, so I just answered all of her questions honestly. I figured it was the best way to be really and if she didn't like one of my answers then she had the right to turn me down, I wanted this horse badly, but I wasn't willing to be disloyal to my heart just to get him. Anyway, she must have liked what she was hearing because she paused and said, "Do you think you would be interested in taking him in" and I said "I wanted him at Clydesdale" and that was the truth, she could have stopped talking at that because everything she told me about him after that was just garnishing really. Then she said he's not pure. And when I thought about it he wouldn't have been would he because you don't get too many pure Clydesdales being used in riding schools, plenty of crosses, but very rare to get a purebred because they are just too big. My heart sunk a little when I heard that, because you can get a lot of crosses that really don't have much Clydesdale in them visually. And I was ok about a cross, but I truly wanted my horse look like a Clydesdale, it just had to because my heart had been set on that for such a long time, the adult in me loved all horses but the little kid in me still wanted her Clydesdale and at that point no other horse was going to do.

Now it was me who was asking all the questions. And the very first one was the most important one to me. "Does he have feathers" in my mind a Clydesdale is nothing without those beautiful fluffy feet. "Yes" came back her answer and I breathed a huge sigh of relief. I pictured him trotting around my green paddocks with his fluffy white feet and I was happy. "What colour is he" I was hoping for black, but he was brown, no biggy, the most common Clydesdale colour really. "Height" pause, "13.2", an alright height for a horse for me after so many years without them and that was the size of Lisa, my very first horse. But if he was that small he had to be crossed with a pony. "What kind of pony is he crossed with" I asked "Welsh Mountain" came back the reply. Well, I almost fell off my seat on hearing that, to me it was a sure sign because they are my favourite kind of pony, it's their long manes that get me in, they are absolutely stunning looking ponies. "How old did you say he was" I asked wondering if she'd said and I'd not lodged it or if she hadn't said at all, my mind was spinning so she could have already told me, as it turned out she hadn't yet, and I think she was holding off because she thought I may have considered him too old. "Year of birth" and there was a long pause before she said "1992" I seriously could have put the phone down and done cartwheels in the front paddock I was so happy. I thought to myself oh this just keeps on getting better and better, 1992 was the year me and David got married, that to me was yet another sign that this was the right horse for us. She went on to say that he was a miniature Clydesdale, he had the belly splash, the roman nose, the socks, the feathers, just a shrunken down version of the real thing. I could no longer sit still on hearing this, it was all far too exciting for me, I started walking around the house while listening to her talk and I was constantly thinking to myself "I have my horse, I finally have my horse". She said "Oh I forgot to ask you an hour ago but is your farm clean" I answered "Absolutely" she said "Good" I said "Clean and clear" that seemed to put her mind at rest. A lot of people have what I call messy paddocks, paddocks that are a danger to any animal living in them. Their land is not fit for horses because they leave old half rotted fence posts laying around as well as nails, screws, bolts, old bits of tin and barbwire, fallen tree branches, all sorts of things that can be dangerous for horses, get in their hoofs, wrapped around their legs, poke them in the eye, and due to having old pugs we had none of that here, our property was neat, and even if we didn't have old pugs we still would have had clear land, nothing would have been unsightly because I wouldn't want to be looking at that. And also, you don't want to leave things laying about that snakes could hide in or under as that's not good for anybody, well I suppose it's good for the snake because he can be hidden from his predators but it's not good for us, so no rubbish gets left laying around here. Then came another question from her "Do you want him for riding" She asked sounding a bit concerned. "No, not really" I answered then added "I've never needed to ride a horse in order to get joy from it. Caring for them, being around them or seeing them out in a paddock grazing is more than enough for me". She seemed happy with that answer. Then merely to make conversation she asked if I'd had a fall or something, was that what had put me off riding and I said that nothing had put me off riding. That I'd only ever had the one fall. I told her how I'd gotten my foot caught in the stirrup but it quickly came out, so I wasn't dragged along that far. It could have been much worse, a lot of nasty injuries are caused this way, getting trapped under the horse or hitting your head if the horse won't stop running. But I was lucky because my foot soon got free then Lisa did a loop of the paddock and came back to see if I was ok. I then told her all about the elderly pugs we take in, she'd been able to hear them barking in the background while we talked, and I had to put the phone down once to go help Ruby to her feet but I hadn't yet told her why we'd bought the farm in the first place and what we actually did here, but now it was time to. So, I told her everything in a rushed voice because she was paying for this long distance phone call and we'd already been talking for quite a while. I told her how I rode more when I was younger, but I've never considered myself a great rider. I can't roller-skate either. I've been blessed with the balance of a drunk without the joy of drinking. David says I will trip over an ant if it's in my path and he's right. I go ass over head over anything, trip over a matchstick if I don't see it in front of me and sidestep in time. We were friends before we started actually going out together and David couldn't believe how easily I would trip over, we'd be walking along talking and the next moment I'd disappear from view, and he'd find me flat out on the ground and look back and not be able to see anything that could have caused me to trip. He said he'd never known anybody fall as often as I did, and I'd say to him that it was just my natural talent I guess. When we first started dating David lost count of the amount of times he saved me from actually falling down, we'd be holding hands and he'd feel me slipping and it was only his quick actions that kept me from hitting the ground. I told her that for a person such as myself I knew how quickly accidents can happen and if I'm injured or worse then who is going to look after my elderly pugs, David has to work, he can't be in two places at once, I need to look after myself so that I can keep looking after them. In all honesty I think these days I have far better balance then I did years ago but still, you just never know do you, so I think it's far safer for me to have my two feet planted firmly on the ground and love my horses from down here. Some people are born to be on horses, they ride so well it's almost like they are part of the horse, me, well, I am not one of them. And if I fell I'd fall hard, I just know I would, I wouldn't bounce, I'd thud and I don't need to be doing that. Also, I'm not in my teens or early twenties anymore, I wouldn't recover as well as I once did so that is in the back of my mind too and I told her all of this. She said Gerald was a wonderful horse, but he still had some trust issues when it came to men and I said that he'd be ok here because I married a gem. She laughed at that. But I failed to inform her that this gem still wasn't 100% on board with me having a horse and it was at this point I realised that I might want to get that situation sorted out fast.

 The lady went on to say that Gerald was gotten for her children, but he didn't like being ridden. He wasn't nasty, he just used to sit down whenever somebody was on his back and then try to roll them off. Her children were only little but they were experienced riders, so nobody ever got hurt. As soon as he began to lower himself to the ground they'd quickly jump off before he got round to rolling. He'd even roll with a saddle on, which must have hurt his back. But he didn't care, he'd be out on trail rides and decide he didn't want anybody on his back anymore so he'd stop, he'd lower and he would roll. And there was no way anybody could stop him, they'd pull on the reins and he'd resist them. Again, not nasty, just stubborn and very much wanting to not have anybody riding him and in that I thought he was perfect for me. For her part I bet she was having a bit of trouble rehoming him, from the sounds of things she had been looking for the right home for as long as I'd been looking for the right horse. She said everybody wanted him until they found out he was not good for riding, and I would come to find this out for myself because once he arrived here all sorts of people would come knocking on the door wanting to buy Gerald, they saw his beauty and couldn't drive past, they were wanting him for pony clubs and that would have been the most agonising life for a horse that didn't like being ridden. I had a lady knock on the door one day and she had a pure Clydesdale, a very big one and she wanted something for her daughter so they could ride together, look nice together, and when she saw my little miniature Clydesdale grazing by the front fence she couldn't put the brakes on fast enough. Due to their combined excitement both her and her daughter knocked hard on the door sending the pugs into an absolute frenzy. But they went way with long faces after they found out about Gerald's party trick. First she wanted to lease him and there was no way I was going to let that happen, then she started offering money and kept upping the price and I kept saying no. I had been living with Gerald for so long that I'd forgotten about the rolling thing and when it came to mind I told her and that was the only reason she left, no doubt the idea of her daughter getting squashed by a horse didn't appeal to her. It happened another time with a man, he came to the door a few times, he wanted Gerald for pulling a cart full of kids at parties and social events, that was his business, and I said "well if he doesn't want a saddle on him what do you think the chances are of him wanting to pull a cart around all day long?" He stood there thinking for a second or two then said "Not good" and I said "Exactly" and that was the last I ever saw of him.

So here I was with this lovely Clydesdale arriving on the weekend and as yet David knew nothing about it. And I was going to cook his favourite meal to soften him up, but I knew he'd smell a rat, I've done the favourite meal thing a good many times over the years to the point where he always knew I was up to something whenever the plate was placed in front of him. I decided the best thing to do would be to come right out and say it, blurt it out fast like pulling off a band-aide, so he walked in the door, and I just went for it. I didn't tell him I had a horse coming at first, thought I'd leave that little tidbit of information for later on. I just said that I'd found a really good one and sweetly asked if I could have him. Dave said "How much is he going to cost? I said "He's free, well free to me anyway, we just have to pay the cost of petrol for the owners to drive him here, that's all they've asked for, it's more about the home than the money" and it was, I think they were just covering themselves really because they didn't want to come from the other side of the city then find our home was not suitable, that I'd lied about the state of the land, I knew this lady loved this horse, if our home wasn't right she would have never left him here, she probably wouldn't have even unloaded him, just turned the float around and driven back through the gate and that would have been the end of it. I was talking a hundred miles an hour telling David all about this horse, his name was Mork back then and he said, "As in Mork and Mindy the tv show" and I said I didn't know that's just what he'd been called at the riding school. David pulled a face and I said, "Don't worry I'm not happy with the name either". So far things were going pretty good because he hadn't said no yet. I remembered the conversations we'd had about horses in the past and they didn't go very well. I think the reason he didn't want horses was because an estate agent had told him that they ruin the land, and I could have slapped that agents face for saying that because I felt he had ruined any chances of me ever being able to share my life with a horse again. This guy was a cattle farmer as well as an estate agent and he had very different ideas about horses than I did. So, there I was talking about Gerald while my husband sat listening to it all. David knew I had started looking for a horse, but I don't think he actually thought somebody was going to give me one as beautiful as this one for free and he knew I wasn't going to settle on anything that wasn't a Clydesdale. I believe he thought he wouldn't have to have this conversation with me so just let me go on my merry way assuming that'd be the end of it, but it wasn't. When we first got the farm Dave said horses weren't something he was all that keen on. And I said to him "Well then I think you and me have a problem here because there's no way I am going to live the rest of my life without them". He started talking about why a horse wasn't a good idea but I wasn't listening, I could see his lips moving, knew he would have been parroting off the estate agents words but wasn't paying attention to what he said because all the while in my head I was amusing myself with a mental image of me and David grabbing each other in a headlock and rolling down the hill in the front paddock until one of us gave in. Over and over again it played like a video until I realised David had stopped talking. But he wasn't quiet for very long, now the mower was being brought into the Gerald conversation, and I knew it was coming because it always came when I brought up horses. A ride on mower would be far less work than a horse. You only need to put petrol in and get it serviced every now and then, but with horses you have to feed and worm, you have to make sure they have fresh water, shelter, shade, regular hoof trims and dental work done. I could see where David was coming from, but I dare not let on that I agreed with him. Instead, I said that I didn't think it was right to have a mower slicing through the grass when there were so many horses around that were starving. I could see this discussion wasn't going anywhere but round and round in circles and unbeknown to David my Clydesdale was arriving on Saturday, so I didn't have a real lot of time to waste. I suppose I could have just brought the horse here during the week and hidden him from my husband, and I'm good but even I am not that good. I'd hidden the occasional price tag off a dress when we were first married but this was a horse, and you can't hide something that big for very long. During winter David only gets to see the paddocks on the weekends, he leaves for work in the dark and gets home in the dark so I could have had a horse here for at least five days without him knowing about it but as soon as it got around to his day off I would have had to come clean especially if he opened the blinds and saw a horse staring in at him. So, I said to him "Look how about I get the horse and you can name him whatever you like" I dreaded what I'd just said because I knew I was in for a name I wouldn't really like. This seemed to make him happy though and his reply came back instantly, he didn't even have to pause and think about it. "Ok I'm going to call him Gerald" Well with that we both burst out laughing. And I said "Ok then, Gerald is arriving on Saturday" Dave looked surprised then said "And when exactly where you planning on telling me this? I said "About half a second after you said I was allowed to have him, which by the way is exactly what just happened"

The reason we laughed about the name Gerald was because my husband's hobby is building aeroplane models. He's been building model kits all his life, remote control cars as well and he raced his cars years ago when we had more time on our hands then we do now. He builds both Sci fi model spaceships as well as sensible planes and by sensible I mean real plane kits and jet fighters too. Well, the kits all come with a pilot, and of course they would do because they are not toys for little kids but miniature replicas, exactly like the real planes, these kits are amazing. I've never built one, just don't have the patience, nor the interest really and besides all the little parts would do my head in if I was to give it a go. He finds them relaxing but I know they would have the opposite effect on me. I have watched David put many kits together over the years and marvelled at the skill it takes building these things. So, one day he thought he'd name one of the pilots that came out of a Sci-Fi model kit. He doesn't normally name them, just sticks them in, because he's more interested in the plane itself then the driver. But this one driver had a big odd shaped head and of course he would because he was an alien and we both laughed when David brought him over to show me. And we laughed all the more when he said he was going to call him Gerald. It just seemed like the most stupid name for a big-headed alien. But it kind of suited him too so it stuck. Well from then on Gerald the alien became the butt of a whole lot of jokes around our home and he got blamed for a lot of stuff too. Like if something was misplaced it was always Gerald the alien who took it and when it finally turned up we'd say things like "Oh Gerald has finished using it now" And we'd laugh and back and forth a few funny comments would be made. If I accidently burnt dinner well Gerald the alien would get the blame for that too. I'd tell David that I'd asked Gerald to stir the pot for me while I was off tending to one of the pugs and I'd say that his long thin fingers must have had trouble wrapping themselves around the ladle and then I'd go a step further and poke fun at him saying that for an advanced and supposably super intelligent species that he wasn't too smart, that he should have been able to use his mind powers to make that ladle move round and round. I'd then say that perhaps we just got one of the dumb ones and laugh my head off as I scraped the burnt meal into the rubbish bin. Even at the cinema Gerald would make an appearance and it was usually the person sitting in front of me. We'd arrive early and find the most perfect spot to sit and then ten or so minutes into the movie a person with the hugest head you'd ever seen in your entire life would wander in and plonk themselves down right in front of me and I'd not be able to see the full screen. I'd turn to David and say, "Oh great Gerald's here". It used to be so annoying, a country cinema, loads of spare seats and yet time after time the person with the biggest head in town was always drawn to the seat directly in front of me. It was like I'd been jinxed. I once had a lady with her hair piled on top of her head in a bun, and I thought to myself, who does that when they are going to the cinema. I thought it was a very ignorant thing to do. Surely she could have worn her hair down.

Clearly she gave no thought to anybody else when she stood in front of the mirror that morning. She may as well have gone all out and worn a cat in the hat type of hat and totally blocked my view.

David would hide Gerald the alien in all sorts of places round the house. I'd find him as I was doing the housework and ring David at work laughing and he'd say "I wondered how long it was going to take you to find him" sometimes it took days, other times only hours, but I bet on the occasions it took a while that my husband was priding himself on finding the most perfect hiding spot for our little alien friend. I was never looking for Gerald mind you because I didn't know he'd been hidden, that was all part of the joke. I'd be going about my business and then spot him and burst out laughing. I'd find him in the most unusual places sitting there with that huge alien head of his. Sometimes I didn't even see him the first time because he was so small, I'd visit the area a few times before I set eyes on him, but the funny thing was I always felt kind of weird when I got close, almost like I knew I was being watched. And I'd glance up and there he would be sitting level with my head. Sometimes I'd pull something out of the laundry cupboard and poor Gerald would go flying through the air, hit the ground, be pounced on and then carried off by one of the pugs. I'd have to race after them fast and try and pry him out of their mouths because I didn't want them choking, and sometimes it was a battle for them to give him up, I'd have to shake the treat jar a few times before they actually handed him over. It all depended on the pug, some would give him up freely, others would want a trade off before they'd even consider letting go. So the treat jar got shaken hard and all the little flat faces would come running from various parts of the house and line up in front of me and the pug who had Gerald would spit him out as soon as they saw what the other pugs were getting, and I'd have to grab him up quickly before somebody else decided that they too would like to chew on him. Gerald's head and shoulders ended up with a few tooth marks in them which I thought made him look like he had flown his spaceship into battle and come off worse for wear, like he was a little alien hero or something.

I rather fancy those full-sized aliens myself, how lifelike they are, some are even taller than I am and some of them come holding balls which are lights, for years I've envisioned one of them standing in the corner of the lounge room. I think they'd look pretty cool too because when you turn the lamp on it'd cast an eerie shadow over the alien's face giving it an unnerving glow. It'd no doubt scare the heck out of me until I got used to seeing it. I imagine myself quietly creeping through the house half asleep in the middle of the night with a pug tucked under my arm who is bursting to go to the toilet and no doubt coming face to face with a life-sized alien that I forgot was there would give me a bit of a fright, but I reckon I'm up for it. Every now and then I think about getting one and then some news report will come on about somebody thinking they've seen a UFO and I think to myself "Well perhaps not, perhaps I'll just wait until all this has died down a bit first" I mean I shouldn't really worry because most of the UFO sightings are from farmers in overalls with straw hats and missing teeth. And they usually come after they've been drinking some of their home brew. But I don't take any chances because knowing my luck a ship will be flying over our farm on a night that I've left the blinds open to look at the stars. It'll see my alien lamp, do a quick u turn, land and unload thinking it's one of their own who's been left behind on last times mission and they'll be tapping on my windows trying to get in and no doubt it'll be on one of those rare nights that David isn't home. I told my husband my thoughts on this, told him how I'd envisioned this alien ship landing in our front paddock and a pile of aliens walking up to the house and tapping on our windows and he just calmly said to me that they won't be knocking, and I asked "Why not? And he said because they'll be able to cut a hole in the glass with their fingers and let themselves in. And I said "Great, thanks for telling me that, now I have one more thing to worry about". So no, I think that for now the corner of my lounge room will remain empty.

Saturday morning arrived and there was much excitement in the air, I'd been telling the pugs all week that they were getting a new brother and that he was a big one, I said it in the most excitable voice so they realised what was going down was something very special. I couldn't wait for that float to come up the driveway. There'd never been a horse float on the farm before, a horse either and very soon that was going to change. My friend had told me that you get an awful lot of people lying to you when rescuing horses so I was a little worried that I wasn't going to get exactly what I'd been promised, he may have been calm and he may have had Clydesdale in him but he may not have looked that way and I really wanted him to, needed him to, because I think I would have been gutted if he wasn't, especially seeing as I'd built this moment up in my mind for such a long time and now it was finally happening and I wanted it to be perfect. Around noon there was a toot of a car horn, and I knew what that meant, so we secured the pugs inside the house and shot out the door. The people were nice and friendly, they got out of the car smiling. I guess the farm being so neat and tidy was pleasing to them, I'd not embellished anything when telling them how the place looked, now let's see if they'd done the same thing when telling me about their Clydesdale. I tried to peer inside the float as I walked by, but it was too high up. I asked if they needed us to stand by the ramp in case for some reason Gerald lost his footing and stepped sideways instead of backwards, I knew a gentle placing of my hand on the side of his rump would have made him move over instead of slipping off the ramp halfway down and possibly hurting his leg. They said he'd be fine, that he was a good traveller and that they'd be ok unloading him themselves and so they set about doing that while David and I went and stood by the fence. The man was dealing with the outside of the float and the lady shot inside to untie the horse. She was doing all the horse handling which told me that yes Gerald was not all that thrilled with men.

I held my breath as the husband opened the safety chains and began lowering the ramp. It was only a single float that'd come up the drive and that did have me worried as when talking to somebody about transporting a Clydesdale a while ago they had said they were far too big to fit in a single float, it'd have to be double or a truck. So, I thought to myself either she's right and he is a mini Clydesdale or he isn't a Clydesdale at all and I've been fooled into taking in something else. The ramp was fully down now but for a few moments nothing happened, and I knew that was because some horses like to gather their thoughts first before unloading. They've been in that enclosed area for a long time and suddenly it's time to vacate, some like to pause for a bit, sniff the air, look out the window, see where they are before stepping backwards and that was what Gerald was more than likely doing and the lady was wise in letting him, the worst thing you can do is rush a horse from a float, they can rear up and hit their head and then start freaking out and sometimes thrashing about and nobody wants that to happen, you want the experience to go as calmly as possible and so you wait patiently until they are ready and when the time is right they will let you know. The waiting was killing me, it was only a couple of minutes, but it seemed far longer and then suddenly I saw the float rocking and heard the clunking of hoofs. I saw a back leg appear followed closely by another one but he was wearing floating boots to protect his legs so I couldn't clearly see if he had feathers or not. My eyes moved upwards focusing on the rump. I'd been looking at photos of them long enough to know that well rounded form was that of a heavy horse breed, I was standing too far away to see if he had a belly splash or not, but he was beautiful and shiny, healthy, well looked after, his coat glistened in the sun. He was all the way out of the float now, he'd unloaded nicely and started snorting and looking around. He was calm but very interested in his new surroundings. I looked at his face and saw the blaze and the roman nose, everything she'd said about him was right and it was there and then I realised that the gods were shinning upon me because this horse was an absolutely spectacular creature. I had the biggest lump in my throat when looking at him, so overcome with emotion. He began picking at the grass but all the while taking in the sights as horses in new situations tend to do. She allowed him to get a big mouthful of grass then lifted his head up and made him stand still while they undid his boots. The first leg traveller took a while to undo or maybe it didn't, perhaps it just seemed that way because I was waiting to see what it would reveal. Gerald stomped one of his wonderful sturdy Clydesdale legs then bent his head down and rubbed his face against the boot, it was like he wanted those boots off as much as I did. I wanted to see if he had feathers, but he wanted to be off exploring his new paddock and knew he wouldn't be able to do that until all four boots were removed. When the boots finally came off and those feathers appeared well I could have leapt for joy because right there standing in front of me was the horse I'd been collecting since I was a little kid, only this one wasn't made of plastic he was real and so incredibly beautiful. And that smell, the horse smell I love so much, well that was only a few steps away from me now, but I didn't go and hug him like I desperately wanted to, he was calm, but his nostrils were flared, I felt it best to let him settle in a bit before a stranger went and threw her arms around his neck. And that did happen about half an hour later after we'd taken him for a walk around the back paddock and showed him every inch of his new home. He was calmly picking at some grass and seemed very contented and happy, so I went over and hugged the heck out of him and he didn't even raise his head, just carried on eating and let me wrap my arms around him. I had my arms as far as they would go around his tummy, I rested my head on his back and I stayed there like that for a little while, feeling his coat against my cheek, smelling that horsey smell. His owners stood by watching me doing this, the woman paying more attention to me than the man. I inhaled deeply as I hugged him, he smelt magnificent. Oh how I had missed that horsey smell.

The four of us stood in the paddock talking with Gerald in the middle of us chomping on grass, I felt sad that he would be the only horse here but grateful for the Palomino living next door, sure they weren't in the same paddock, but they could talk to one another over the fence and such a thing would be nice for both of them. When we'd taken Gerald for a walk his head kept turning in one direction then the other and I wondered if he was looking around for another horse and if he was upset because he couldn't see one. I looked towards next door to see if Topaz was anywhere in sight, she wasn't, and really I already knew that because if she was she would have been hanging over the fence seeing what was going on. I caught sight of our neighbours standing on their veranda, I'd told them Gerald was arriving on Saturday and clearly they'd come out to see him for themselves, they gave me the thumbs up both of them before disappearing back inside their house. I asked how Gerald was on the trip down, she called him Mork when she answered, and I swear David physically flinched each time she said it. She went on to say that Mork was fine, and she knew he would be, she told me she had thoroughbreds, who are well known for being edgy, she said even when Mork wasn't needing to go anywhere she always put him in with the thoroughbreds because he had such a calming influence on them. He had an amazing ability to bring them into a state of complete calmness and kept them that way throughout the journey, so he was always put on the truck whenever the highly strung horses were being moved. Hearing this pleased me because I'd been to a few race meetings in my youth and seen how those horses behaved and if this little guy could calm them down then there was something very special about him. After a lot of chatting had been done they said it was time to leave, they had a long journey ahead of them, I started to hand over the petrol money, the amount we'd agreed on, but she wouldn't take it off me. She said it was fine, that they didn't mind bringing him, I think she was just so relieved that he was in such a nice home, a clean clear well treed paddock with caring people to look after him. She said she liked how I was with him, how gentle I was when touching him, not heavy handed like some folks are with horses she said, "I knew all I needed to know about you on seeing that warm loving touch".

Because we had been standing around talking for so long Gerald had wandered off and was now grazing by the trees at the opposite end of the paddock. And I think it was fitting because it gave them time to say goodbye to him on their own. I knew it would be a hard thing for them to do, especially for the wife, they hadn't had him very long, but they were definitely horse lovers, her more than him. I motioned for David to come and wait by the gate with me so they could say goodbye to Gerald alone. They didn't need an audience; they needed to be able to be free with their emotions and free with whatever their final words to Gerald were going to be. Things like that are private. We had no business being involved, no right either, if I was in that ladies' shoes I would have wanted to be shown some respect and so that's exactly what I did with her. She would have been upset, they had a lot of horses so I think he was glad to have one less mouth to feed but I could tell the final goodbye was going to be difficult for her. David and I were talking by the gate, well I was talking he was listening, listening to me saying how I couldn't believe that I finally had a Clydesdale. I would have asked him to pinch me but knowing how strong he is I decided to refrain. The pugs were going nuts at the back door, banging on the glass, jumping up and scratching, desperate to come out, so Dave and I walked over to make sure they were all ok. When Gerald was being unloaded I could hear the pugs barking, it was like the only two sounds that could be heard were a horse snorting and the growly little woofing of snuffly faced dogs. The couple were taking a while saying goodbye to Gerald, so we let the pugs out to have a run around and they made a beeline straight for the horse poo, up until Ruby started eating it I hadn't even realised that Gerald had relieved himself. It showed that he had a bit of nerves going on and naturally he would have done, everybody does when big changes are taking place in their lives. After a while I heard voices so walked back over to the gate and opened it to let the couple through, her eyes were red from crying, I gave her a hug then looked her firmly in the eye and told her that she had my word that I would love and look after Gerald for the rest of his life. She said she knew that and thanked me for being able to put her mind at ease, she said "I know I've only just met you, but I completely trust you" I nodded my head, I knew what she meant, sometimes you don't need to know somebody long or well to know who they are. She knew I wasn't going to sell her horse on, make a quick buck out of him, she also knew that he could be happy being himself here, that I was not somebody saying they were going to do the right thing by him then forcing him into pony club or trail riding a week later. Before getting in the car, she turned to me and said that if I ever needed help with anything or had any questions that I could ring her anytime. As the empty float rattled down the driveway Gerald barely looked up, he was too busy eating in the shade by the trees. He had foundered once while in this lady's care so I would have to watch him for that. But for now, it was summer and the grass wasn't too full on. Spring would be the time I'd have to really keep an eye on him for foundering, the percentage of sugar in the grass. But I knew that by the time Spring came he would have some company in the paddock, some extra mouths to help keep down the grass. I knew I'd be carrying heavy by that time so I probably wouldn't have to pen him off like he'd been penned in his previous home. But Spring is Spring, and it is not at all kind to horses that are prone to foundering. This lady and I kept in contact for a couple of months. I'd ring her to let her know how Gerald was doing or she'd ring me if she was missing him. Gerald was everything this lady said he was and more, so well behaved, you'd give him the signal to do something and he'd do it, no trouble at all. I used to lunge him a fair bit when he first arrived, and he was lovely to watch running around like that. His conformation was absolutely flawless. Those big fluffy feet trotted around nicely, he had a beautiful way of lifting his hoofs up. He was a dream for the farrier too once he knew he could trust him, the farrier we had at the time was a wonderful man, very good and gentle with the horses, a true horse whisperer and Gerald could sense that about him, a lot of the time he'd close his eyes whenever he was getting his hoofs trimmed, you'd almost expect him to be snoring by the time the farrier was packing up his tools. Then the farrier and I would stand around talking, he'd say he always looked forward to coming and doing Gerald's hoofs because he was such a great horse to work with, he said not all horses were and that sometimes he dreaded visiting some farms because he knew the trouble that awaited him. He also liked the fact that Gerald wasn't as big as purebred Clydesdales are because they can be hard on a farrier's back, lifting those big heavy legs up can hurt you if you are prone to back trouble which I think a lot of farriers end up having as they age. The real good thing about Clydesdales is that they are blessed with such kind docile natures they just stand there and let you do what you need to do. Can you imagine if they were born with the same temperaments as some of the littler ponies have, I truly don't think there'd be as many of them around if they were because nobody would want to do their feet. It'd be hell trying to hold onto those big legs if they were constantly trying to pull away from you or nip at you while you had your head down. Some ponies never get used to having their feet trimmed and it has to happen so often that you think they would be well used to it after the first year or so of life, but no they spend their entire lives playing up and I was so glad Gerald wasn't anything like that. I had such trust in this horse, he was both beautiful to look at and beautiful in nature, he was in fact the most perfect horse.

Gerald got stuck in the shed once, well he actually snuck in the shed and managed to get himself trapped behind a large glass outdoor table setting that I was storing in there. When I saw he was trapped I thought to myself that this isn't going to end well, I envisioned glass smashing and legs being cut. David was at work and the table was too heavy for me to move on my own. And if I went next door for help Gerald could have hurt himself while I was gone. I knew I had to sort this situation out by myself and do it fast. I was about to try and get in front of Gerald and make him walk backwards, which was easy to do, you'd just point your finger above his shoulder and say "Back back" and he'd start walking backwards right away. I stood there for a few seconds trying to decide which side was my best chance of getting in front of him, but I didn't need to worry about that because he looked over his shoulder and on seeing me standing there called out a soft greeting then gently started to move backwards on his own. He was so calm, didn't rush things, just moved his big body so delicately, he felt his way back with his big fluffy white hoofs, patted at the air, found the ground and placed each hoof down beautifully and did it time and time again until he had cleared the glass table. And all I could do was watch on in awe of this wonderful intelligent creature in front of me. I assumed he must have gone in search of food, there was no other reason for him to have squashed himself in beside that table and the shed wall. Perhaps a bird had flown in with a bit of bread or something equally as tasty and left some of it behind. Gerald wasn't starving but no horse is going to not investigate some interesting smelling food. Our neighbours at the time were always feeding crows and magpies and they were constantly flying over our property dropping things. Half-eaten bread rolls and stale slices of bread mainly and I would run ahead on seeing them in the paddock before the pugs got there because I didn't want them choking on those dry crusty bits of bread. This would be the only reason Gerald would have gone into that area, this explanation was the only one that made any sense. I remember David saying not long after Gerald arrived that he was just like a dog and I said yes some horses are, I don't know what he expected from a horse but really they can be just like dogs for following you around and searching for food and interacting with you, the only difference is they are so much bigger than dogs are. Gerald spent most of his time in the horse paddock but occasionally when the pugs had been given their morning walk I'd go and let him out onto the front. The front paddock wraps itself around the house, so Gerald was free to wander as close to the house and decking area as he liked and there'd be a pile of flat little faces watching every move he made, it seemed they were as mesmerised with him as I was. Also, it was a thrill for me having him interacting with us like that. I liked him being around us as much as he possibly could. I'd be going about my housework and see him standing at the windows looking in. The sound of the vacuum cleaner seemed to lure him over, he would be off in the distance grazing, and I'd turn the vacuum on and the next moment I'd look up and see his face peering in. He would follow me from room to room as I vacuumed and me and the pugs got a real buzz out of that. They would be jumping up at the windows barking in a frenzied manner and they'd see where I was heading and know if

I was going that way Gerald then was too, so they'd race into the room ahead of me and be already barking at the windows by the time me and the vacuum cleaner made our way in. Gerald didn't care that he was being barked at, it neither thrilled him nor scared him, he was rather neutral on the matter because the pugs were not what he had come over to see and to be honest neither was I, the vacuum cleaner was, he seemed quite fascinated by it. Then I'd turn it off and that was it, he was already back out in the middle of the front paddock grazing by the time I wrapped up the lead.

After Gerald arrived here it was like this little farm became even more precious to me, our land now had a presence, the paddocks sat right. The house was already full of life and love and happiness but there was something missing in the paddocks. I felt it each time I was wandering around the place. It felt like a ghost town out there, David didn't seem to notice it, but I sure did. There were birds chirping and the sounds of animals in places nearby but our land only echoed loneliness, it was like the wind was constantly whispering the word "Barren" in my ear and I didn't like having that kind of atmosphere out there. The paddocks were not only empty but there was an emptiness that saturated everything for me. It hung in the air, wrapped itself around the trees and cloaked the grass. It was as if the land was constantly unhappy, a real sadness hung over the place. I felt it every time I set foot outside the door. Sure, it was a joyous time when the pugs were all sniffing about, they always seemed to have a happy little cloud hovering above them, but when they moved on so did the cloud leaving an empty spot where it had just been. I'd be following on and became more and more aware of it each passing day. And then Gerald arrived, and things instantly changed. He put his big hoofs on the ground and suddenly everything outside sprang to life. It was like he had blessed our land. Life became even more magical for me here. Now the land was exactly like the inside of the house was. There was joy out there, real joy. Gerald would be trotting around the place looking absolutely magnificent, big fluffy feet moving so beautifully across the green grass, mane and tail flowing, voice echoing on the wind. I loved watching him out there, it didn't matter what he was doing I loved watching him do it. He'd call out to me and the pugs each morning when we were going for our walk, and I'd glance over at him and often have to do a double take especially in the first few weeks of his stay. At times I couldn't believe my eyes, I think because I had wanted this for so long Gerald it was like he was a mirage. Like my eyes were playing tricks on me and I was too scared to blink in case he disappeared and didn't come back. I'd smell his scent on the breeze and feel lucky, just out and out lucky to have him. He made friends with the cows at the back of our property and friends with Topaz next door, he wasn't short on company. He'd hang his head over the fence talking to them a lot of the time and if they were off grazing he'd be fine with that as well, he'd take himself off and have a bit of grazing time too and they'd be calling out to one another just making sure everybody was still there. Even at nighttime I'd hear them talking to one another and it was a nice sound to hear. Or I'd be laying in bed and hear thundering hoofs, Gerald on our side of the fence and Topaz on hers, it was like they were amusing themselves by having races at midnight and I'd fluff my pillow up and wonder how many of those races my lovely boy won. Friends would drop by and rib me about Gerald, they'd ask me if I believed he was real yet and I'd laugh and then be honest and tell them it differed from day to day. And it did, sometimes I'd walk out there and be looking for him, very much aware of him being here and always wanting to know where he was and what he was doing then other days I'd come outside, and he'd be so beautiful standing there that I still couldn't believe he was truly mine. The child in me that had been dreaming about owing a Clydesdale all her life still couldn't fully believe that she had actually gotten one. But I had gotten one hadn't I, Gerald was real, Grace Farm now had a reigning monarch and what a magnificent King he was.

CHAPTER FIVE

Horton

Well you'd think after writing an entire book about Horton that I wouldn't have anything else to say about the little guy wouldn't you, but you'd be wrong. There were a couple of things I forgot to mention in The Joy of Horton, well didn't actually forget because they are still in my mind all these years later, but they were not forefront in my mind when I was writing Horton's book. They only came to me afterwards, once the book was in print and they are lovely stories, too beautiful not to share with all of you who truly loved Horton. So, I'll go ahead and tell you these stories later on in this chapter. But let me first talk about Horton's book. After I finished writing The Joy of Horton I decided to sit on it for a little while because I wasn't sure if I was ready to share his story with the world yet or not. I guess in a way I was trying to keep him to myself for a little bit longer, he was so precious to me and I wasn't yet ready to let the book go because it was part of him, well it was more than part of him it was him, 100% him and I wanted to keep him close to my heart for a little longer so that's what I ended up doing. And then when I felt I was ready to let the book go I did, and this time I found it very easy to do because I'd had that extra little bit of time and I guess I needed to have it. But now I wanted to share this lovely little boy's story with everybody who loved animals and that brought about its own set of problems. I found the promoting side of things extremely difficult and of course nobody knows you have a book if you don't tell them, and I got really stuck on that. I am quite shy and self-conscious. That's who I am, that's who I've always been. But what I needed to be in order to get Horton's story noticed and read, was bold, forward and outgoing. And that bothered me a lot. I mean you can't change your personality just because you've written a book.

I was born in England and raised in Australia. The English are quiet and reserved and the Australians don't take themselves too seriously and if you do people think you are full of yourself and of course being the person, you are that is the last thing you are being. What you'd really love more than anything else in the world is for somebody else to promote the book for you. But you don't have a publisher and you don't have a literary agent. You just have yourself and your husband who is more or less the same personality as you are, well shyer than you are really. So here I was with this beautiful book about a beautiful little boy who meant the world to me, and I felt stuck. It's like you know people are going to love Horton's book once they've read it and that thought fills your heart with joy, and you know telling his story is the right thing to do because you know it will help other little dogs born just like him, but then your thoughts get in the way, and you start feeling insecure. Normally I am promoting my dogs and that's the easiest thing in the world for me to do but with my name up there I started to feel incredibly uncomfortable. I was writing the first of the Grace Farm series of books at the time. Well trying to anyway, but due to pressure I put on myself with promoting I found that I'd lost my writing voice and at one point wondered if I was ever going to get it back again. I tried hard to keep writing but found I just couldn't do it, I wasn't sitting comfortably in my life, I lost my flow, my world had changed and that caused my words to dry up. I had nothing to say, no stories to tell, well of course there were stories to be told in a houseful of pugs there always are, but they weren't what was on my mind at the time, they were being pushed aside to make room for everything else I was feeling. And you just cannot write under those circumstances, well I find that I can't anyway.

David came home from work when I was having a particularly rough day. I was standing in the middle of the kitchen in my pug pajamas, pug slippers, hair piled on top of my head in something that barely resembling a bun and if it was a bun it had definitely been demon possessed and was in the middle of being exorcised at the exact moment my husband walked through the door. So, I'm standing there ramming chocolate biscuits down my throat at an alarmingly fast rate. I looked like a deranged woman and was very much acting that way too and as is always the case there was a cloud of old pugs at my feet looking up at me longingly. I was meant to be giving the pugs their dinner and the bowls were all lined up on the countertop ready, but they remained empty. I just spotted the packet of Tim-Tams and figured "Why the hell not". David walked in and found me there like that. It was summertime so still daylight and I still had to go out into the paddocks and feed the horses and sheep, but my pajamas were already on and I didn't even care that they were. At that point in time I reckon I could have done a Hugh Hefner and lived in my pajamas for the rest of my life and not cared one single bit what anybody else thought of it. David was coming in the door cheerful as always and stopped dead in his tracks when he saw me. He asked if everything was alright, and me being the sarcastic little turd that I can be at times snapped back at him with "Does anything about this scene look even remotely alright to you" I felt sorry for him that night and even sorrier for myself and I knew Horton wouldn't have wanted that for his parents or his family. I was short tempered and snapping at somebody who really did not deserve it, behaving as far away from how I wanted to be behaving as I could get and I just thought to myself "This has to stop and it has to stop right now" I wondered how it had gone from David lovingly squeezing my hand and telling me he was proud of me for writing Horton's book to me standing there in the kitchen acting like an absolute idiot.

I remembered the day David loaded "The Joy of Horton" onto Amazon, he had to do it because I couldn't, I've never been good with computer type things so it was best for him to do all the tricky work for me otherwise I would have driven him insane with all the questions. So, David loaded our son's book up and when it was done we sat there holding hands as he clicked the key to put Horton's story out there. We were both excited and a little nervous too, well I was anyway, my husband was cool calm and collected like he always is. Just before he hit the button he asked if I was ready and I took a deep breath and said "As ready as I'll ever be" then I closed my eyes and said a little prayer, I prayed that The Joy of Horton would reach those it was meant to reach. Then I heard David say, "Ok done" so I opened my eyes again and looked over at my husband, we both smiled at each other and he said "Well done baby", he told me that I was now officially an author. But I didn't feel like an author, not then and still don't now even though I have written a few books. I'd call myself a storyteller if anything and the stories you are reading here are the same ones I'd be telling you if you'd dropped by my little farm house and were sitting across the kitchen table from me with a biscuit and a cup of tea. There'd be a pile of old pugs sleeping by your feet and elderly sheep and horses grazing outside the large windows. If it was winter the fire would be roaring and you'd probably be looking over at the flames while listening to me talk, summer and the sound of ceiling fans would be heard whirling in the distance. Between sips of tea, you'd glance around the room, point to a pugs face in a frame and ask me who that was and I would begin telling you their story and maybe the kettle would have to be boiled again and the biscuit tin given another rattle. But we'd talk and we'd laugh, and we'd talk some more and really that's how this has always felt to me, like I'm sitting down with likeminded people talking about my pugs. I remember when Horton's book first came out a lady wrote to me asking what the secret was of writing a book. I was out in the paddock with the horses when my phone went "Ding" so I leant against a fencepost while I fished it out of my pocket and read the message and the first thought that ran through my mind was "What is she asking me for, how the heck would I know" and the second thought came rather quickly after that, as I watched the sheep and horses happily wandering about I thought to myself "Oh yeah that's right I wrote a book didn't I". So, I wrote back and said "Let your heart lead you, be true to yourself and be honest, you can't go wrong if you do that". Rules of writing and rules of life are pretty much the same I think. I answered a few of her other questions too but never heard back from her so don't know how she went. Although having just said that I don't feel like an author has reminded me that I did try and play the author card once, it was a day when there was a particularly large and very messy dog poo in the middle of the lounge room floor. I smelt it way before I saw it but as soon as I set eyes on it I realised that it was Ruben John Comer who was responsible because he had a way of managing to do almost horse sized poos. I looked down at it and instantly knew it was something I did not want to be dealing with in that particular moment, so I called over my shoulder to David. I said "You'll have to clean that one up because I don't do things like that now I am an author" to which he very quickly replied "Yes, but you are a Mother first so get on with it" so I sighed and dealt with the issue at hand and grumbled the entire time I was doing it but I never again tried to get out of doing my job because I knew Dave wasn't going to put up with it.

The day after what has now become known around here as my "Tim Tam meltdown" I decided the best thing I could do was take a step back from promoting and get my inner peace flowing again and didn't feel bad about doing that because I knew Horton would understand. I knew he wouldn't want me stressing out and making life for all those who relied on me here at Grace Farm miserable. So I went back to doing that which makes me the happiest, being around my animals. I stuck to my quiet little daily routine of walking the pugs, feeding the pugs and looking after the pugs and I was happy, but the writing didn't come back as fast as I thought it would and you can't push it, it has to come naturally. Instead, I just focused on the pugs and figured one day I would feel like writing again and until that day came it was no use worrying about it. So lot of squeaky toys got squeaked and a lot of pug snuggling was done, and the outside windows were totally free of cobwebs for once and that went on for quite a while. The weeks were flying by, and you start wondering if you are ever going be able to write again, like it's been so long that you wonder if you may have even forgotten how to string a sentence together. I would sit on the deck in the mornings with a cup of tea and sometimes I'd be wondering if today would be the day that the keyboard got tapped and a chapter would start to form and other days that sort of thing was the furthest thing from my mind. I was proud of Horton's book, and I figured if it was going to be the only book I would ever write then that was more than enough for me, sure writing about my pugs has always brought me joy but if I couldn't do it anymore then I knew I could be ok with that. I now had a record of Horton's life and that meant everything to me.

Another thing that meant a lot to me was when I started getting letters from people telling me how much reading Horton's story meant to them. Some hadn't even finished his book before they started writing, three or four chapters in and they said they just had to contact me and tell me how much they loved Horton and that really touched my heart. I felt blessed that people loved him, felt blessed that my little boy's story was touching people, I think if he'd come into this world and gone out of it without anybody knowing who he was, well, that would have been a great tragedy. I also heard from a lot of people when they had just finished the book, when their pain of loss was raw and I fully understood how they were feeling, they had only just lost Horton, I had stood in their shoes, I knew exactly what that was like, but for me I was years on from it now, I was in a different place but I knew the stage they were in and my heart went out to them. Over and over again I was thanked for sharing Horton's story and in a way that's what began making the promoting side of things easier for me. I got a letter from a lady one day and she was telling me how much she adored reading The Joy of Horton, but she also said something that really struck a chord, she said she'd come across the book by accident. She was sitting in a doctor's waiting room and decided to do a google search for a new book to read and that's how she found out about it, well I didn't want my lovely boy's story being found accidentally. He was too precious for that; it was then I realised that I needed to get out of my comfort zone and start promoting. David and I were talking about it one evening and I said I guess it's like a little corner shop having a beautiful product that people are going to love but how are they going to find out about it if that little corner shop doesn't advertise. I was telling this same lady how hard I was finding the promoting side of things and she said, "Look Andrea you didn't write this book for nobody to read did you" and I said "No" and she said "Well get out there and promote the heck out of it" so that's what I did and like most things in life the more you start doing it the easier it becomes. And this lady was wonderful with me, she started promoting the book herself and I was grateful to her for doing that for Horton and for me. The more people read the book the more correspondence I received. I have some lovely letters from people who said reading Horton's story changed their lives. I like that he had an impact on people. I also found it fascinating where these people lived, what part of the world they were in when reading about Horton's life. Here was this little paraplegic pug that lived his entire life on a small farm in Australia and suddenly people from vast and faraway places knew his name. People said Horton was now part of them, that for the rest of their lives they were never going to forget him, and I thought that was a really beautiful thing. All I ever wanted was for people to feel that they knew who Horton James Sparky Comer was, to get an essence of him and what he achieved in his short but wonderful life and from their words I knew they had done just that. Before Horton I'd certainly never come across a being that small with that much strength, determination and courage dwelling within, nor that much personality either and people got that about him and loved him for it and I was such a proud, proud Mum. Never underestimate how much your words can mean to a person, because they certainly meant the world to me. And when people started giving The Joy of Horton five-star reviews, well my eyes welled up and the tears overflowed. I cried because he was lovely, I cried because he was no longer here, and I cried because I was so happy that people were taking him into their hearts. They were giving the little guy a huge thumbs up for what he had accomplished. To me every star was saying "Well done little one, very well done". I was reading those reviews one day and a quick thought shot through my mind, I thought "Little man I hope you can see all of these from heaven" I think Horton would have gotten a kick out of reading those reviews, but you know what I reckon he may have even been sitting right bedside some people as they were reading his book, in my mind I pictured his little face looking up and watching their reactions and that would have been a real nice thing for him to be doing. Somebody wrote and said the book should have been called "The Little Pug that Could" because that was how they felt about Horton. And I thought wow that's great, they really understand the true heart and soul of Horton and I was overjoyed because I felt like I had done this little pug that meant the world to me justice, I'd captured his spirit with my words and that's what I most wanted to do.

I was talking to somebody one day and they said five stars wasn't too bad at all for a little pug that couldn't walk and a lady who couldn't read and that comment hurt my heart, it settled on the surface and seeped deeper and deeper in over the next few days. It was meant as a complement I know it was, but it hurt my feelings all the same. It upset me that they referred to Horton as merely being a pug who couldn't walk, that was offensive because he was so much more than that. To reduce Horton down to those few words wounded me more than what she had said about me. Those words were about his condition not about him. Not about all he was. To sum him up that way after everything he achieved was truly upsetting. And bringing up the fact that I'm dyslexic, well that can be hard too because you always feel like such an idiot when people say those things to you. It can be shattering. My early years of schooling were the hardest, knowing you are different to all the other kids makes you feel incredibly insecure and being a shy kid made it all the worse. It was like everybody else in my class was part of a special club that I had not been, nor would I ever be, invited to. It was like they had all been given this secret code and that code was the written word. To look at that blackboard and not see what everybody else saw, as a kid you sit there wondering "Why me. Why do I have to be the dumbest kid in the classroom, what did I do that was so wrong that I was afflicted with this". But I wasn't stupid at all it's just that my brain was different to theirs. And I was very good in the area of creativity, and I liked being that way. I used to get top marks in art class and some of the brains of the class used to amaze me because they were so smart and yet they drew like kindergarten kids. I used to stand next to their easels and stare at what they had painted in utter amazement. But I came to realise that we are all made differently, nobody excels in everything. I thought because the smart kids were brilliant at English that they would be better than me in all areas and they weren't. These days I am far more accepting of being dyslexic because it's part of me, it makes up who I am and I'm fine with that because I like who I am. I still have the fear of being thought of as stupid though but nowhere near the mad panic I used to have because I've had a lot of losses in my life, I've lived through grief, I've suffered heartache, being dyslexic isn't that, it's just a few letters being seen backwards and a few words that I am always going to get mixed up, it's not what is important in life, it's difficult at times yes, but it's not all that significant, you learn to cope, you learn to live with it. And at the end of my days, I doubt very much I'll be giving a second thought to having been dyslexic. Of course, I'd be rich if I'd been given a dollar every time a school teacher called me stupid growing up. And naturally I've heard all the dyslexic jokes a hundred times over and then some. I'd say the dyslexic Devil worshiper who sold their soul to Santa is probably the funniest one I've ever heard though, that is my all-time favourite. But yes the fact that I am dyslexic and was often called an idiot has made me a little insecure and at one point while writing Horton's book I stopped typing mid-sentence and thought to myself "What right does a dyslexic have to write a book" but because Horton was important to me I quickly snapped myself out of it and carried on typing. I knew I was only thinking that way because of what had been said to me throughout my school years and if I didn't keep going, keep on telling Horton's story then those school teachers and classmates of mine would have won wouldn't they. And I wasn't ever going to let that happen. These days they wouldn't be allowed to treat a child that way, but things were very different when I was at school. Being left-handed as well also brought it's challenges as far as school went, one teacher in particular took great offence to it, she used to smack my hand hard with a ruler and yell at me to use my proper hand and well I just couldn't make my right hand form letters, I probably would have had more luck writing with my toes. My right hand didn't seem to know what to do with a pen, yet my left hand wrote beautifully and drew beautifully, so I'd swap back to my good hand until the ruler was brought down over my knuckles once again. Thank goodness I only had to put up with that teacher for a year. I never liked school anyway, but that year was the hardest one for me and it was all due to her being so unreasonable. My art teacher by the way had no issues at all with me being left-handed.

One thing I did do due to being dyslexic, well, felt was the best thing to do, was get a professional editor and proofreader to go over The Joy of Horton once I'd finished the book. And I found it to be both a good and a bad thing to have done. I got a few good pointers out of it, learnt a bit with the feedback given and was grateful for that but what I also found was the changes they made spoiled the book. I write like I talk and the way I talk is uniquely me, my traits and personality all woven in there. There are parts of me being English and parts of me being Australian, when people hear me talk they can generally figure out I'm Australian but the odd words come out and you'll see their mind ticking over, it's like they are trying to figure out what my other accent is because it's not broad English, although it can be at times especially when I get with other English people, I can snap right back into talking the way they do and half the time not even realise I'm doing it. I was sitting at the kitchen table having a cup of tea with a friend one day when Dad dropped round. He stayed and had a cup of tea with us and then we all walked him down to the gate. As he drove off my friend looked at me bizarrely and said, "What the hell just happened" and I said "What do you mean? She said it was like being in an episode of the twilight zone, she said that I would talk to Dad in a very broad English accent and then turn to her and talk Australian. And she said as much as she wanted to burst out laughing she felt she couldn't in case Dad thought she was being rude. It was the first time she'd met him and so of course the first time she'd experienced this. In my childhood all my friends used to witness the same thing and became quite accustomed to it, we'd walk into my house after school, and I'd instantly switch accents on crossing the threshold and then pick my Australian accent up again when I walked back out the door. I do occasionally get asked if I'm from New Zealand, but the funny thing is when I'm talking to somebody from New Zealand they never think that, after a while they'll have to ask where I am from because they can't quite pick it. They say I talk mostly like an Aussie but keep dropping words from somewhere else entirely and they are trying to figure out where that somewhere else is but when guessing they never say England. Anyway, when the book was sent back that was all gone. Of course, the story was the same but my writing voice and style had been replaced. I had been erased, the words didn't sound like they had been written by me anymore. They'd completely altered my way of talking. So, I had to go back in and change everything to how it was in the first place and that took a bit of time, but in doing that I found they'd also replaced a few words with the wrong word. I got David to double check in case I was seeing it wrong and being dyslexic that can happen, so I needed him to check too. I'd highlight the sentence and pass the laptop over to him so that he could have a look. Time and time again I did this and time and time again he said I was dead right in picking up the mistake. It wasn't just different words used in different parts of the world either, but more that the sentence written no longer made any sense. It seemed we'd paid good money for somebody to remove my voice and alter words that didn't need altering. It was all a bit of a mess really so after that we decided not to get a professional to proofread but to stick with us, I know how I talk and David knows how I talk and we were the best ones at understanding how I wanted things said. Naturally both of us had read and reread The Joy of Horton numerous times before sending it to the proofreader. But I guess my insecurities made me think we needed to do more than that and as it turned out we really didn't. Now a days we have a small group of people proof reading for us and of course David and I will have read the book a few times before handing it over to them. Also, there was even talk about the very last paragraph of the book being pulled, the part where I talk about grief being like floating in a sea of pain, and I said "Absolutely not". There was no way known I was not having that in the book. I thought it was a perfect way to end The Joy of Horton. And I was very proud of writing that paragraph because it summed up exactly what grieving is like for me. But not only that it was written at lightning speed, no need to do over, no need to add or subtract, it was all there, I nailed it, I felt it perfectly described the grieving me. And it was written under enormous pressure too. I have a few areas that I write the books in, it all depends on the state of the day. But one thing that's always the same is that I write with all the pugs sleeping peacefully around me because I love hearing their slumbering snuffles as I type, plus if I pause while typing as I sometimes do, then I can glance all around at my little blessings and feel incredibly lucky to have them in my life. If the sun is shining we'll go out on the deck, and I set myself up at the table we have out there. Sometimes I write at the kitchen table but a lot of the time I write sitting right in the middle of my bed with the split system running hot or cold depending on the day. I like being on the bed because it means I can have more pugs up level with me and we all seem to like that, David made me a small wooden table to set the computer up on and I'll have a pile of cushions behind my back and there will be pugs to the front, pugs laying across my legs and pugs on either side of me and I'll be typing away happily until it's time for them to have a walk and be fed. Sometimes I'll be late getting set up to write, on busy days I only get to write a paragraph and a little one at that, but if I am on top of all my chores that allows me to get stuck in early and on those days I can get a fair bit done. It all depends on the blessings really and what they need me to do for them that day. If somebody is not feeling well then there's no need to get the computer out because I'll be constantly tending to them. They always come first, they have to, they are important and precious, and I won't allow it to be any other way. People often ask me how much writing I get to do in a week and my answer is always the same, "As much as the pugs let me" because that's the honest truth, and no two weeks are exactly the same. Writing for me is a little treat I give myself when all the pugs and other animals have had all their needs met, when they've been fed and walked and I'm sitting in a good position with the never ending pile of laundry. Some days I'll have a tiny bit of time to write and others days it's just not going to happen and sometimes that can go on for well over a week but I've gotten to a point now where I don't let it bother me, if I've got say ten or fifteen minutes to write I just put my head down and start typing for that ten to fifteen minutes and then pack the computer away, go off and do what I need to get done not giving it a second thought because I now know all those ten, fifteen and twenty minutes of writing are important, they mount up and in the end you'll have yourself a book. Although if I'm only going to be on the computer for that small amount of time I don't set myself up properly because it's kind of pointless, I'll set up on the kitchen bench instead, running on battery and because I'm in the kitchen the pugs think it's dinner time and they'll be pushing their faces into my legs trying to get me moving or a little blind face will appear at knee height so I'll be typing with one hand at those times while the other hand is hanging down patting the little old blessing's head. Once I even wrote by candlelight during a storm, running on battery, again one handed because I was cradling and soothing an old dog who is terrified of thunder. I suppose I could have simply left it for another day and once the power went out I did think of doing just that, then I thought well with all this rain I can hardly walk the dogs so I may as well type out what's in my head. So I grabbed a candle, scooped up the little girl who was trembling and started tapping at the keyboard, Lumen was sleeping in her cot nearby and the candle cast a beautiful glow across her fluffy black and white head.

Anyway, I was writing that bit about grieving and I was almost finished what was in my heart and was pretty happy about that because I was late with the afternoon walking and feeding and was well aware of that fact, but everybody was sleeping so peacefully that day and nobody seemed to be aware of the time. Then all of a sudden I saw out of the corner of my eye one little body rise up, and she stood staring at me like "Well what are you waiting for, I'm up, walk me and feed me" but I was so close to the end of the book that I chose to ignore her and because I'd ignored her Amber started walking around the bed, well stomping really because that's how she generally walks when she isn't happy. So I'm typing away and I see another little body rise up and before I know it they are all wide awake, all surrounding me in a half circle with their eyes fixated, most of them swaying a little to get my attention, some were doing little growly woofs as well because they didn't like being ignored, they have me well trained I don't normally ignore them, I normally put them first, shut the computer down fast and take them for a walk. But today I knew how close I was to finishing Horton's book, so I wanted to keep going. And I'm like a racehorse in the last leg of the Melbourne cup, only I'm not looking up at the track in front of me like they do I've got my head down typing like crazy pretending to be invisible. Then I do look up and they are all there growling, swaying and groaning, it's like a scene from a zombie movie and I'm thinking to myself there is no way known I am getting out of this alive. They were getting so impatient and the more impatient they got the more they were swaying and the louder their noises became. But my head is down and I'm typing, typing like crazy, feeling the heat but still typing, typing like I don't even know they are there and then that's it, it's done, finished, perfect. And it was like "Lift your hands from the keyboard now Andrea and walk away, there is nothing more to be said here". So I start to close the computer down and as it's shutting down the pugs know what's happening, they can see what I'm doing and start jumping up at me and giving kisses and I'm hugging them and tickling tummies and lowering them to the ground and the love in the air is like electricity and we all file through the back door, go down the ramp and out into the fresh air and it was a glorious moment. The book, his book, was finished and I felt I had done Horton proud.

 The fact that I could write a book at all, well full credit has to go to my Mum for that because she was the one who got me through all those hard days at school. She was the one who never gave up on me, who found ways to help me when the school teachers couldn't. I remember one incident in my early days at primary school very clearly. My teachers didn't understand why I couldn't see any difference between the letters "b" and "d". Using capital letters I was ok, that was a bit easier, I could see the difference there, but not with lower case writing. No matter how much they tried to tell me those letters were different I just wasn't getting it. Because the truth of the matter was that I couldn't see it, being dyslexic they both looked exactly the same to me. After weeks of frustration my teachers called Mum in to explain to her what was going on. The next day I went in, and I was "cured" as one of the teachers put it. They couldn't believe that Mum had done in one single night what they had been trying to do for weeks. But me and Mum had a secret. Mum had gone home that night and made up a verse to help me out. And to this day that verse is still in my head, it went like this.

"b" is a boy with a big fat tummy.

"d" is a duck with a big behind.

Mum kept repeating that verse to me as I sat watching her cooking tea. And we chanted it together as she walked me to school the next morning. As we said goodbye at the gate Mum just said "Ange whenever you have to write a "b" or a "d" stop and say our verse in your head before writing the word, so that's what I did. I never once had a problem with those two letters after that. I thought Mum was smarter than all of my school teachers put together.

Perhaps me feeling insecure about being dyslexic added to the stress of releasing my first book and what caused my Tim Tam meltdown. I remember David forced me out the door with the instruction to go spend some time with the horses and sheep while he took over feeding the pugs. So, me, my pug slippers, my pug pajamas and my deformed bun went out and stood in the paddock and kissed Gerald's nose and hugged Whisper's neck and put some feed buckets down and sat on the ground watching everybody eat. And as I watched I felt the tension slowly slipping away. I wasn't thinking about trying to promote Horton's book or about David and the pugs, I just sat and watched everybody in the paddock chewing and snorting and glancing over at me when they lifted their heads. I cleared my mind of my worries, I let go of it all and concentrated on the scene in front of me. I smelt the horses and the sheep and the feed and had a beautiful time out there. When they'd all finished eating I fed Gerald and Whisper the apples I had stored in my pajama pockets. Ok I was a mess, and I was being forced out the door by my husband at lightning speed but before I was discarded from my own home I still had the mind to go over to the fruit bowl and shove as many apples as I could fit into my pockets and I was so glad I'd done that because they were really enjoying them. And as I closed the paddock gate I thanked all the animals for restoring my spirits. I walked back into the house feeling like a huge weight had been lifted off my shoulders, hugging horses and patting sheep tends to do that for me, animals are remarkable beings. That's why I always seek them out when life gets too hard. David glanced up at me and smiled when I came through the door and all the pugs ran over to me in greeting and just like that, I was back to being ok again. Well on the inside I was anyway, the outside of me still looked slightly deranged but I chose not to concentrate on that, my heart felt happy and that to me was all that mattered. Also, while I was sitting in the paddock I had been lucky enough to hear a Kookaburra laughing in the distance, from my spot on the ground I couldn't see it in the trees, but I could hear him loud and clear and the sound of him made me smile really wide. It also made me think of Ruby and how much she enjoyed listening to all the birds here on the farm. It made me think of Horton too and the time we had a Kookaburra come sit in the nearest olive tree to our house. From his spot on the deck Horton could see the middle of that tree very clearly and it was he who drew my attention to the fact that a Kookaburra had landed there. Me and all the pugs rushed to Horton's side when he began doing his little excitable woofs. At first I didn't see the Kookaburra but I knew it was something special that had gotten Horton's attention, so I began slowly looking around, taking everything in. And not just big obvious things either I had to look for things that were not really of much interest to me but things that my little boy would find appealing, with Horton it was a lot like seeing the world from a child's point of view, he took joy in things that an adults eyes, a busy Mum's eyes, would merely skip over, so I let my eyes linger, began looking all around trying to see what a little puppy would have found interesting. And Horton saw everything with those huge eyes of his, nothing went unnoticed by him ever. So, I was looking for insects and ants on the deck and I was looking for insects and birds flying through the air. I was gazing slowly at the grass, looking for leaves and branches that had perhaps just recently been blown across the paddock, if it hadn't been there the day before then it would have been exciting for Horton seeing it now especially if the wind had decided to pick it up and play with it again. In the end I had to get down to Horton's eye level in order to see what he saw, and I was just as excited as he was with the find. This Kookaburra was looking back at us all like we were the weirdest things he had ever seen, but I guess a woman laying full length across a deck and a pile of snuffly dogs weren't considered threatening to him because he wasn't for going anywhere in a hurry. So I watched him for a little while, took in his beauty, he wasn't laughing just staring at us all but being so close to him was amazing. And the entire time we were out there Horton was doing his little puppy woofs. Perhaps that's why the Kookaburra remained silent, maybe he was giving my baby boy a turn, I guess he thought if that tiny black pug was happily entertaining people then so be it. As I was laying there watching our new friend I suddenly remembered that I had some mincemeat in the fridge. I knew Kookaburras liked such things so raced inside the house and the Kookaburra turned his head watching me go. I began rolling the meat into bite sized balls as I made my way back out to the deck, big enough so he could see them when I threw them on the ground but not so big that they would be hard for him to get down. I tossed one ball towards the olive tree and the Kookaburra saw it land but didn't go after it. I shrugged my shoulders, figured I'd gotten it wrong, figured he wasn't interested and began sharing the balls with the pugs, who by the way were incredibly interested and had been since they heard the fridge door open. The Kookaburra saw what I was doing so spread his wings and flew to the ground. He ate the mincemeat fast and looked up at the deck for more, but I didn't have any more because by this time the pugs had gobbled everything up. So back inside I went but when I came out again he was gone. But the next afternoon I heard Horton woofing again, and again it was his super excitable woof, so I rushed outside and there was the Kookaburra sitting in the olive tree, exact same tree exact same branch. I don't believe they like olives, so I don't know why he was there, perhaps he'd been watching us for a while from one of the gum trees and thought he'd fly over to have a better look. So again, he was fed a small ball of mincemeat. The day after he was back and the same routine was carried out. No laughing ever, in fact never any noise from him at all. This went on for about four or five days, it was always Horton who alerted us, always the olive tree he chose to sit in and always one small ball of mincemeat eaten and then just like that he stopped coming. A year or so later I read an article in a magazine that said we shouldn't really feed mincemeat to Kookaburras, well any kind of food for that matter, it said that mincemeat didn't provide the right nutrients for them. Being carnivores, they should be eating mice, baby lizards and small snakes. Eating the entire thing bones and all is what the article said because that'd give them everything they needed to remain healthy. It said if they become reliant on food from humans they will be missing out on calcium and other nutrients that are vital for their overall health. Mincemeat for a Kookaburra was like a cheeseburger is for us, ok to have once in a while but not good to live on. The article said that the only thing we should be leaving out for Kookaburras is clean fresh water, especially in the summer months. So, I bought a bird bath and never fed a Kookaburra again. And that was an easy enough thing to do because we never had a Kookaburra come so close to the deck again, plenty in the surrounding trees and one sat on the TV aerial once but never interacted with us and he only sat the for a short amount of time, never looked at me like he wanted feeding, never really paid all that much attention to me or the pugs. Perhaps he was just resting and once he caught his breath off he flew. The birdbath is still out there and to this day blackbirds and sparrows gather round drinking or splashing about in the water, it can be particularly entertaining for us on very hot summer days, seeing them all out there sharing is a lovely thing to witness. Well, the blackbirds and sparrows share it anyway, the Indian myna's never do, but then again they share nothing with anybody, it's just how they are, they are very territorial and nasty because of it, that's why I've never been overly found of them. Not a particularly attractive looking bird and no traits that I find appealing, so they are not really the birds for me.

For a long time after Horton died people still walked into the house and looked for him. They knew he was gone, everybody was very well aware of that fact, but they still did it because they were so used to doing it and I understood perfectly because I found myself doing the same thing a lot of the time. And of course, once you realised he was no longer here it sure did sting, I felt a twinge in my heart when it hit me and I could always tell the exact time it hit visitors too because their faces would change. I'd watch them come in smiling, patting the pugs, happily calling out all their names in greeting and then they'd lift their heads ever so slightly and start scanning the room, looking for that sweet little darling to come scooting along. Horton used to come in in almost a cat like manner sometimes and they'd be there, eyes darting all over the place looking for their special boy then realise he was no longer with us and it was like "Ok, and there it is, and there we have it" and we'd look at each other and they knew I knew what had just happened and sometimes we'd half smile or nod and sometimes we'd give one another a hug. No words spoken, no need for words really, just a soft hug in silence and then we'd carry on with what we were doing. And it wasn't just friends who were affected by the fact that Horton was no longer here. People who'd only met him once seemed to be upset when they found out we'd lost him. One of the tradesmen who met Horton on a previous visit asked about him as soon as he walked in the door, and it was a good two years since he'd been at the house. He met Horton as a pup and said when he noticed the address on the job sheet that he was really looking forward to seeing him again, he said he'd often thought about him and wondered how he was getting on. I do remember this man taking a lot of notice of Horton and Horton taking a lot of notice of him. But Horton was like that when we had workmen here, he seemed totally captivated by them and what they were doing. He always followed David around when he was doing jobs on the weekends. I've got a lovely photo, the image of which has just shot into my head, it's of David fixing the bottom of the flywire door and Horton sitting next to him looking on. No doubt one of the pugs had been scratching and torn the flywire, it may well have been Horton himself who did it as he was one for pounding on the bottom of a door when he wanted out. I remember as David was fixing it he kept holding his tools near Horton's little face so he could have a sniff at them. Horton seemed to like being part of everything and the more he could be involved the happier he was. And ok his Daddy had time to hold up every tool and only take it away once it had been well and truly sniffed but the workmen we had here were on the clock so didn't have time for it, yet Horton followed them around all the same. If they were working inside Horton would shuffle along after them seeing what they were doing to his house and once a reminder to watch where they were putting their feet was given I knew I could allow him to do that without coming to any harm. But if the men were working outside then Horton would have to be satisfied with watching them from the windows or the glass sliding doors. When our water heater died David bought a new one and put it in place himself, but rules stated that you needed an authorized electrician to wire everything up, so a local guy was brought in to do the job. He turned up in a ute with a beautiful golden retriever sitting up front on the passenger side, I could see her through the window as they pulled up and as soon as he opened his door she flung herself across his knee and sprang onto the ground. She was only young I could tell that by the way she ran, fully grown but giddy and silly and galloping about in a very excitable manner, limbs flopping around all over the place. She looked a bit like a cartoon dog, where everything is exaggerated for comical effect. She crossed the front paddock in no time at all and then came racing back to tell us what she'd discovered. I could hear my pugs barking at her from the window, her antics were keeping them amused. He was going to tie her up to the side of his ute, but I said "Don't do that, she'll be fine running around" I think he was as happy about that as she was. The idea of tying a big bounding beautiful dog up for hours on end didn't sit right with me. I knew she couldn't get into the back paddock to chase the sheep and I was keeping all my dogs inside so I couldn't see any reason for her to be bound. I brought her out a bowl of water and she lapped at it then went hop, skipping and jumping round and round the front paddock and then she'd come back to check on her owner and fly off at full speed once again. She was having the most wonderful time and my pugs were having the most wonderful time running from window to window watching her. Her name was Poppy, and she was just over eighteen months old. I could see Horton inside the house running with his brother and sisters and every now and then when they quietened down I could hear him doing his puppy woofs. When I came inside Horton followed me into the kitchen but the others stayed where they could keep an eye on this strange dog, by this time Poppy had discovered that if she stood on the back veranda and peeped in through the glass she could see a pile of pugs circling and dancing and then flinging themselves at the glass close to her face, this seemed to startle her the first time they did it, which made the pugs want to do it more and more. But when she started doing it back it wasn't as much fun for them, so they stopped, and she stopped, and they all lay down looking at one another through the glass. I think they wanted her to always react as much as she did the first time they flung themselves at the door, it was funny to watch, in my mind I could see exactly what was about to happen, but it was even funnier seeing it for real. From the kitchen I could see her coming up the back ramp sniffing and investigating. No doubt she could smell that there were dogs living on the property. She paused by a flowerpot and was distracted sniffing that, she hadn't seen the pugs getting closer to the door, they weren't barking at this point, I did think that perhaps they were all barked out. But then they threw themselves at the glass and started barking like crazy, Poppy heard the slam and flew down the ramp, but only half way down and her tail was wagging madly, and when she realised they couldn't get out she started sneaking back up slowly. She'd woof and they'd woof, and she'd jump back and they'd feel powerful for making her do it so they'd fling themselves forward again and again until the novelty wore off. And it took quite a while for that to happen.

Horton moved from the kitchen into one of the dog beds, the one that faced the back door, he watched what everybody was doing for a little while and then settled down the sleep. The others came over and found themselves beds of their own, they were exhausted, Poppy and her antics had worn everyone out. And because there was no longer anybody staring back at her Poppy went and slept in the shade of the ute. Everything was quiet now, the electrician's dog slept, and my dogs slept and the only sound to be heard was him tinkering away at the side of the house. A part was needed that he swore blind was in the back of his ute but after opening and shutting multiple metal boxes twice he said he must have used it on the last job so called his office and got a young bloke to drive the part over while he came inside and had a cup of tea. It was then that he discovered Horton, he was aware of the pugs being at the doors and windows watching him, but he mustn't have looked too closely, not close enough to realise that one of the pugs had special needs. When he came up to the back door and pulled on the handle he found it was locked and I think he thought I was locking him out, the look on his face told me that he thought I was being rather rude. Then when he saw Horton I started explaining to him how strong this little pug was, strong enough to slide the door along and let himself out and he seemed amused by it but I'm not sure if he fully believed me or thought I was just making up an excuse for having the door locked. I told him that I reckoned Horton could take on a Great Dane in an arm wrestle and win hands down and he laughed at that. I said, "His front legs are very strong, he can open all the doors by propping himself on one leg and hard pushing with the other, so I have to keep my eye on him as he's quite the little escape artist". Again, the look on his face told me that he kind of believed me but kind of didn't. But a little while later he got to witness how strong Horton was for himself. He watched on as Horton scooted over to the door and slid it open a crack, not much, just enough for Poppy to stick her entire nose through, which is exactly what she did and the electrician shot up from his chair, pushed his dog's nose back, slid the door shut again and this time locked it himself, then he patted Horton on the head and walked back to the kitchen table with a huge grin on his face.

He was fascinated with Horton and wanted to know all about his condition and when he found out he said that it didn't seem to impair him at all. Horton sat in the middle of his bed woofing when the electrician came over for a better look and he allowed the large rough hand to stroke his head and when he stopped stroking and moved away Horton flew out of his bed and went and sat beside him because he had a new friend now and wanted to be near him. And besides he smelled like Poppy, so Horton and the other pugs took some long lingering sniffs of his legs and boots. When the part finally turned up there was a big chorus of barking and Poppy, recognising somebody she knew flew at the young bloke at full speed and he must have been used to her doing this because he braced himself for the impact while my lot looked on from the house. As big as she was she flew into this guy's arms, gave his face a few licks and set off again running round the paddock. When the electrician finished the job he came back inside and sat at the kitchen table while I wrote out a cheque. Horton once again scooted over and sat beside him, he asked if it would be ok to pick the little fella up, so I put my pen down and lifted Horton and settled him in a comfortable position on the electrician's knee and they spent some time together. I think he was looking forward to doing that again on this visit, but of course that couldn't happen.

David and I both lost our way a bit after losing Horton and it took us a long time to come back round again. I remember one morning a week after Horton died. I came out of the house to take the pugs for their morning walk. As we set off down the driveway I glanced across the paddock and saw David sitting on some sleepers a few feet away from Horton's freshly dug grave. He looked like an old, old man sitting there hunched over like that and yet he had not long turned forty. But I think his body was reflecting the week we'd just lived through, it was like it had aged him by decades. And the closer I got to him the older and more worn out he looked. He said he'd been unable to sleep so had come out early to spend some time with his son and of course Ruby and Grace's recently dug graves were nearby too so he was spending time with all of them. He looked so sad and so alone in that moment, and of course he was sad, and he was alone in that moment. None of the other pugs were with him, they were all with me. And it's very unusual to see either one of us without at least one or two pugs by our side. My heart went out to him. He had crept from the house, left the rest of us sleeping, because his broken heart prevented him from getting any rest. I would have liked to have known what his exact thoughts and feelings were as he sat there on his own like that. That's just how I am, I like to analyse everything, or over analyse everything as David often tells me. But that morning I decided not to ask, not to make him talk about it because some things are private, and he was allowed to have that moment alone beside his young son's grave without any interference from me. I was respectful of both my husband and his feelings. If he wanted to talk about it later on he would seek me out and I would be there for him. But I guess I already knew what he would have been feeling and what he would have been thinking about because those same thoughts were clinging to me daily as well. When me and the pugs finally reached him I sat down next to him, I didn't say anything, I just gave him a hug. The pugs had already smothered him with a good many kisses, they bounded ahead of me, so he was feeling well loved by the time I got there. I had watched them take off as soon as they became aware that David was there, when we first came out they hadn't seen him, being so close to the ground he wasn't as visible to them as he was to me, I'd glanced across the paddock and found him in no time. But the pugs just went about their business, sniffing the ground happily and weeing on one spot after another like they do on every walk. I knew once they saw him it would be different, and they didn't disappoint, they flew at him as fast as their little legs could carry them, it was nice to see them giving him that warm loving welcome, it was much needed today, oh the pugs didn't know that because they always gave him the same huge excitable welcome, but I knew it and I paused and watched as one by one they raced full speed towards Daddy and smothered him in love. I witnessed a blind pug sniffing the air as he drew near and saw Arthur's little curly corkscrew tail going ballistic when he finally got to his Dad. I watched them as they twirled and danced and begged to be picked up and when they reached his face they started snorting and snoting and licking and kissing and when they were put back down on the ground again so excited were they that they gave a giddy jig. There was nothing left for me to do but join in on the loving, they flew from David to me and back again so fast. I guess they are used to walking with me when David is at work, and I suppose that's where they thought he was when we'd first come outside. I can only imagine how they must have felt on stumbling across him, coming across somebody you love with all your heart when you are not expecting to see them is always a wonderful surprise. So, we sat there like that enjoying the moment, me and David not really talking that much just picking up and hugging one excitable pug after another and then once I felt Daddy had gotten his fill of loving and the pugs had all settled down to normal breathing again we moved on, carried on with our walk. As I neared the corner of the house I turned and saw David wasn't following us, he was still sitting there, once again alone with his thoughts. So I took the pugs inside and started getting their breakfast ready. It's what I normally do after their morning walk, and they know our routine well. The pugs were all happily chowing down when David finally came through the door, heads lifted from bowls for a few seconds, eyes looked across the room, faces acknowledged he was there and a tail or two wagged then they carried on eating until their bowls were clean. As I went round picking up the empty bowls I glanced over at Horton's little gravesite, at that point we didn't have anything marking the spot which I think made the grave look even more sad, but at the time I couldn't do anything about it, I was still trying to get through each day as best I could.

Today things are different, today Horton's grave has a lovely lion statue on it, but that statue was a long time coming, it took me quite a while to be in a place where I could put something on his grave. A lion was very much the right choice though because to me they signify bravery, courage, confidence and most of all strength and Horton was all these things and more. The day I went to buy a statue I had no idea what I was going to buy, I did have an angel in the back of my mind but that's about all. I figured a little chubby cheeked cherub would do just fine but then I started thinking that a chubby cheeked cherub had absolutely nothing at all to do with Horton. So now I had to look for something else, something that bore testament to everything he was and had been all throughout his life. We looked at a few garden centres nearer to home, but they all seemed to have the same old things, and nothing that really caught my eye and then I remembered passing a place on the way to visit David's brother some years ago, it was a bit of a distance from home and halfway there I began hoping that the place hadn't closed down. It was on a busy main street in a heavily built up area and I'd only gotten a quick glance at it as we'd sped by but there seemed to be a whole lot of different statues in there, the place was spread out over three or four house blocks and I remember thinking as we were driving along that if this place didn't have anything for us then I didn't know what we'd do. We pulled up outside the statue centre and I thought at the time how lucky we were to have found a car space right out front. I figured we would have had to park some distance up the road or down a side street, but as we were looking for the place a car pulled out in front of us, and David quickly slid our car into that spot. As I was getting out of the car a lion statue caught my eye, it was sitting right by the high mesh fence directly opposite my car door, although it was in amongst a pile of other statues it seemed to stand out to me, I really couldn't have not seen it if I tried. I walked over and had a closer look, and it was nice, but this place was huge, it had hundreds of statues for me to look at and I thought well I'll keep that lion in the back of my mind but I wanted to see everything else this place had to offer first. I wanted the statue that was going to be marking Horton's grave to be perfect, it had to be perfect it was too important to me not to be. So I dragged my poor husband round and round that place and he was getting rather bored by the end of it, he'd asked me if I wanted him to go pick up the lion statue when we first arrived. We'd both stood there together looking at it and he said if you like it I'd best grab it as soon as we get inside, I think he thought he'd carry it around with us while I looked about but I believe when we finally got back to the car he realised that such a thing would have been a mistake because the statue was made of pure concrete and I hadn't exactly been in a rush when looking. All that concrete was too heavy to be carrying around for any length of time. His arms would have been ready to drop off by the end of it. Dave said to me "But what if somebody else comes along and buys it while we are looking round" and I turned to him and said "Then it isn't meant to be ours" I think in a way I was expecting to be guided to something, which I believe I had been due to it being right there where we had parked the car and in hindsight I guess we could have been in and out of that place in a matter of seconds but if we'd done that I think for the rest of my days I would always be left wondering if there was something more fitting for Horton if I'd only spared the time to look. They had a few of that same statue scattered around, well the same mould just different colours, but the lion we bought had something special about it and I don't think it had anything to do with it being the first one I saw. I just had a very real feeling it was the one we were meant to have, I mean we could have parked somewhere else and if we had of done then I would never have seen this particular lion because once you got inside the place it was concealed from view, if you didn't know it was there you would have never seen it. David had to climb over countless statues of all sizes to get our lion and the sales assistant wasn't too impressed by that. I think she was worried that we were going to break something or that David would fall, she kept saying there were others exactly like it that were easier to get at, but I said that no they weren't exactly like it, and she looked at me as if I was nuts, I said it had to be the one by the fence, that was the only one I wanted. And David knowing what I am like just carried on trapesing in until he had it in his arms. Lucky I am married to a very patient man, he never said a word about what I'd put him through, even though I had dragged him round that statue place a good many times he never once complained about it. I think he knew how important this was to me. When we were paying David put the statue down right near two others that were from the same mould and our little lion simply shone, stood out from them very clearly even though the others were lighter in colour, and it was a bright sunny day. I just think that particular statue was special, and I can't say exactly why, but it was, and it still is today. And as soon as we placed the statue on Horton's grave I felt it was the most perfect thing to have gotten, I had a real peace about it. The lion is in a laying down position, his face is slightly tilted to one side and he's resting his head on his two front paws. I have gotten a lot of joy from looking at the statue whenever I walk by. I've stood at the window watching rain falling on it and felt contented, I've seen it shining in the midday sun and smiled. It has faded over the years, the colour became all patchy and uneven and I didn't like it looking shabby like that, so last year David painted it, not in the same shade it was because we couldn't match it perfectly so it's a shade lighter but still beautiful and I still smile whenever I see it because it reminds me so much of Horton and the courageous little package that he was.

Horton's lion has a flat base, it's part of the mould, it's like the lion is resting on a platform, we have had some heavy rains here, but Horton's lion has always stayed firmly in place which has not been the case with some of the other statues. The statues are heavy and after days of rain the ground gets pretty soft. One winter we had so much rain, just one downpour after another and it went on for days on end, some of the statues kept teetering a little and I would put my raincoat on and dash out and straighten them up. Then one afternoon after I'd just finished giving the pugs their dinner I noticed that Ruby's angel was face down in the mud. I meant to go out and fix it up right away, but it was raining so hard, I thought I'd nip out as soon as the rain stopped but it never stopped so I got busy with some inside jobs and it goes dark early in winter here, it was a cold night, so I drew the blinds and put some more logs on the fire to keep everybody warm. I hated seeing that angel face planted in the mud like that, I knew it was made of concrete and didn't have feelings but it just seemed like a very undignified thing for that little angel to be doing and I certainly didn't mean to leave her there like that for long, but one job got done and I soon found myself presented with another and David was due home soon so I began making dinner so he could have a nice warm meal waiting for him when he walked through the door. I dashed outside to the shed for more wood a few times, but Ruby's angel wasn't on my mind at the time. I stood at the back door waiting for a break in the rain and when it didn't come I ran to the shed loaded my arms with wood then ran back inside again as fast as I could. I made sure none of the pugs followed me out because I didn't want them getting wet, but each time I came inside I was sopping and left a trail of water from the back door to the fire. Mopping up the water and cooking and keeping the house warm was what my mind was full of so I didn't remember about the fallen angel until about eleven o'clock that night, and because I'd been busy I couldn't recall if I'd asked David to go pick her up when he came home from work or not. We'd been in bed for about half an hour, and I was doing my settling down to sleep thinking thing that I do every night, I like to run through my day, going over all that has gone on and only then do I find I can settle down to sleep. All of a sudden I remembered about the angel so shot out of bed, grabbed my torch and shone it through the window and yep sure enough there was the poor little thing still splatted in the mud only she now looked wetter and sadder than she'd looked when I first spotted her all those hours ago. I didn't want her left there all night. During the day was bad enough, in daylight she had looked like the most wretched little thing laying there like that but thinking of her doing the same thing in pitch blackness made it all the sadder for me, from my position by the window I was telling David all this. The house was in total darkness so I couldn't see his face but God bless him he didn't tell me off for not reminding him when he'd first gotten home. No instead my wonderful husband got an enormous flashlight, put his raincoat and boots on and trudged out there to fix Ruby's grave up and I stood peeping through the blinds at him with the pugs all snoring softly in the background. That ground truly was soft because he kept picking the angel up and positioning it and it just flopped right back over again as soon as he took his hands away. I went outside, stood on the deck shouting down to him, asking if he wanted me to go look in the shed for a large flat piece of wood to use as a base. I figured if the angel had something flat to sit on she would be able to stay in place. I couldn't hear what he said with the sound of heavy rain pelting down on the roof, but he held up a bit of wood in the air, clearly he'd thought about the wood the exact same time I had done and shot round to get some, that's why I'd had trouble seeing him when I first got out there, I thought it was the rain and the darkness that concealed him from me but it wasn't, it was because he wasn't even out there at the time and I was shouting over to nobody in the distance. So, the wood was slid underneath the angel and David came back inside looking like a sewer rat mumbling something under his breath about it being lucky that I didn't remember about Ruby's angel at two in the morning.

About a year after Horton died I was looking round a store, not really wanting to buy anything, I'd only gone in there to kill some time while waiting for an appointment. I saw some ornaments in the gardening section of the store so wandered over for a closer look. My eyes were glancing over a pile of not very nice ornaments, and I was just about to turn and walk away when I spotted something that made me stop dead in my tracks. It was a little cement dragon, instantly my heart skipped a beat and leapt for joy all at the same time. Now this dragon had nothing to do with Horton at all except that its back legs and feet were curled up in the exact same position Horton's did whenever he was fast asleep. It was like an instant shot of elation had been injected into my system. I was once again looking down at Horton's legs and feet and I hadn't seen those little feet of his for such a long time. I picked up the dragon and held it to my heart, it wasn't a fierce dragon, just a sweet little baby dragon curled up sleeping with a very peaceful look on his face. I studied it closely, yes those back legs and feet were held exactly the same way Horton used to hold his feet and legs, exact same curl, exact same position, the feet especially were the splitting image of his. I held the baby dragon to my heart for a few moments longer soaking the happiness in and then I couldn't get to that cash register fast enough. When I showed David my find he smiled. I didn't even have to point the feet out to him, the look on his face let me know that he'd seen the resemblance too. If the dragon had been facing a different way I would have simply walked off without knowing it had feet like my son. It looked like somebody had picked it up then carelessly placed it down again facing the wrong way round, well it was the wrong way round for everybody else to be looking at it, but it was the right way round for me. And it was the only ornament like it in the entire store. I felt very blessed to have come across it. For about half a second I did think about putting it outside on Horton's grave because it too would have been fitting, I mean dragons are just as brave and fearless as lions are aren't they. But whereas a lion symbolized Horton this little dragon looked exactly like him, not the face or body, just the back legs and feet but that was enough for me, I knew I couldn't ever leave it sitting outside getting cold and being rained on, no it was far too precious to me for that. This little concrete gem was going to be well looked after just like the one who had the same little feet had been well looked after, so I painted it and sat it on our marble coffee table, and I still smile today and am filled with such tenderness and warmth every time I look at it. I see it as a gift because I may have forgotten exactly how those feet were over time, of course I have photographs, but they are not the same as having a statue and this statue looks like it could have been cast from a mould of Horton's feet and that makes it all the more special. From time to time, I run my finger over those little feet and feel very happy doing it. I open the blinds each morning, see the lion and I remember Horton's strength, bravery and determination then I turn round and there is my sleeping baby dragon with its little Horton feet and those little feet make me smile. Then again all memories of Horton make me smile these days. Sure, it wasn't always the case but these days it is and it's a nice place to be in.

It took me quite a while to pack away Horton's pram and Tinkle Trousers. They sat in the corner of the lounge for the longest time. I knew I didn't need them anymore, but I couldn't bring myself to pack them up. I guess I was holding on to everything of his and to not have them in view was like losing another part of him and I couldn't bear that. Sometimes I was sad when I looked over at the corner, but I knew I would be sadder still if they were no longer there. I'd already lost Horton, having them out of sight too was more than I could handle at the time. During the day I'd sometimes go over and hold Horton's Tinkle Trousers, hug them to my chest, and I'd touch his pram, touch where Horton used to be, where he used to sit. I was doing all I could to be close to him. And, of course, there were days when I had to walk past them real fast and not look down. Every day was different. No two were exactly the same and I just took each one as it came because that's all you can do really. In the end David had to pack Horton's things away for me and I couldn't be in the room when he did it. From memory, Horton's pram and Tinkle Trousers sat in the lounge for about six months. It wasn't as if I needed them to be left there to remind me of Horton because he was on my mind all the time, but everything I put away of his was like removing another trace of him ever existing and soon there would be no sign of him ever having been in our home. I had Horton's photo in frames all over the house, but they weren't something I could touch and hold, you know, physically hold, that were part of him, something he wore or played with or rode in, something that smelt like him. Then it got to a point where I knew I would be all right if they were no longer in view. I didn't want to give them away, I wanted to keep them forever, but I knew I would be okay with them being in another room. Besides, we had taken in a new pug with limited vision, and she kept walking into the side of Horton's pram. I didn't want her injuring her little black eyes on the knobs or brake pedal. That wouldn't have been at all fair to Amber so I asked David to pack them up while I was busy doing something else. To watch them being packed away would have been hard on me, but to walk into the room and have them no longer there was something I thought I could cope with. But I was wrong. It took me a few days to stop looking for them. They are stored now in our walk-in wardrobe, ready and waiting should one of our future pugs need them. The swimming pool we bought for Horton, the one he never got to use, was never packed away, his siblings used it the very next summer and are still using it now, each summer it's brought out and a pile of little old pugs get gently lowered in by David or myself and they splash about and get wet and cool down and their faces change, and they are happy. And I stand watching them and laughing at them and yes, thinking about Horton because it was his pool, but I don't reflect on him with sadness when the pool comes out, how could I when seeing the joy it brings to my elderly blessings. And Horton was not a selfish pug, he was a good sharer, I think he would be happy that they are all using the pool now and that the summer months are more bearable for all of them because of it.

Even today there are constant reminders of Horton all around the farm. I think about him every time I see a dragonfly flying through the air, Horton loved Dragonflies, he was fascinated by them, well once he got used to them he was anyway, the first time one flew at his head he ducked but after that he loved watching them and woofing at them. After he died for weeks and weeks whenever we were out walking the pugs one or two dragonfly's kept flying around our heads, following us as we walked, it was the most amazing thing and we felt it was a sign from him. I occasionally think about pushing Horton round the farm in his pram and I do miss doing that, miss watching his reaction to things. I remember him being with me when I was out collecting sticks for the fire, he'd be pouncing on dry leaves amusing himself. No matter what I was doing around the place Horton would be there making a game out of it and I loved watching him do it. He would chew on the odd stick, clamp down on it and gnaw like mad and all the while he would have his eyes on me, watching what I was doing in case I found something of interest, and if he thought I had he'd quickly spit the stick out and shuffle over to get a better look. Horton played like a puppy his entire life and I liked that about him because I think he would have enjoyed life more because of having such an attitude. But out of everything around the farm and everyone living on it Gerald reminds me of Horton the most and that's not because they were similar looking but more due to the special bond they shared and how much they loved one another. When I see Gerald out there in the paddock I think about David lifting Horton up so he could give him a kiss on the nose. I think about Horton racing to the fence and woofing for Gerald to come over. I think about Gerald leaning down and wrapping his tongue around Hortons little chin. And although he's no longer here and no longer joining in on them David's homecomings remind me a lot of Horton because I can still picture my husband coming through the door of an evening and picking Horton up because he didn't want him to get knocked about in the stampede. But Horton wasn't bothered, he was there jumping up, well jumping as much his little body allowed him to jump, he jumped with his front paws only and they'd get a fair distance off the ground as well. I can clearly see this image now of Horton doing his special jump and David bending down and scooping him up into his arms. Then Horton would give what seemed like a million kisses before finally settling down enough to go back on the ground, then it was time for everybody else to have a turn. Horton knew this so he'd come over to me so I could pick him up and together we'd watch the others getting their hugs. Sometimes if I was talking to David, telling him something about my day, I'd be concentrating on what I was saying and not realise Horton was there at my feet, at those time he became rather impatient and started to crawl up my leg, much like a kitten on a flywire door. He could get pretty high if I let him, his front legs were so strong and so powerful, he'd elevate himself higher by gripping onto the top of my boots, he would have hurt himself if he'd fallen backwards so whenever I felt him there I'd stop talking, pick him up and continue with whatever I was saying, usually with Horton kissing the side of my face as I spoke. He loved being up close to either one of us and he liked being up high because he could see everything that was going on from there. The Daddy homecoming is a lovely thing to witness, it was back then with Horton and it's still just as lovely for me watching it today. The pugs start getting excited as soon as they hear his car turning into the driveway and we have a long driveway, so from the time Dad pulls up to the gate until he walks through the door must seem like an eternity to the pugs and a huge frenzy starts building. And to tell you the truth I couldn't get in front of them if I tried, they wouldn't let me, they are too excited, so I have learnt to watch on and wait my turn. I know he's only been missing for a day but the pugs act like he's been gone for a week and then the next night they are there giving the exact same excitable greeting. And David loves it as much as they do.

When I am running my errands I think about when I used to take Horton out with me and the people we used to meet. There is a bench by a shop that I walk by often and I sometimes recall sitting there with Horton. I like old people's faces, women's faces in particular because they seem softer than men's, men can be more guarded and so to me their faces appear harder, it's like they've lived a lifetime putting up walls, but women's faces seem to reveal all. The lines, the wrinkles all tell a story, a journey, the life they've lived. I think you can tell a lot about a person by the lines on their faces. You can spot a life-long worrier a mile away, deep thinkers have faces that I recognise instantly and warm to because I'm one of those myself. And it's easy to spot a laugher, the folk who've not taken life too seriously. Those lines are deeply engrained, very well earned, like they've had a fantastic time getting them. Mischievous people I think have the best faces of all, doesn't matter if it's a man or a woman if they are mischievous it's evident with one quick glance. They seem to have the ability to appear childlike, well you look at them and it's easy to see how they would have looked as children because a lot of that is still there, they've kept that youthfulness, that cheeky spirit. It's not only in the lines but the eyes as well and no matter how old the face gets the eyes remain the same. You can be five or eighty-five but if you've been blessed with mischief your eyes don't let you down they are there twinkling, sparkling away, always on the lookout for the next bit of fun and they give themselves away to a stranger in an instant. Boring people, glass half empty people have the worst faces of all, they can be incredibly pleasant looking, good for their ages even, but their faces are uninteresting to me, their expressions blank, there's nothing there, so those folks are the ones I'll try to avoid. Horton had a fascination with people's faces too. I saw this in him quite early on. He seemed to study them, not just glance over, but actually spend time taking their features in and I thought he was really cute doing it, intelligent too. I would have given anything to know what he was thinking while looking at them but of course that was something I'd never fully know, I would try and gage his thoughts from his expressions, I'd watch on as his eyes moved over people's faces, lingering a bit and then moving on to another part, he was really human like in the way he did this and if the person he was studying actually looked down and spoke to him, well he'd go nuts in my arms, he loved being spoken to by everyone.

One particular day stands out in my mind. I didn't have Horton's pram with me that day I was carrying him instead. It was a cold day and what I had hoped was going to be a quick trip out, so I'd wrapped him in a blanket and left the pram at home. My sister decided to go look in another shop and I'd already had my fill so decided to sit this one out. I'm always in a rush to get back to the pugs so more often than not I dash in and out, get what I need and then leave, or in other words I shop like a man which pleases my husband no end. But my sister, well she's a real shopper, likes to pick everything up and ooh and aah at it and in knowing that she would be a lot longer than I would have liked her to be I looked around for somewhere for me and Horton to park ourselves while we waited. Horton was getting heavy, I'd been carrying him for some time, I needed to rest my arms and while they were resting I thought it'd be nice for Horton to have a look around, I chose a seat with the best view of the street for Horton because I knew how much he enjoyed looking at things, he was a little observer and I knew the goings on in the street that day would be of great interest to him. I'd been sitting for only a few moments when I heard footsteps approaching, from the shuffling sound I figured they belonged to a much older person than the one who eventually sat down next to us. She sighed as she lowered herself into the seat and I figured she'd be making a similar sound when she got up, I've found in life that people who sigh when they sit down generally sigh twice as hard when they get up. Horton and I looked over at her at precisely the same time, she smiled down at him but completely ignored me. And that was fine, living in the country isn't all about scones, cups of tea and long conversations, not everybody moves out here for the country spirit, some people come because they want to get away from everything and that includes people and in figuring she was one of those types I respected her for it and didn't try and strike up a conversation like I would normally do with somebody who'd come to sit alongside me. Maybe she wasn't here for a chat after all maybe she was merely tired and wanted to rest her legs. I didn't even say hello. In the small glance I took of her I noticed she was slightly turning her body away from me, like one does when being made to sit next to somebody they don't really like. I'm big on body language, I think because I spend a lot of time observing my animals for signs of them being unwell or any changes in their bodies that I automatically do the same thing with humans without even realising I'm doing it, either way I could read this lady like a book and decided that I would let her sit and enjoy her silence. Horton though had other ideas, he had his eyes on the street a lot of the time because that's what was capturing his interest the most but every now and then he would look at the lady beside us and give her a little woof. I thought it was sweet that he was trying to engage her, I'd not seen him make such an effort with somebody who didn't want to talk to him before. This went on for a little while with the lady not taking an ounce of notice of him, me I would have definitely given up, decided that it was this persons loss for not wanting to get to know us, but Horton wasn't giving up so easily. I had long lost interest in the idea of talking to this lady, all my attention was on Horton, watching him watching the street, seeing what he was woofing at, and a lot of the time was spent trying to make him more comfortable on my knee. Because he was bouncing around a lot I figured his legs may have needed repositioning. I lifted him out of the blanket, rearranged it, then put him back down and wrapped him up again, the whole time I was doing this Horton was not looking at me he was more fascinated with the woman next to us. I was now aware that she was watching what I was doing, sort of sneaking a look, head not fully facing us more looking on from one side, a thing I felt she had probably been doing for a very long time because she was quite good at it, the fact that she was watching Horton didn't surprise me. I kind of expected it because Horton had a way of drawing people in, even when he is wrapped in a blanket and his legs are not visible he just seemed to draw people to him with his expressive little face. When I finally had him sorted I turned and looked closer at the lady, she was now turned a bit more towards us, like we had suddenly become of great interest to her. Being able to see a little more of her features I realised that this lady had suffered a stroke and the effects of it were written clearly on her face. One side, the side nearest to us, was perfect but the other side was bunched up, very noticeable, very obvious that something had gone on. I now realised this was the real reason she had turned her body away from me when she'd sat down. She was concealing herself. I was trying to think of something to say to her but then she quickly spoke to me. "You sure do love that little dog of yours don't you" it wasn't a question, more an observation but I answered her anyway, I mean this was the first time she'd spoken to me the last thing I was going to do was ignore her. "With all my heart" I said smiling over at her. She then started talking a bit more, we spoke about the weather first, then she began talking about Horton, she said it was a good idea keeping the little fella wrapped up on such a cold day. I explained to her about his spine and how that affected his legs, told her his story and in turn she told me about her dogs. She didn't have them with her so I could only assume they'd died, I didn't ask though, I figured if she wanted me to know I'd find out soon enough. The whole time we were talking this lady never fully faced me and it did make me feel kind of sad that she felt she had to hide. But I guess people can be cruel and even if they don't mean to be their reactions tend to give their thoughts away and perhaps she'd had enough of dealing with those kinds of looks. I don't think Horton gave much thought to why this lady wasn't fully facing us, he was pretty fascinated with what was going on in the street, he wasn't scared, just sat on my knee watching everything from the warmth of his cocoon. Every now and then he'd glance up at the woman's face like he was actually listening to her talk, like he understood what she was saying. I spent a lot of time talking to Horton and I feel if you do this they begin to take on an almost human like interest in people's conversations, they get to understand human language more so then if we are always speaking to them with doggy terms.

We had been talking for quite a while and the street was becoming windy, I pulled the blanket up closer to Hortons's face trying to shield his eyes from the wind, I didn't want grit from the street getting into them. When I did this he snuggled in closer to me which gave him a better view of the lady next to us, all of a sudden the wind rose up again and swept her hair across her face and in trying to sort that out she let her guard down and faced both of us full on. I carried on talking, never reacted, never let my side of the conversation skip a beat and when I did this she smiled, our eyes met and I noticed just how beautiful they were, not in colour although that was nice too but more in warmth, there seemed to be something really special there, like she was the most wonderful kindhearted soul and this shone out through her eyes. Horton was once again back to concentrating on the street, he hadn't noticed the lady next to him had changed position and now sat more relaxed. Her whole body had shifted round to face me, and we were now having a proper conversation. And I was so deep in that conversation I forgot that Horton hadn't seen her entire face yet, suddenly he turned round, the lady had laughed, and I guess that was what made him look up at her. Horton liked laughter a lot. There's something comforting about the sound of laugher, I've always found that, and I suppose that's one of the reasons why Horton liked it so much. We couldn't laugh in the house without him wanting to know what we were laughing at, it was usually about him so that was fine but when it wasn't, and he heard me and David laughing in the distance he would come scooting over fast to see what was so funny and sit there bouncing up and down on his nappy while listening to the laughter. Maybe he associated laughing with joy or maybe he just liked the sound of people being happy. Either way he was drawn, his little head spun around, now his eyes lay solely on this woman. I knew he would soon notice that one side was somewhat different to the other. I kept on talking but I was also keeping a close eye on Horton waiting to see if he would have a reaction. And he did, he seemed to pause, sit there for a few moments staring at her, his huge glossy eyes searching her face, moving all over it, from her eyes to her mouth, he took all her features in and then he did something I'd never seen him do before, he leaned slightly closer to her, stared her firmly in the eye and gave a series of little woofs with the last one turning into a long slow howl. It was really unusual for him to do that, he'd answer me and David with a woof sometimes and he'd howl sometimes as well but never quite like this. She reached up again to move some more hair from her face and Horton's eyes followed her hand. If he knew she was a bit different he didn't seem to mind because his eyes didn't linger on the right side of her face, they just brushed over it, like he'd made note of it but decided it was nothing to bother about. After that he went back to looking up and down the street. Honking horns and people walking by drew his attention away for a little while but he always came back to the lady and what she was saying. He woofed at her again once or twice and I still don't know why he did it or what he meant by it, and I think the fact that he did the leaning in thing made it all the more unusual, but he'd lean over, come slightly out of his warm cocoon look her directly in the eye and woof, he actually reminded me of a cuckoo clock the way he did it. Then once he'd woofed at her he'd go back deeper into his cocoon and back to gazing at the street again.

 A boy on a bike stopped and said, "That's a cute puppy you've got there" and I said "Yes he is". A lady who was in the shop Horton and I had recently come out of came over and said how nice she thought it was of me to make sure he was kept warm on such a cold day and before I could say anything our new friend started telling this lady all about Horton, his entire life story. And she got it right as well, practically repeated word for word how I'd told it to her, but I noticed that she sat side on to the lady as she said it, she was once again back to shielding herself. Horton loved getting all this attention, but he was also bothered because the lady standing in front of us was blocking his view of the road. He kept leaning sideways trying to see round her, I made sure I had a good grip on him so he didn't fall. Our new friend picked up on what was going on and made mention of it to the lady. Mentioned it in a more abrupt way than I would have said it, but I think by this time she was in love with Horton and didn't like him having a view that was bringing him so much joy stolen from him. The lady in front of us must have felt uncomfortable, she said she was in a hurry then quickly scurried off and Horton was once again happy sitting watching the view. I thought it was nice that she was looking out for him, sure it was only a view being blocked but she wanted the puppy to be able to see the road, that's what she had told the other lady and she seemed proud of herself for sending her on her way. This lady and I carried on talking, by this time she was treating me like a trusted friend, so she talked, I listened, and all the while Horton's eyes kept going from the road to the lady and back again. When she laughed, a thing I noticed she was now doing a lot of since letting her guard down, Horton's little head would shoot round to see what she was laughing at. I was glad Horton gave this lady some of his attention, she deserved it because she just seemed to love him so much, she kept stroking his head. When she first started doing it he turned and looked up at her every single time but after a while he got used to the hand constantly reaching out to caress him, in the end he didn't even take his eyes off the road, just leaned into the stroking hand and tried to position his head so she was actually rubbing his ears. Horton was happy and I was happy, we sat there in the middle of the street on a cold winter's day him wrapped in a blanket, me with thick coat on, listening to what this lovely person had to say. And she wasn't miserable or wanting people to feel sorry for her, she was happy and funny, and it was nice spending some time in her company.

At one point she paused, looked out into the street and said "Will you get a load of that" my eyes instantly began searching for what it was that I was actually meant to be getting a load of. I looked over at her for guidance, for a clue, to see if I could tell by her gaze what it was she thought was worth our attention but by that time she was already looking down at Horton and patting him again, so I was left with looking up and down the street. My eyes first fell on a man smoking a cigarette while looking in the butcher shop window, middle aged, average height and build, no nothing special about somebody trying to decide if they wanted a chop or a steak for dinner so my eyes left him and went looking for something else. There were a few kids on bikes riding up and down, a group of older ladies stood talking by the entrance of the bakery, a man in an expensive suit paused on the edge of the curb as if not knowing which way to go, further up the street an elderly couple walked together hand in hand and I smiled when I saw them because it always warms my heart when I see things like that, to know that a couple have been able to spend a long time loving one another is very special. A lace curtain began blowing out of a window on the second story of the bakery. I hadn't noticed it before so either the window had just recently been opened or the wind had just this moment reached in and dragged the curtain out, either way I sat enjoying the view. I've always liked seeing things blowing in the wind and this lace curtain was a very pretty one, meant to be white but yellowing a bit which made its pattern stand out all the more, it reminded me of days gone by. I like to be reminded of such things. And if my new friend did too then maybe this was what she wanted me to look at, her face told me otherwise, so my searching continued. Up the street in the opposite direction a few mothers with prams were walking along, one talked on a mobile phone as she pushed, another tried to hold onto a wayward toddler with one hand as she steered the pram with the other. None of these things seemed worth drawing someone's attention to. Sure, the man in the expensive suit looked slightly out of place in this country town but there were always visitors coming through the area for one reason or another. Again, I looked back at my new friend trying to figure out what she would have found fascinating, I mean if the scene in front of you isn't giving up any answers then you have to start looking more closely at the source. But I hadn't known her long enough to know where her interests lay, if I was sitting there with David or an old friend there wouldn't have even been a need for words, one look would say it all, but there were no such familiarities for me here. I glanced up and down the street again, seeing if there was somebody or something I had missed. Maybe somebody new had appeared on the street, somebody she had seen through a shop window who was now out and about carrying a heap of bags, I looked up half expecting for that person to be my own sister because she had been in that shop long enough to have filled a dozen bags by now. Or had she skipped out of that one shop and quickly shot into another one on seeing me happily talking to a stranger. Feeling I had got it right I turned to the lady and said "You mean the herd" she laughed heartily at my terminology. Our eyes were both now resting on the group of older ladies. "You know them do you" I asked expecting that she did, she didn't talk but nodded her head in response. "Which one do you think is the boss" she asked. I looked over paying a bit more attention now, there was one who was really tall and loud, hands gesturing all over the place, black pants and a bright floral top, holding court she was and not letting the others get a word in, next to her were two average looking ladies, no fuss ladies, casually dressed, figured them to be farmers wives at one time, there was also a little lady standing to the side quietly, much smaller in statue to the others, next to her was a lady with a poodle type perm, home job, badly done, I know that because I had a similar perm in the 80's, worse hair mistake of my life and I couldn't wait for it to grow out. Next to bad poodle perm was another lady wearing a tracksuit, her long grey hair pulled back in a ponytail. I watched on for a few moments longer before giving my answer, sort of sizing them up, trying as best I could from this distance to get a feel for them. "The little one is" I said and then once again moved Horton into a more comfortable position. In a shocked voice she said "How the heck did you figure that out in such a short amount of time" she said it'd taken her a few weeks to figure it out for herself and she'd been sitting in amongst them while doing it. I said it was easy, again I meant body language but didn't tell her that otherwise due to my honesty I may have blurted out that it was the same way I'd figured out that she wanted absolutely nothing at all to do with Horton and me when she'd first sat down. In my observation I had noticed that the other ladies were facing slightly more in the little one's direction and that their eyes kept glancing over at her every now and then for approval. She said that she felt sure I was going to say the tall one in the floral top, and I said "No". To me she was the least secure of them all because she was seeking approval from the little one the most. She went on to tell me a bit more about these ladies, they lived in the same block of units as she did, she didn't have to tell me the units she meant because at that time we only had one set and they'd knocked down an old store to make room for them. I was sad about that because I liked the old store a lot, not for what it sold but the details in its features. Old buildings have so much character, souls, and I thought it was a real shame that it was no long standing there in all its beauty for me to look at whenever I went into town. She said life in the block of units was not as nice as it could have been due to the old ladies and their little clique, a clique I could only assume the lady sitting next to me was not part of. I looked over at the ladies again and saw the years being stripped away, it was like they were now a bunch of teenage girls cruelly rejecting anybody who didn't quite fit in. You'd think they'd have learnt some lessons along the way, but I guess they had raised their families, lost their husbands, sold their homes and were now back to having nothing better to do with their time then form a clique and make a deserving soul feel inferior. It said more about them then it did about the lady stroking Horton's little ears. She said she was better off without them, happier keeping to herself and spending time with her dogs. I was glad that her dogs were still with her. I told her that her dogs would be much better company as far as I was concerned. She nodded her head again then looked at her watch, muttered something about medication, said it was nice meeting us and I am a 100% sure that by "Us" she meant "Just Horton". Then with a big groan she was up on her feet again shuffling off in the direction that she came. The clique of elderly teenagers barely gave her a second look by the way, even though she was in clear view of them. Horton and I saw her several times after that, either she'd wait on the seat for us, or we'd wait for her and it was always nice having a chat. Then one day she wasn't there, and she never showed up again, I figured she'd either died or that the cliquey herd of elderly teenagers had finally become too much for her so she'd sold her unit and moved on. Either way I had a silent wish whenever I walked by the empty seat, that wherever she was and whatever she was doing that she was happy. Even today whenever I walk by that seat I still think of her and still offer up that same silent wish.

Another story that wasn't in The Joy of Horton involved chicken nuggets and a stretch limousine. I can't believe I didn't put this tale in Horton's book because whenever I think about it it always makes me chuckle. David used to travel overseas with his job, did it quite a lot at one time but once Horton entered our lives he didn't want to be away from him for too long so started suggesting other people in the office to go instead of him. When David was away he would ring home to see how we all were and of course if I answered the phone he figured I was alive and well so got on to the real reason he'd rung, Horton, he always asked how Horton was first because he was our most needy pug and once he had the answer to that question he'd go down the list of everybody else. He missed Horton a lot, missed all the others too, especially Ruby, but Horton must have been on his mind a lot of the time he was away. David loved hearing Horton's little puppy woofs and so I would try and get Horton to bark down the phone, I figured if it was me who was away then hearing my little boy woofing would make all that time sitting in a lonely hotel room a tiny bit more bearable. But Horton wouldn't do it, no matter what I did he just stared at me with those big glossy eyes of his and didn't say a word. He was giddy, he was happy, and he was excited because I was talking to him, but none of that used to make Horton bark. He just wasn't the type of dog to bark over nothing, there had to be something interesting going on for him to have a woof and a phone being held in front of his face and his Mummy's high pitched encouraging voice simply wasn't doing it for him, he looked at me like I was a complete idiot at times, and he'd lean closer and give the phone a good sniffing at but that was about it. Still David got to hear Horton sniffing and he laughed at that. I got a few of the other pugs to bark down the phone by doing things I knew they liked to bark at, and David was happy to hear them all. I think it made being away from his family that little bit easier to handle. I pictured him in hotel rooms, on planes and in conference meetings wondering what we were all getting up to on the farm. If I was in his shoes I wouldn't be able to concentrate on what I was doing, such would be my longing to be back where I belong.

David's company has always been very good when sending him overseas, they look after him pretty well and me too should I have ever needed their help while he was traveling the globe. I never once did but I knew they were only a phone call away should I have needed something. They always sent a driver to pick him up and take him to the airport and of course the same company would have a driver waiting to bring him home again. They even came all the way out to the farm to pick him up and David's company covered the bill. The pugs and I would stand and wave David off and I reckon he wouldn't have even turned onto the main road before we all started missing him. He had a few different drivers over the years, and they were all very nice people, always on time regardless of how late or early the hour and always helped him with his luggage while he went around picking up pug after pug giving them one last hug and one last goodbye before getting in the car. He got one particular driver quite often so they were on a first name basis, got to know one another quite well, he would leave the partition down and chat all the way to the airport whereas some of them would keep the window up not bothering to talk at all which can make a long drive seem even longer. He was a short round faced happy guy with glasses and took off with the suitcases at high speed then sat in the car waiting patiently while David said his goodbyes. He always wore a suit and tie and a chauffeur's cap, it all seemed like a very posh set up to me, way too posh for us simple farm folk that's for sure. One day we were waiting by the gate and down our long country road came this stretch limousine. It was a cold day, so Dave had said goodbye to the pugs at the house and left them in the warmth while we went and stood out on the street waiting for his ride. David and I started joking about it being his car and we were having a good old laugh about it until the stretch limousine slowed down and turned into our driveway. I said to David "No, this has to be a mistake", but the guy got out and said, "Mr. David Comer" and sure enough the limousine was for him. Well, we just didn't know where to look, so much for living in the country and being inconspicuous. It was broad daylight too, not even a night-time pick up where we would have been more hidden. And to make matters even worse the driver accidently leant on the horn as he was getting out of the car. In that moment I wished the earth beneath our feet would have parted and swallowed me, David, the driver and the limousine up in one enormous gulp. I don't like attention being drawn to me, I much prefer to fade into the background and a stretch limousine at the front gate isn't exactly fading into the background. And with the size of the thing, we couldn't have hidden if we tried, if we'd known there was a stretch limousine coming for David we would have had the front gate wide open so it could have come up the driveway and been hidden by all the trees. Then David could have jumped in fast and sped off making it look like the limousine had merely come up the wrong driveway and on realising the mistake instantly turned round and taken off again, but no, here was this long shinny white limousine stretched out for everybody to see and a few of the neighbours came out for a closer look. I don't know whether they saw it going by their front windows or actually heard the horn being leant on, but I glanced around and there they were staring at the car. I didn't even wave to them like I would normally do. I just wanted to pretend this wasn't happening. I think they thought we had some big celebrity coming for a farm visit and wanted to know who we knew from the world of showbiz. I think they were very disappointed when nobody interesting got out and only their long-time neighbour David ended up getting in. I guess if you are expecting a huge celebrity then your shy slightly geeky and slightly boring neighbour can be a real let down. David said it was just as funny at the other end too, he said when they pulled up a lot of heads turned and a few young people even held up their mobile phones to capture whoever it was that was about to get out of this big, beautiful car, he said he's never seen mobile phones lowered at such a speed in all his life. Some did give him a good looking over trying to figure out if they recognised him or not. And when they didn't, they seemed rather annoyed by the fact. I said to him that if there was a Star Trek convention in town he could have gotten away with being Brent Spiner and maybe even signed a few autographs because a lot of people have told him over the years that he resembles Brent and at first we laughed about it, but I have since looked at him on certain angles and yes I can certainly see what they mean. Take his glasses off, paint his face gold and he could easily pass for the android Lieutenant Commander Data.

 On the way home from that trip, we were both relived that there was a normal car waiting for David at the airport and his normal happy talkative driver too. Dave rang me and said he wanted to get the pugs some chicken nuggets on the way home. This trip had been the longest Dave had been away from us and he wanted to get something special for the pugs as a little treat because they had been without him for so long. That was another reason we were glad a stretch limousine hadn't been sent to bring him home, imagine all the fuss it would have caused at the drive through. When David asked the driver to pull in for some nuggets he just laughed and shouted "No worries" over his shoulder. Because the driver knew us he didn't even have to ask who they were for. It was winter and a cold night but David asked if I'd bring Horton out first so he could have a snuggle with him and give him a nugget before doing the same thing with everyone else. I was a bit reluctant due to the weather but decided it would do both David and Horton the world of good to spend a few moments alone after so long apart. And the other pugs were all sleeping when I wrapped Horton up in a thick blanket and tiptoed from the house, so I didn't feel guilty about leaving them behind. I slid the back door open very quietly so nobody would be disturbed. A few saw me going out, but none got up to follow, they were warm by the fire so were pretty much contented to stay there. Plus, it was way past their normal bedtime so they were quite sleepy. It's always hard to get them to go outside for a toilet break in the middle of winter. They probably just thought I was taking Horton out for a quick wee and were relived I hadn't asked them to come along. Of course, he wore a nappy so didn't need to be taken outside for a wee but I don't think that thought even entered their minds when they saw us creeping out the door. Dave asked the driver to drop him off at the front gate and he would walk the rest of the way up with his luggage, but the driver wouldn't hear of it. He said he'd bring him up to the house which was a nice thing for him to do because the top of our driveway takes a bit of getting out of when you are not used to it and in the dark it's even harder, lots of reversing and mucking about if you are sticking to the path, which in the middle of winter you always try and do so you don't get bogged in the mud. The driver knew all this and yet he still brought Dave all the way up. I don't know if it was because he was looking after his passenger or if he just wanted to see a pile of pugs eating chicken nuggets. I stood in the carport with Horton because it was warmer in there and also so he could see everything that was going on, the porch light was on as was the shed light, so the top of the driveway was as well-lit as you are going to get it. Dave leapt from the car as soon as it pulled up and took Horton out of my arms. And Horton was very ready to go, he had been doing his little woofs as the car came up the driveway and when it stopped he waited to see who was going to get out and when he saw his Dad, well he just couldn't contain himself, he started doing his little dolphin type noises and bouncing about in the blanket. The driver unloaded the suitcases then came over to watch Horton eating his nugget. I guess David had told him that the little paraplegic one was going to be brought outside to get his treat first. He seemed to be enjoying watching Horton eat, chicken nuggets are given as a treat, they are not for every day eating so the pugs really go nuts for them. Normally I would have brought the nuggets inside to feed the other pugs but the driver was so happy witnessing the event that I went and let the barking blessings out so he could see them all enjoying themselves. "Can I have a go" he asked, so David handed the rest of chicken nuggets over to the driver and he bent down and fed the pugs and had the biggest smile on his face while he was doing it. We then all waited around for everybody to have a wee and when they had all waddled up the back ramp and disappeared inside the house I went and shut the back door behind them. Then me, David and Horton waved the driver off. I think he would have been very happy to be the one who got that late night pick up. I think he will remember being part of our funny little pack for those few moments that night. The pugs jumped up and splatted his nice clean trousers with their wet muddy paws, but he didn't even blink an eye at it, just patted each old head and popped a bit of chicken into their open mouths. That was one of David's last trips overseas and to this day we still laugh about him going out with a bang, what better way to end things then with a chicken nugget feeding frenzy.

In 2011 we put Horton's photo on the Christmas cards we sent out and although he had died eleven months earlier it didn't seem at all odd for me to be doing that. And if people thought it weird that a dog who had been dead almost a year was on our cards well they weren't for saying so. I don't think they dared. I'd already taken the photos the Christmas before and had fully intended to use them for our 2010 cards but then went with one of the older pugs instead because they were getting on in years and I wanted to have them on a card while they were still here. Of course, I thought there would be plenty of time to use Horton's photos while he too was still with us, but I was wrong about that. But there was no way I was going to leave those photos lying flat in a drawer, never to be seen by anybody just because he had gone, they were too beautiful for that. I knew I would eventually end up using them at some point so what better year than this. I did it as a way of honouring him and all that he was, and I did it because those photos were pretty cute and he looked adorable in them. I remember trying to get the most perfect shot and giving Horton some lovely treats in order to get it. It is hard to get a good photo of a black pug's face, the lighting has to be perfect otherwise you end up with no features showing at all. I popped a tiny Christmas hat on Horton's little head, then sat him on a cream blanket to help shed light and then happily clicked away hoping for the best. And I wasn't disappointed with any of the photos taken, they were taken at the right time of the day so the lighting in the house was good, it shone on his little face and captured all his mischievousness. He looked up at me with those big baby eyes of his and bounced up and down for the treats I had in my hand. It was an enjoyable time, a happy time, I'd talk to Horton, and he'd bounce and I'd give him a treat and he'd chew away happily, then be there all bug eyed looking around for more. There were old pugs coming over lining up for their treats because we never give them out to just one, treat time is a family affair here and they knew that so stomped around my feet. Horton was actually sitting on the couch and David was crouched down in front of him making sure he didn't fall off. And he had to be there because Horton was so excited that he was flipping himself in one direction then a quick flip over and off he'd go in the other direction running along the couch and Dave was there following along with both hands out ready to catch the little guy should he get overly excited and take a dive. The Christmas hat stayed in place on Horton's head no matter how boisterous he became because I'd sewn a little elastic strap onto it that was perfectly measured because I was afraid of making it too tight, I'd rather have had no hat at all and just given him a pile of tinsel to play with than have him be uncomfortable in a hat. I must have gotten it right though because from the way Horton was behaving it was like he didn't even know it was there or if he did know he didn't care. It wasn't a heavy hat, barely any weight at all as I didn't want to be putting any pressure on his head or neck. There were old pugs barking excitedly and the treat jar kept getting the lid taken off and I'd grab another handful and off we'd go again. "Look over at Mummy Horton, look over at Mummy" I'd be saying and when he did it was a case of click, click, click. Ruby was stomping round the room woofing with joy, doing her little penguin walk fast and woofing away like crazy as she went, she was really enjoying herself you could see it on her face. Sarah stayed by my side because she knew I had the treats so there was no use racing around expelling excess energy if she didn't need to. And besides if Horton should drop one, well she was right there ready to pounce on it before anybody else had time to. Emily kept bounding onto the couch and being lifted down again because we didn't want her accidently pushing Horton off. Harper was slumped over by the corner of the couch, tongue hanging out, eyes looking up and blinking at the goings on. Little Grace was darting about all over the place, to the windows to bark at the birds then back to the area of the lounge room where all the activity was. She was feeding off the energy in the room and going absolutely ballistic, she was our oldest pug but she sure wasn't acting like it. Arthur was in the kitchen circling and doing that faint growly woof he is well known for, sometimes he'd come into the lounge and join us, but being blind he could smell the treat jar sitting on the countertop and each time the lid got lifted the aroma filled the area and he wasn't about to leave that too often. He was smart, he stayed where the biggest amount of food was and whenever I went for a refill I'd bend down and pop a treat or two into his mouth before racing off again. Tommy was rolling around on the floor on his back, he'd get up when another round of treats got dished out but then he'd be back to rolling again pawing at whoever walked past with those big paws of his. It was a wonderful time, a delightful happy family time for everybody and all of that was reflected in the photos and captured perfectly on Hortons little face.

Today when thinking about Horton I think a lot more about his great achievements than I do about his final days. Yes Horton's life was short, but he lived it well, he packed a lot into those three years, and that should be celebrated. I believe he actually lived a lot bigger and better life than a lot of dogs in this world do. I don't like or agree with it, but I know it happens, I know you have dogs who are bought and then left to live out their entire lives in back gardens because their family quickly loses interest in them or think that because they are dogs they belong outdoors. And some of them do go on to double figures, and yes they may live longer days than Horton did, but I don't believe they live as happily or as well as Horton did. And that's a poor reflection on their owners because they should give their dogs much better lives than that. Nobody wants to live their entire lives on the outside looking in.

But for Horton each day was a celebration, his entire existence was a festivity of joy, he was happy, and he was healthy. I've since come to learn that he was a lot healthier than some dogs born with hemivertebra are. Horton didn't have reflux and he never had to go on oxygen, well not daily, not all throughout his life he didn't like some do, he was only given oxygen the one time and that was in those last forty-eight hours of his life. He didn't have congested lungs and he didn't have to be on daily medication, in a nutshell he didn't have a lot of the things that other dogs who are born like him can have and I don't know why that was, I just don't. But I am glad he didn't as that would have been hard on him and hard for me to witness. Maybe it was because he did live a full life and was not restricted, well yes restrictions were put on him due to him being how he was, we had to look out for him and look after him and we did that but we also didn't keep him confined, we protected him by always being there for him, watching him should he ever need us to jump in and help, but we did step back a lot, we allowed him to be independent, be out and about on the farm exploring, he had a full and interesting life, and he was fit and healthy because of it. Maybe some of the other dogs who suffer these conditions do nothing but lay around on a blanket all day, not much movement. Or maybe they are worse off than he was, I mean Horton was a classic case of hemivertebrae, an extreme case actually and I know that because he is not the only pug with hemivertebra that I have shared my life with. I always said should I ever have the opportunity to take in another pug like Horton that my hand would be in the air fast, waving around shouting "Me, Me, Me" and I did just that, to date I have had a few dogs who have been born with various degrees of hemivertebra and many dogs that have spinal conditions. So I have had a lot of experience there and I'm glad I have it, I'm grateful to have shared my life with these special needs dogs, taking care of them is such a joy and a real privilege too. No two of my dogs who had hemivertebra were exactly the same though, each one was slightly different. Maybe Horton was just lucky in that he didn't suffer other afflictions, he was the worst case of hemivertebra we have ever had but he didn't spend his entire life being ill. And again, I have to say that I'm incredibly grateful for that, but again I also have to say that I don't one hundred percent know why that was. The only way I would ever be able to know for sure if the lifestyle we gave Horton caused him to benefit would be if I had two dogs who were born exactly the same way Horton was and allowed one to live like Horton did and the other to be more confined and the chances of that happening are less than zero because if I was to ever be lucky enough to be given the opportunity to care for two such souls then you can bet your bottom dollar that I am going to not restrict either one in any way, I am going to give them every opportunity to thrive, in others words I would give them both the exact same lifestyle that was given to Horton. There would be no experiments undertaken in my house. I would give both of them the very best life possible and my heart would sit right with that. Ok there may be one thing I would do. I would contact the person who wrote to me after Horton died just to see if they really did have some new information for me or if it was all just a hoax. I remember getting the email and them saying they knew of a way that Horton could have lived longer and when I asked how that could be they said they wouldn't tell me now, but should I ever get another pug exactly like Horton that they would give me the information then. And I thought that was a weird thing to say, I mean why not share this information with somebody who is constantly taking in and looking after elderly and special needs dogs, if you genuinely have information to help why hold back. But anyway, they wouldn't budge and so that did make me think it was just somebodies idea of a cruel joke. But if I should ever find myself caring for a dog who is exactly like Horton again then I will take the chance and contact them, how could I not, I would be wanting to do everything possible for this little pug in my care so would definitely risk being the butt of somebodies joke just in case they were in fact telling the truth. I would also hope that should I ever be lucky enough to share my life with one like Horton again that technology will have found a way of being able to help them more. When Horton was born there was nothing they could do but that was over ten years ago, let's hope there will be some form of change in the future.

I am actually quite proud of myself for how I handled Horton's death and for what I've gone on to do since losing him. Yes I fell apart when he died, fell apart for a long time, that was clear enough for everyone to see, but I also picked myself up and carried on, carried on doing my life's work, carried on rescuing and helping needy animals. I'm proud that in one of the saddest hardest darkest most heartbreaking times of my life I reached for the light because it could so very, very easily have not been the case. I could well have given it up completely and anybody who witnessed how bad I was at the time wouldn't have blamed me one little bit, to be honest most expected it. They say it's not what happens to us in life but how we respond to what happens and I never thought about that much before, but since losing Horton I do now think that saying is one hundred percent correct. I was extremely affected by the loss of Horton, affected like I've never been affected by anything in my life before, but I did not let it destroy me or my life. I had a choice to make, and I made it and I have helped a whole lot of animals in the years since Horton left my side. And I'm proud of myself for that and I think Horton would be proud of me too.

I used to think that one day when I am very old and maybe living in a nursing home that on the anniversary of Horton's death I would bolt upright in my chair just with the sheer memory of that heartbreakingly sad day. Well, I don't think that anymore. Yes I will remember it, no matter how old I get I am always going to remember that date because it's just what we do. But I more think now that the longer you live the more dates you'll have that are memorable, and for so many different reasons too. Some will be sad, most will be happy, a few will be heartbreaking and a whole lot will have you sitting there with tears rolling down your cheeks from laughter, and you won't be sitting there alone with your memories either, you'll more than likely be telling the other nursing home residents about them, and they'll be laughing too and sharing their life events with you. I was going to say that I'd undoubtedly be peeing my pants from laughing but stopped myself short because, well, I'll be an old lady in nursing home won't I and such things will probably be a lot closer to the truth then I'm comfortable thinking about right now.

I do think that Horton James Sparky Comer is always going to be very special to me, I do think he's always going to be a lot more than just a little paraplegic pug I shared my life with between 2008 and 2011. I am grateful that he came, I am a different person for having known him, but I also think I am a stronger person for having known him. Stronger than I ever thought I could be and it's Horton who I have to thank for that. It's like you start out as a form and your life experiences chip and whittle away at you until you are unrecognisable as whom you once were. Well inwardly you are anyway and sometimes the outer you is affected too but not as much as what's inside. That's very much how I felt after losing Horton and how I felt after that first week of January 2011. I changed when I lost Horton in so many ways and some of that came back to me over the years and some of it hasn't and I don't think it ever will. And some days I am alright with whom I have become and other days I think to myself that it'd be nice to go back to how I once was. When I lost Horton, Ruby and Grace I also lost the ability to live in a carefree manner, I can no longer live that way now because I know that bad things can happen, will happen and do happen and so I've become an over worrier. I tend to worry a lot more then I used to do because I now know how quickly so many things that are precious can be taken away from you and that knowledge does alter how you live your life, it effects your days and effects the way you think even if you don't want it to. It's like it's always there in the back of your mind haunting you. And I try hard to be different, try not to dwell, and sometimes I succeed and sometimes I don't, it all depends on what's going on with the pugs at the time. But I also know that I can go through these incredibly traumatic times and come through them. And having such knowledge has helped me. It was beneficial in helping me cope with my Mum's death because I knew no matter how I was feeling in that moment, it wouldn't last forever, things would change and that I would go on. With Horton's death I didn't know that, I felt like I was always going to be in the depth of its grasp, always going to be sinking with no glimpses of the surface but I now know that you will at some point come up for air and be able to breathe again. Grief is forever changing, it's a journey just as life is a journey. You just keep on doing whatever you have to do to get yourself through the day until you feel strong enough to do differently. When I lost my Mum I was deeply, deeply grieving, but I knew the path it would take me on because I'd walked that path before. And so, for that reason Mum's loss was just that teeny tiny bit easier for me and that was due to Horton and the lessons I learned there. It was a hard way to learn this lesson but really it's the only way you can.

The other day I was going through a cupboard and found a magazine at the back of it. I thought it was a recent one I'd shoved in there in a hurry but no it was actually from 2011. A copy of my favourite magazine dated January 2011. I must have tossed it in there after Horton died because I had no interest in reading it at the time. So, I grabbed it out and was about to put it in the bin because I thought it would be full of old celebrity news, but before I did I decided to flick to the horoscope section because I was curious as to what it was going to say and how accurate it would be. And as is the case with these things some of it was way off but a few lines stood out because they were spot on. It said that the old me was going to disappear as fast as my 2010 calendar. It also said that me changing would be uncomfortable for people who were used to being around the old me, and that was pretty much spot on too because I was so full of sadness that being around me would have been painful. And I did lose a few friends who couldn't deal with what I was going through, and I didn't mourn their departure. I was relieved to see them go because it meant no longer having to put the energy into keeping those relationships alive, it was a gift really because I just didn't have it in me to do what I once did, in my eyes it was one less job and I believe if you think of a friendship as a job then that friendship has run its course.

I'm glad I took so many photos of Horton and videos too. Sure, they were hard to look at at first but now it's like I have so many images to look back on and they are a lot more than just images, they all tell the story of how well he lived his life and in years to come if I have forgotten how much he achieved I can look back on those photos and videos and witness it all over again. And be thinking "Oh you wonderful little daring boy, look how you shone, look at what you accomplished, look at how many lives you touched and how brilliant you were" I still have a heck of a lot of respect and admiration for Horton. And sometimes when I feel myself wavering, I think about him and all he did with what he had, and I gain enormous strength from that. Today I smile when walking by his photos in the house, I look down and think "Now weren't you just something extra special" and I believe that's the way I am going to go on thinking about Horton for the rest of my life. And then that'll be it, lights out for me, and I'll see his gorgeous little face once again and what a wonderful reunion that will be. As I write this, we are a few months away from the eighth anniversary of Horton's passing and I do see things differently to how I once did, time has allowed me to do that. I can't look back on Horton's life and see it as a sad story, I just can't do it, yes the ending was sad, all endings are sad. But oh, how he lived, oh how magnificently he lived and what he achieved and how wonderfully special he was.

ABOUT THE AUTHOR

Andrea Comer is an Australian author with a talent for being able to tell a story as though you are actually standing right beside her seeing exactly what she is seeing. She has the ability to take you onto Grace Farm with her, making you feel that you are part of her magical life, caring for and loving her beloved animals. Andrea's books have been read and loved by people all over the world. Her first book The Joy of Horton was published in 2016 and she has gone on to write more books since then and is still writing. Andrea was born in the United Kingdom and migrated to Australia when she was six years old. From a very young age she became aware of the way animals were treated in this world and vowed that one day she would create a place where elderly animals could live out their natural lifespan without knowing fear, feeling pain or enduring suffering. Andrea lives with her husband and a cloud of elderly pugs, sheep and horses. Her days are spent taking care of her large four-legged family, but sometimes in the late afternoon when the pugs are sleeping, she has time to write.

Books by this author

The Joy of Horton	ISBN 978-0-9953904-0-9
The Divine One	ISBN 978-0-9953904-5-4
Grace Farm - Senior Pug Sanctuary	ISBN 978-0-9953904-1-6
Grace Farm - Always and Forever	ISBN 978-0-9953904-3-0

www.ingramcontent.com/pod-product-compliance
Lightning Source LLC
Chambersburg PA
CBHW062146080426
42734CB00010B/1584